The Inheritance

The Real Journey of Life—
Out of Ourselves and
Into God

By John & Lyza Clarke

THE INHERITANCE
John & Lyza Clarke

Copyright © 2003 by John & Lyza Clarke
ALL RIGHTS RESERVED

International Standard Book Number
1-894928-43-1

Printed in the United States of America

Contents

Preface

It feels like this book took as long to get into print as it took the story to unfold—forever! In actuality, it has been almost three years. Since God takes a lifetime to form his life message in us, it must be okay to take time and put loving care into a creative project such as this book.

Our church family has been so faithful to us through all the years and patient with us as we have laboured to finish this work and get it published. Although we cannot name you all here, we are so grateful for your support of us and your belief in the message of this book. However, I must mention those in the church office that laboured on the manuscript, deciphering my sometimes-illegible handwriting. Special thanks go to Patsi and Darlene for all their help, and to Theresa, my personal assistant, who guided the project to completion from the office with such skill and efficiency—typing, organizing, and generally managing me and all my idiosyncrasies with such grace.

I also want to acknowledge the contribution of our family, especially our children: Dave and Lori, Julie and our soon to be son-in-law, Chris, Matthew, and Ginette. They have all been vulnerable to the Lord and to us as we have found our way together on this path of our lives. May our grandchildren—Irelynn, Finn, and Tate—as well as descendants not yet born be blessed by this part of the family story.

Although I had the guiding inspiration and essentially wrote the story, my wife Lyza's and my collaboration brought it to fruition. This cooperative effort reflects not only how we wrote the book, but how we have lived our lives, and I am deeply grateful to God for the helpmate He has given me for both undertakings. My writing would be hopelessly wordy and my ideas overly complicated without her deft touch. Lyza, an excellent writer herself and an English teacher to boot, was 'editor-in-chief' of this enterprise and even wrote several sections of it. We decided together to risk sharing the inner workings of our lives and some quite personal aspects of our marriage relationship in order to encourage others on their journey into God.

Writing it in narrative form and interweaving personal tales with Bible stories rather than just pontificating about spiritual truths was risky, too, but I believe it was part of the creative plan. It is our hope that this work will help define the spiritual heritage for the people who have been part of our lives as well as for others who are inheritors of this greatest legacy of all.

John Clarke

Pitching Our Tent
on the Promise

The Inheritance, Genesis 12

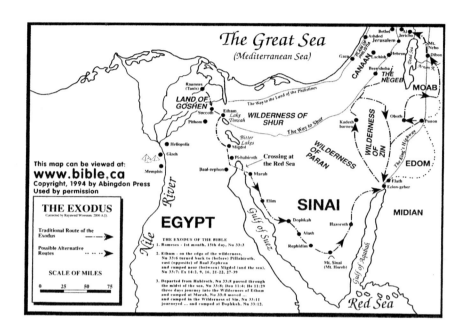

The Great Sea
(Mediterranean Sea)

The Way to the Land of the Philistines

LAND OF GOSHEN

WILDERNESS OF SHUR

The Way to Shur

CANAAN

THE NEGEB

MOAB

Raamses (Tanis)
Succoth
Pithom
Etham
Lake Timsah
Migdol
Bitter Lakes
Pi-hahiroth
Baal-zephon
Marah

Crossing at the Red Sea

WILDERNESS OF PARAN

WILDERNESS OF ZIN

Kadesh barnea
Oboth
Punon
EDOM

Ezion-geber
Elath

Heliopolis
Gizeh
Memphis

Elim

SINAI

MIDIAN

Dophkah
Alush
Rephidim
Hazeroth

Mt. Sinai (Mt. Horeb)

Gulf of Suez

Gulf of Aqabah

Red Sea

Nile River

EGYPT

This map can be viewed at:
www.bible.ca
Copyright, 1994 by Abingdon Press
Used by permission

THE EXODUS
Corrected by Raymond Wiseman, 2000 A.D.

Traditional Route of the Exodus

Possible Alternative Routes

SCALE OF MILES

0   25   50   75

THE EXODUS OF THE BIBLE
1. Rameses - 1st month, 15th day, Nu 33:3

2. Etham - on the edge of the wilderness,
Nu 33:6 turned back to (before) Pillahiroth,
east (opposite) of Baal Zephon
and camped near (between) Migdol (and the sea).
Nu 33:7; Ex 14:2, 9, 16, 21-22, 27-39

3. Departed from Hahiroth, Nu 33:8 passed through
the midst of the sea, Nu 33:8; Deu 11:4; He 11:29
three days journey into the Wilderness of Etham
and camped at Marah, Nu 33:8 moved ...
and camped in the Wilderness of Sin, Nu 33:11
journeyed ... and camped at Dophkah, Nu 33:12.

Bethel
Ai
Ashdod
Jerusalem
Jericho
Mt. Nebo
Gaza
Lachish
Hebron
Dibon
Beersheba
Arnon R.

The King's Highway

Chapter One

I slowly opened my eyes and tried to focus. My senses told me it was probably morning, but it was hard to know in the darkness of the basement. I could have felt claustrophobic waking up in this dark vault with no windows, breathing the coolish stale air; instead I felt a tremendous sense of exhilaration as I remembered why I was sleeping here. For the next year, this house would no longer be our home. My son and his wife now occupied our spacious bedroom upstairs with the view of the pond and the woods and mountains in the background. We cheerfully relegated ourselves to the basement since we would be on the move most of the year.

This was actually an amazing and liberating thought because we were really and truly out—out of our house, out of all our routines, out of White Rock, British Columbia, and possibly out of our minds to cut ourselves loose from thirty years of committed pastoral responsibilities to wander the earth as vagabonds with no fixed address or job. Today was the first day of our yearlong sabbatical.

I savoured it again in my mind. First we would live at our cabin on Nelson Island for a couple of months. Then in the summer we'd fix up the old sailboat and travel up the Inside Passage to Alaska and back. After that we would head for the east coast to explore the Canadian Maritimes in the fall and investigate some family roots in Maine. Then, (and I almost felt too decadent about this one to relish it), a friend had offered her condo in Hawaii to finish off the year. After living all my years on the west coast, we were in for a major change and a real adventure.

"Must be nice to be a pastor. You got a year vacation!?" I could hear it now. I had already heard it and I couldn't blame people—I would be jealous, too. But, as I said to myself, it's not really a vacation; it's a sabbatical.

Until about a year ago I didn't really know much about the rationale of sabbaticals for pastors. But what I did know was that I was ready for this break no matter what it was called or what people thought. I was weary of trying to live beyond 'what people think' after twenty-eight years of serving a congregation of four to five

3

hundred members. The elders approved it wholeheartedly, the congregation blessed and released us and we hardly heard a discouraging word.

I resolved to myself, "I'm not going to lose one day of this precious time to guilt, self-doubt, or recrimination. God orchestrated the details and events of our life up to this point, so this sabbatical chapter will be the same." I determined to suck the marrow out of each day without rummaging around in my overactive, self-examining soul (I was always a little prone to wearing the camel's hair).

As I ruminated awhile on the whole concept of God's orchestration of life I began to look forward to the opportunity to write. Tendrils of story line from our lives, from the scripture, and from the opportunity of the year ahead wove through my thoughts and my anticipation grew. God would surely weave it all together as we went.

"Lord, You and me. We're going to write a book. You're gonna just bring me my daily bread and it's all going to work out somehow, right?"

The time had finally come. The outline for this book on the inheritance had been in my mind for at least twenty years, but I always knew it had to be the right timing. It had to be fully cooked. And, it would be fun. I felt the inner assurance of God's voice.

I'm going to have fun, too, son. I'm looking forward to having you all to myself for a while. You and me. We'll have an adventure. We'll talk. Now is the time. You'd better get on with it. There was a certain urgency to the matter.

A whole year. What would it be like? Time enough for time not to matter anymore. I was enmeshed in an unhealthy way and I knew it. Pastor, counselor, preacher, administrator, father, mediator, school overseer, vision maker, discipler, evangelist—be all things to all men, live above reproach, be an excellent husband... so many parts of me were invested in so many things that I wasn't sure which piece was me anymore.

Even my marriage seemed enmeshed. We were both involved up to our ears in ministry and our relationship was feeling the strain. We couldn't even go on a date without at least an hour of debriefing the week's intrigues and sometimes two when our personal buttons got pushed and we'd end up falling into old patterns of conflict and overflowing emotions. We understood it all, knew better, but did it anyway. We were still desperately in love, yet bruising each other.

In all aspects of my life I was reaching down deep for something more and coming up empty. I felt like a cooked battery—you charge it up, but it doesn't hold the charge and before you know it, it's in the red again. As I lay in bed next to Lyza, I looked into the basement gloom where all our boxes were stacked with household stuff that needed to be gotten out of the way, and I asked myself, "Can I really take all my responsibilities and just pack them away, stacked up in the basement for a year? What will they do without me?"

Yes, what will they do without *me*, incredible me? Some adjustment in my own mentality, if not that of other people, was definitely in order. What if I were dead? Almost all my spiritual mentors were dead in their sixties, and they didn't seem to apologize for it. Life moved on. God somehow ran His kingdom without them. I needed to really know that it didn't all depend on me. A year would be enough time to find out just how dispensable I really was.

At that moment the next altogether new sensation suddenly hit me. It was April 4, 2000, the first day of my sabbatical, and my father was dead at eighty-eight. How uncanny! Yesterday my brother phoned me to say Dad had passed away that afternoon. It felt like the passing of an era.

My father was the patriarch of the Clarke clan for more than fifty years. My grandfather died young and I never knew him, but Dad was always the rock. Now it was me, my four brothers, and my sister left to support Mom and carry on. I was glad I would have time to really embrace this event in my family's life without rushing back to other pressing affairs at church. Next weekend was the memorial and we would spend at least a week in Seattle with time to reflect.

In ancient Israel, every fifty years was declared a year of Jubilee—a time to release everyone from their debts and a time for a man to return to his ancestral lands and start fresh. I would turn fifty this year. Time for me to renew my sense of heritage and take stock of my spiritual and ancestral roots. I have learned through the years that God has prepared a great inheritance for those who seek Him. God's inheritance is a mystery, a secret that is hidden in life, in history, and in the scripture, but discoverable to those who discern it and prepare for it. After thirty years of pastoral ministry serving the spiritual inheritance of God, and after fifty years of living in the heritage of my natural family, it was time to make a contribution to the understanding of the eternal inheritance. That is what I would write about.

Probably the first time I actually thought about an inheritance was when I was faced with the possibility of losing one…

"You want to what!!!?"

"Lyza and I want to get married and move to Canada."

My dad's face expressed incredulous disapproval, the look he wore when a situation challenged his very firmly set worldview. When my announcement had fully penetrated, he started in.

"John, you're only nineteen years old. You're not ready for marriage. You've got so many good years ahead of you, and so much to learn. When I was your age, I didn't even think about such things. I was just enjoying life and having fun and when my father told me to go to school, I went to school and then to law school. My dad was the smartest guy that ever lived. Came out to the great Northwest, built on Mercer Island, started the law firm, built the *Nor'wester.* I didn't marry your mother until I was thirty." I wondered how my grandfather's move to the west coast from Iowa went over with his father.

"I know, Dad, but I think you just don't understand who Jesus Christ really is and what He has done in my life. Lyza and I want to give our lives to Him. We want to preach the gospel. I've seen miracles really happen!"

My dad looked at me blankly. In my youthful pride I knew he didn't really comprehend these things. If only he could see what I'd seen, and feel what I had felt. I loved my dad. I wanted him to 'get it'. The passions were rising high in a number of dimensions in my young heart and his sixty years of living and his lawyer's perceptive mind were not ignorant of my youthful idealism.

"Son, this doesn't make any practical sense. You're not ready to take care of a wife. Where will you live? How will you support yourselves, finish your education? You can't just head off to Canada."

I stood stoutly before him declaring my faith. I felt my inward trembling so much that it affected the edge of my voice and I was emotional, which was unusual for me. To stand up to my dad and talk like this? I never would have dreamed of talking back to him. It was hard even to disagree with my dad. You just didn't do it. Even if you did disagree, you nodded and kept your secrets. I thought to myself that this newfound bravery must have come from God. I was empowered to do His will.

"God will provide for us, Dad. He answers prayer and if we're supposed to do this, He'll take care of us like He did for the apostles." The same blankness met me. He was trying to understand me.

"How's He going to do that? I believe in God, John. This is very good for you to believe in God, but I still had to go to work, go to school, learn. What is God going to do? Have dollar bills float down out of heaven?"

He just didn't get it. I would just have to do it. He would see... somehow. And I marvel at it now—I didn't feel fear or trepidation, just blind confidence. I was full of spiritual zeal and youthful idealism and I don't think I had a clue of what I was getting into, either. Growing up in an affluent home I never experienced hardship or want.

"Dad, we've prayed about it and we've put a fleece before God."

More quizzical looks. Had his son joined some cult? The 'Christianese' language was beyond his scope. What was a fleece before God? Where did all this religious talk come from? He was getting more disturbed by the minute.

"We're going to work this summer. Lyza has a job at Seattle Center in a donut shop and the ministers in White Rock have hired me to be the 'Man on the Beach' for June, July, and August. If we have two thousand dollars by the end of the summer, that's confirmation we're supposed to do it."

"Do what?"

"Get married in September, move to White Rock and work with young people. Young Life will give us a partial support (I didn't tell him it was only one hundred dollars a month) and they will try to find us some place to live."

My dad's face clouded over. Generally a positive and cheerful man, these wild plans were getting out of control and his patience was running out. I felt the dread of Dad's disapproval and the fear that he would lose his temper made my heart beat in my ears.

"All right!" It was one of those conversation-ending, put-your-foot-down kind of expressions. He looked at me with those penetrating blue eyes that said, "God Almighty, you better not be hiding anything," and sputtered momentarily, trying to find words for the rising emotion. He didn't know how to deal with his son who was slipping out of his hands, becoming incomprehensible. I'm not sure he really knew his son that well in the first place. It was not like we were great communicators of inner things in my family.

"You're not going to do anything like this. You know I've always respected you and I don't tell anybody what to do. But this is crazy. You can't do it. If you do this, you're on your own. You're going to have to pay your own way through college. I'm not supporting you and a wife. You'll have to take care of yourself."

I saw the inner turmoil. The great provider never dreamed of his children paying for their own education. It was a major struggle for him to threaten to cut me off. He only applied pressure tactics as a last resort. Respect for his wishes usually carried the day, but it wasn't working this time.

"Dad, I'm not expecting you to keep supporting me. God is going to be our Provider." This statement translated, "You don't need me, you're not listening to me." It took me years to appreciate the pain I caused my parent with those words, but the die was cast. On September 18, 1970, Lyza and I got married. We left our families and our country to settle in Canada with our scraped-together fortune of two thousand dollars and the promise of free rent in a church camp counselor's cabin.

At first sight of the cabin, Lyza burst into tears. Far from a cute honeymoon cottage, it was a filthy shambles when we arrived with all our worldly goods in the back of her parents' van. But her mom, a veteran of many adverse circumstances in her life, put her arm around Lyza's shoulder and walked her off down the path, talking softly about all the possibilities for the little place. By the time they returned a few minutes later, Lyza had rallied and just dove in, chattering in her usual enthusiastic fashion about what curtains here and a rug there could do to spiff up the place. I don't think I was ever more grateful for Lyza's mom than at that moment of parental support. Only now as I remember the incident does it occur to me what it must have cost this mother to cheerfully look on the bright side knowing she had to leave her only daughter in such a place.

Seemingly cut off from my earthly inheritance, we set forth to discover a spiritual one.

> *By faith Abraham, when he was called, obeyed by going out to a place which he was to receive for an inheritance; and he went out, not knowing where he was going.* (Hebrews 11:8)

Since we didn't know where we were going either, Abraham was a good role model for us. The life of Abraham marks the beginning of the inheritance promises in the Bible. The Bible chronologies begin with Abraham (who was as much a nobody as anybody), living in the land of Ur of the Chaldeans around 1850 BC. He became the father of Isaac, who was the father of Jacob, whose name God changed to 'Israel'. Jacob had twelve sons who eventually became twelve tribes. Abraham was the father of the Jews through Isaac and the Arabs also claim him as their father through Ishmael, the son of his concubine. Christians call him the father of faith as well as the natural progenitor of Jesus Christ. This was quite some 'nobody' to have had such a profound effect on everybody right up to the present day. Why him? Why did God make the promise of inheritance to Abraham? We don't really know why, but God had to begin with somebody to reveal the mystery of His inheritance.

> *Now the Lord said to Abram, "Go forth from your country, and from your relatives and from your father's house, to the land which I will show you; and I will make you a great nation, and I will bless you, and make your name great; and so you shall be a blessing; and I will bless those who bless you, and the one who curses you I will curse. And in you all the families of the earth will be blessed." So Abram went forth as the Lord had spoken to him; and Lot went with him...* (Genesis 12:1-4)

The promise to Abraham if he would leave his father's house contained two specific things. Those two things are the primary ingredients of any inheritance. God promised him land and He promised him a seed (or descendants). Land is the foundational base of wealth and children are the means to preserve it. A true inheritance involves land and seed. For Abraham, the land promised was Canaan, which encompasses the land of Israel and Palestine today, and the seed was the line of descendants of his miracle son, Isaac.

These two foundations for an inheritance take on a spiritual application for Christians, which will be explained as we go along. Suffice it to say that just as Lot went forth with Abraham to a strange country, so Lyza went forth with me to White Rock. At the time we had no thoughts of obtaining an inheritance from God nor did we even know that there was one.

White Rock was then a little Canadian beach town on Semiahmoo Bay in the southwest corner of Canada, facing Blaine, a border town on the northwest corner of the United States. God may not have sent us very far into another land, but it was definitely a foreign country. When we made our move we were not aware of the parallels our lives had with Abraham's journey because we hardly knew anything about Abraham. We were only aware of our love for each other and the exciting life into which Christ was leading us. This new life together actually began in British Columbia, Canada a couple years earlier when we met at a place called Malibu. Both of us worked there in the summer of 1968, just after I had graduated from high school.

"So, what should we talk about today?"

Maurie, our work crew boss, looked ridiculous, reclining in the sun like a beached sea mammal, his white stomach popping out from under his tight T-shirt and a ragged straw hat perched on his head.

"How about masturbation?" replied Lyza without skipping a beat.

"Masturbation! Lyza!" Maurie reddened immediately and tried to suppress his laughter. He'd already learned to expect any kind of frank questions from the pert sixteen-year-old sitting on the end of the dock. I had, too. She disarmed me with her perspicacity and enchanted me with her confidential cuteness. She got around my seventeen-year-old reserve and made a beeline to my heart. We spent hours sitting on the balcony of the dining lodge overlooking the Malibu Rapids talking about ourselves and our newfound faith. It all seemed to go together, faith in Christ, emotional openness and intimacy, honest talk about real values. I couldn't get enough.

Maurie had had quite enough by the time we finished the masturbation conversation, but he, too, was strangely drawn to the candid couple on his month long work crew that June. I say 'couple', but that wasn't really accurate until the last night of our stay when I kissed Lyza for the first time on the golf course, breaking the work crew 'no personal contact' rule. Our relationship grew from that point on and so did the relationship with Maurie. He wasn't going to let me get away with just a summer's effort.

"If you're going to college in Bellingham, why don't you come up to White Rock and help me with the Young Life club this year? It's only a thirty minute drive."

I was only a couple of years older than the Canadian teens, but with that offer I was conscripted into a new purpose for living. That was the beginning of the end for me—the end of living mainly for me. I was soon leading the teens with Maurie and involved with those same vital issues that Lyza and I loved to talk about. Dealing with eternal issues was what I wanted to do. When Lyza enrolled in Western Washington College the following year, we both went north to White Rock as leaders of the Young Life club after Maurie moved to Vancouver to assume a Young Life staff position. The following summer we made the plunge to get married and move to White Rock. Like Abraham, we were going to learn by stepping out on God's promises.

By faith he [Abraham] *lived as an alien in the land of promise, as in a foreign land, dwelling in tents with Isaac and Jacob, fellow heirs together of the same promise.* (Hebrews 11:9)

Abraham pitched his tent on a promise. It was more than five hundred years before any of the actual land he was living on belonged to his descendants, but he followed the voice that called him to faith and he learned to believe in things he could not see.

11

You have to see beyond the natural circumstances when you're living in a tent. We came to know how he felt shortly after we were married.

My nose woke up first, smelling the canvas warming in the sun. Beside me on the propped up bedspring lay my sweet bride of nine months and beyond her in the 9' X 12' tent was a dresser containing our clothes, tilted downhill as our tent site wasn't quite level. A curious raccoon actually stuck his nose in the door the night before to see who the new neighbors were and to assess our worldly possessions. "It must be later in the morning," I thought to myself, judging by the buildup of heat in the tent. Late nights were the norm in those July days as the coffeehouse we started on the beach was generally open into the wee hours of the morning when the youth culture was out in full force.

As Lyza stirred beside me, I felt a few pangs of worry. What was I bringing her to? Our counselor's cabin arrangement came to an unexpected close after nine months (they decided they needed the space for the camp that summer), our two thousand dollars was spent and my only recourse was to borrow an old canvas tent from a friend and pitch it in the backyard of another friend's rented beach cottage. The 'backyard' was a jumble of overgrown fruit trees, a tangle of blackberries and four-foot-high grass. We sat on the hillside in the tall grass, clinging to each other, Lyza crying, not quite sure what would become of us. We didn't belong to any church yet, so there were times when we really felt 'on our own with God'. While hacking out a place to put our tent we discovered the backyard was on a definite slope. We raised the end of our bed with bricks to make it level, put our clothes in a dresser and called the tent home for the next three months. It was a good thing it was summer.

Only one thing really sustained us beyond our love for each other and our youthful naiveté – an Abraham kind of faith that God had called us out to a place where He would take care of us. Now we lived in a tent just like Abraham had, in an alien country. The 'land' was an uneven hill behind a beach cottage and the 'descendants' were an unstable flock of teenagers. I had left my family behind, my resources were gone, my ministry created no revenue, and I couldn't work in Canada on my extended visitor's visa.

(It was the only status we could get in the country while I was still a full-time university student).

The coffeehouse was a miracle gift of charity, which we rented for the grand total of one dollar a year from the Mental Health Association who used the premises in the daytime. We only had to pay the heat and light bills. That was when we found out about supernatural provision. In a way, it was liberating. We were totally dependent. Either we would be disabused of our youthful idealism and go home with our tails between our legs, or we would find out once and for all if there was any substance behind these radical Christian ideas.

Like Abraham, the promises, which we were beginning to grasp, would take years to turn into a provision. In fact, it would be a lifetime process. Sometimes it takes generations. God gives a promise and the promise is usually followed by problems. When God has sufficiently tested us, building our character, and we are convinced that His promises are totally beyond our own ability to fulfill, He brings to light His provision. Promise, problems, provision. Any person used by God goes through this process.

The inheritance promises are not easily perceived or understood. Many give up before the processes are finished. The foundational illustration of this is the Exodus, the central story of the Pentateuch. The Pentateuch is the first five books of the Bible and describes God's preparation of the people of Israel to inherit the land of Canaan (Israel today). God planned this foundational history to serve as an allegory for the spiritual pilgrimage of the soul. As such, it has a timeless quality and a richness of application for all people of all times. The stories and events of this history will serve as illustrations to help give understanding of this pilgrimage into the spiritual inheritance.

The youthful adventures of our early Christian days happened over thirty years ago. Now, here we were in our own house, well established. "Hardly a tent now," I thought, as I mounted the winding stairs from the basement to the bright April morning light flooding the kitchen. A delightful smell of coffee was in the air. My first grandchild, Irelynn, padded by in a saggy diaper and bare feet, eyeing me warily, a plastic toy crammed in her mouth with one hand

13

and Floppy, her bedraggled stuffed bunny, dangling from the other. We were beginning to bond and now I felt a twinge of regret about leaving for the next year. I quickly shifted my thoughts to planning out the next few days of getting our affairs in order.

Soon enough we were driving the freeway south to Seattle for the funeral. I turned onto the familiar roads of Mercer Island and wondered what home would be like without Dad in his chair in the den.

The next morning I found myself sitting in an antique armchair surrounded by the green and brown decor of my childhood home, looking out the window at a blue lake. Seward Park, directly across from my parents' home, was filled with the same forest greens and browns I remembered, as was my mother's yard mixed with the showy color of rhododendrons, her favorite. The snow-draped Olympics guarded the horizon under which the buildings of Seattle's skyline stood in box-like contrast. However, it was the lake that captured my attention in the morning light as the steady breeze pushed the waves south. The water was a constant presence in my childhood, splashing at the borders of my world and lulling me to sleep at night.

Tomorrow I would scatter my father's ashes on the water. As I glanced around at the photographs—images of his many accomplishments and stages of life—the room resonated with warm memories. Today was his memorial service, and tomorrow his remains would sift into the depths of the lake beside which he had been born, lived, and died.

I wondered what would become of all the old landmarks? The big square brick house, the dock, the wood boats, the squash court, the familiar gardens and pathways of my youth. The house and land would eventually be sold and pass into other hands. Nothing is permanent. Only life itself is the constant. These tangible things were only the frame of the picture drawing attention to the real content of a life. My father's frame was gone, but his life force was still in me and was a part of me, the eternal river of life flowing from generation to generation from the throne of God and back again.

My dad kept a folder of poems and writings, and some of his own maxims that he called 'The Basics'. Every one of his kids had a copy and none of us would forget those truths committed to our keeping. I, too, would eventually pass into the blue waters and my children would walk their moment around the shores of this life. It was things like 'The Basics' that constituted the real heritage, the internal things. I hoped I would leave my children with an internal heritage.

Dad had been a robust and happy man. He often said he was the luckiest man on earth. By his confession he had the most wonderful woman in the world as his wife, five strong sons and one adored, beautiful daughter. He lived in the Pacific Northwest, which was, in his opinion, the very best place in the world in the very best country on earth. Ever optimistic, he figured the world had more good people than bad and truth would always prevail in the end because Winston Churchill, his hero, said so.

In his youth (he would say) he had been a nature boy, born and raised on Mercer Island in Lake Washington, just across the water from Seattle. He was proud to be the son and namesake of Fred G. Clarke Senior, an attorney, outdoorsman, marksman and boatsman who came to Seattle in 1906, and was the grandson of George W. Clarke, governor of the state of Iowa in 1918. I felt the rich heritage of our family every day in our surroundings. My father reinforced it continually with expressions of honor toward his father and pride of family, especially his own first cousin, Nile Kinnick, winner of the Heisman Trophy in 1939 as the University of Iowa quarterback.

The war years did nothing to repress Fred's (nicknamed Ted) good humor and zest for life, even after both his Kinnick cousins, Nile and his brother Ben, were lost at sea as navy pilots. Dad served in the war as an intelligence officer gleaning secrets from the Russians amid vodka and caviar. This central chapter of his life included marrying my mother, Lee Vinal, the daughter of another Mercer Island pioneer family. Her sister married his only brother, George, who became a longstanding Washington State senator, and they all raised their families on the shores of Lake Washington. Through all these years, my father and his brother were highly respected Seattle attorneys of their own law firm. Dad also played squash so well he won the Seattle A Squash championship twenty years out of twenty-two. At one time he was ranked the sixth best squash player in the nation.

My dad was a unique character. I remember him even in his fifties doing back flips off the dock piling in front of our house. His physique was naturally like Popeye the sailor man, and he was a physical fitness buff before it was in vogue. Verging on the eccentric, he gave expression to his zest for life with shouts of pleasure, Tarzan yodels, loud greetings to his friends, and singing in a rich baritone hymns of faith or more raucous ditties like Hank Thompson's "Squaws Along the Yukon Are Good Enough For Me".

A person of routine and discipline, he did calisthenics every day while quoting aloud the Basics. Every morning he doffed his hat from his baldpate to affectionately kiss his wife as he left for his work at the Seattle Hoge Building and then charged up the one hundred-yard trail from the lakefront to his car on the driveway up the hill. On the way home he often stopped briefly (and sometimes not so briefly) at the Roanoke Tavern, and then, on arriving home, paused at the back door of the house to ring loudly the ship's bell he installed there, exactly three times as his ritual required. On entering the house, he turned the lights on and off a few times and flushed the toilet just to check they were working and bellowed, "Left, I'm home!" (My mother was left-handed, a fact my father reveled in— hence, the nickname).

He had pet names for everyone and everything and, comfortable in his own skin, didn't hesitate using them at any time, any place, and in front of anybody. For years he sported an African pith helmet in the summer and explored the lakefront in an old seven-horse outboard, standing up in the boat like an acrobat and steering by shifting the weight with his feet.

He had many idiosyncrasies yet was awesomely weighty in presence and opinion, holding court with his family, friends and neighbors, pontificating on the Basics, or his analysis of the Bible, Winston Churchill, politics, or sundry seers, poets and sages. Something about his manner did not encourage discussion or disagreement, even though you might not actually agree with his quite conservative Republican views. My youngest brother's friend, a very left-leaning civil activist lawyer, once said, "Charlie, even I could never dream of taking issue with your father." Yet, whatever your views, you couldn't help but have an admiration for my father who lived what he espoused.

Integrity was his signature value. He told us often the story of an associate of his father coming into the law office saying, "If you can't trust a Clarke, you can't trust God." Such statements struck terror into me, and later, paroxysms of guilt, knowing that I could never measure up to such ideals. Yet, all this was part and parcel of who my father was and it was an endearing, powerful image which lingered over us the day of the memorial. .

The breeze on the lake was cold and the mood was somber under an overcast sky. Rumbling underneath us and into our collective memories were the consoling sounds that only the *Nor'wester* made. The fifty-four foot wooden boat was older than most of us aboard. It played host to our childhood and now it bore the entire tribe, including most of the nineteen grandchildren, on our sad errand. I carried in the crook of my arm an urn of ashes; it was hard to comprehend that I held all that remained of my father in my arm. We read some scripture and poems, we prayed, and I began scattering the contents upon the gray water. Particles of dust carpeted the surface; little gray bubbles played upon the rippled waves. I saw in my mind his merry blue eyes and the stubble of a day's growth on his face just days before the end and I felt warmed by his spirit. "All is well," was the last thing he managed to say to me with a tired smile. I was not worried, but I was sobered. Never had I been so struck by the finality of death. I would never again see him, feel him, or be able to find him anywhere in any place in this world. My father as I knew him was now only dust in my hands.

By the sweat of your face you shall eat bread, till you return to the ground, because from it you are taken; for you are dust, and to dust you shall return. (Genesis 3:19)

No wonder the ancient cultures became so obsessed with death, excavating tombs and filling them with elements of this life, trying to make a bridge, trying to make sense of the imposition of oblivion. I looked up to the surrounding faces of his progeny in grave rapt attention as my mother fumbled with an object in her hand, a little brass bell.

"We bought them for each other in 1981," she confided to me earlier in the day. "I want to drop his bell in the water with him."

I gently grasped her hand as she slowly turned toward the rail.

"Mom, let's have each one ring the bell once for Grandy before you drop it."

At first unsure, her voice breaking under the strain of the long bond now severed, she let me lead her to my brother standing by. A ringing clear note of brass struck the air again and again, as old hand, young hand, tiny hand sounded the farewell note. Only the breeze and the soft swish of wave against hull marked the respectful good byes. All remembered the homecoming ritual, "Left, I'm home!" Gong! Dong! Gong!

When the bell finally came back to her, Mother looked into the depths, and with her own final ring tossed the bell whose note stifled mid-ring as it sank. Mother followed the bell with her eyes as it plummeted into the deep. I tried to fathom the depths of grief in losing your spouse. The expressions on my siblings' faces were far and away and tears rarely shed appeared on cheeks. He was gone.

I remembered my brother's words at the memorial the day before. "I cannot relate to a heaven I cannot see, but I can relate to the dad I see in every one of you in all your faces. He is in us." Coming from his eastern philosophy perspective, I understood him, but I was glad to affirm my own confidence that my father had not just been absorbed into the cosmos. Because my Redeemer lives, because the resurrection of the one Man conquered death, I knew I would see my father again in the person he was and had now become. But for now, my brother was right in a way. The lands, the houses, the boats, the accomplishments were not him. His character, his values, his love is what remained with us. My father's real legacy to us was internal.

Having an inheritance can be a wonderful thing. Most of us prick up our ears if we hear the word 'inheritance' if it relates in any way to ourselves. We think of money or lands coming our way as a gift. Somebody ahead of us has worked and accomplished and stored up and then left it to us. As we struggle to make our way in life, to get on top of the mortgage and carve out a career, an inheritance comes along to smooth our way and make it easier. The cumulative effect of a former generation's good will and thoughtful preparation can lighten our loads.

Most of us have mixed feelings about such thoughts. If gaining an inheritance means losing parents or other loved ones we don't want to think about it too much. At the very least it's not very polite to talk about it. We may have heard of the relatives who gathered like a flock of vultures around the reading of the last will and testament of their rich uncle. It read, "I, being of sound mind and body, spent it all." If we were honest we would admit that an inheritance gained when you still have time to use it is a very desirable thing.

What most of us don't realize very clearly is that God has prepared a very rich inheritance and provided it for every person who can legitimately claim to be a child of God. As has already been mentioned in reference to Abraham, the whole story of the Bible could be said to revolve around this theme. In fact, even the terms 'Old Testament' and 'New Testament' refer to God's last will and testament wherein He describes the conditions under which the people of earth will or will not inherit the future. Therefore, it is to our advantage to read the Bible and discover both the bold and fine print of God's will.

The bold print, in a nutshell, is that the inheritance of God has been granted through the merits, death and resurrection of Jesus Christ. In the same way that we do not earn earthly inheritances but are given them through the merit and labours of someone else, so we obtain the inheritance of eternal life and all that goes with it as a gift simply by believing in Him and surrendering to Him. Paul expressed it this way:

For the promise to Abraham or to his descendants that he would be heir of the world was not through the Law, but through the righteousness of faith. (Romans 4:13)

The promises of inheritance given to Abraham are given ultimately to his descendants by faith. In other words, the natural descendants of Abraham, the Jews, were the only heirs until Jesus came. From then on the descendants are those who believe in Jesus and are born of the Spirit, whether Jews or Gentiles. All who believe are the spiritual children of Abraham and are thereby inheritors.

The fine print of the will goes on to promise and describe the further riches of this inheritance that can be gained by those who diligently seek it. Simply stated, there is a greater inheritance within the inheritance. Eternal life is a gift, but experiencing the richness of that life is the further reward of those who value and look for it. The multitude of references in scripture to rewards and treasures and overcoming are references to a richer inheritance. This inheritance is the greatest secret and mystery of all time.

> *...that is, the mystery which has been hidden from the past ages and generations, but has now been manifested to His saints, to whom God willed to make known what is the riches of the glory of this mystery among the Gentiles, which is Christ in you, the hope of glory.* (Colossians 1:26-27)

This mystery is not easily discerned and is reserved for those who really want to know about it. Just as Christ himself has been undervalued and unrecognized by the world at large, so the inheritance that is in Him has been undervalued and unrecognized even by many of those who confess His name. We need a revelation that penetrates our hearts to really see it. This is why the apostle prays for us,

> *[I] ...do not cease giving thanks for you, while making mention of you in my prayers; that the God of our Lord Jesus Christ, the Father of glory, may give to you a spirit of wisdom and of revelation in the knowledge of Him. I pray that the eyes of your heart may be enlightened, so that you may know what is the hope of His calling, what are the riches of the glory of His inheritance in the saints...* (Ephesians 1:16-18)

This prayer is our prayer over this book. We all have two sets of eyes, one in our head and one in our heart. The heart eyes can only be opened by prayer. When they open they see the riches of the glory of the inheritance. The purpose of this book is to help illumine our eyes by telling stories—the story of the Biblical inheritance, the story of John and Lyza, and the story of a year of sabbatical rest.

Resting in Christ is the end of the inheritance message, and so it is fitting to write about this whole subject while at rest. It is our hope and faith that these three stories will weave together one good illustration of the inheritance message and confirm that God orchestrates the details of life to accomplish a larger purpose.

The Creator has designed life to reveal His purpose for creation. Therefore, all of history, all the Bible stories and all of the details and struggles of our own lives are designed to open up our hearts to perceive that purpose. It is the everyday things that teach us most about it. We do not have to be great intellects to perceive it, just open of heart.

The Generations in Jervis

The Passover, Exodus 12
The First Temptation – The Pressures of Life

The Ten Temptations: **1. The Pressures of Life in Egypt**

Seven Stages of the Spiritual Journey:

1. The Passover in Egypt	2. Red Sea Crossing	3. Mt. Sinai Visitation
		4. Wilderness

Spending the first week of our sabbatical in Seattle at a funeral was not our original design, but then the plans we make in this life rarely turn out as we think they will. Vagrant events and unforeseen complications remind us we're not really in control of much. That's why it is good to have a bigger and wiser Someone in control who is working on a greater design than what we readily see.

Originally we had intended to spend the first couple of months living in the wilderness in our beloved cabin. Only our youngest daughter, Ginette, ten, was to accompany us, and, of course, our one year old yellow lab, Boaz. Now we put our plan back in motion and turned over the house to our three older children—Dave, with his wife, Lori, (and Irelynn, our first grandchild), Matthew and Julie, our two college students. We had a family moot to clarify who was in charge of what in the new sibling boarding house even though their level of compatibility was high. They established separate pantry domains to avoid potential conflict and decided who was responsible for various chores.

Waving them all good-bye we headed north out of Vancouver, to the Horseshoe Bay ferry and up the Sunshine Coast eighty miles to Egmont and the Backeddy Marina. From there we piled our belongings on the *Grady*, the extended family's motorboat, for the last eight miles over water to our isolated cabin site. No access by road, no phone, no electricity, but with running water from our own stream and serenity and scenery unmatched, it was the perfect place to literally get away from it all.

The *Grady* was a great improvement over the *Racer*, which was the first boat my brother Tom and I had when we started building our cabins on my uncle's property seven years earlier. The *Racer* was a smaller 14-foot runabout that had been in the family for over thirty-five years and it hauled many tons of building materials from the Egmont float to our cove. During those years we served as a primary source of entertainment for the patrons of the Backeddy Pub as they leaned over the outdoor deck to catch a glimpse of the latest impossible load my brother or I were attempting to maneuver into the inlet, usually with only three or four inches of freeboard. We loaded on plywood or boards (often hanging out two feet port and starboard) piled clothes bags, stove pipes or the proverbial kitchen sink on top, bags of concrete in the bottom for ballast and finally, the people, perched on the floating barge like inordinately large, colorful seabirds. Due to merciful Providence and brazen seamanship born of the years my brother and I spent as water rats on the coast of British Columbia, we managed not to scuttle the poor *Racer* through all these antics.

This tempting of fate came to an end one October when I invited three pastor friends and their wives to spend a couple of days at the cabin after a weekend of preaching. We arrived in Egmont to find the *Racer* on its trailer, filled with a foot of rainwater because the tarp had blown off in the fall winds. After pumping up the two flat trailer tires and bailing the water, we launched her, some luggage and a couple of pastors, only to find she 'drove very heavily'. That means we couldn't get her into a plane because two hundred pounds of water had leaked into the hidden compartment in the bottom of the boat. The wind was blowing strongly and it took about three round trips to get them and all their stuff to the cabin. After that experience we started looking for a decent ship to transport us to the cabin, not wanting to be responsible for drowning the clergy (or any future grandchildren). Hence the good ship *Grady*, a sturdy 20-foot fiberglass outboard, would be our lifeline to civilization for the next months. Lugging our belongings over rocks, up onto the deck and into the cool cedar-smelling interior of the cabin, we plopped ourselves down and sighed contently. This was home for now.

A tiny island sits in the mouth of this cove, covered with thick moss and three stunted firs. It was a great place to sit and survey my domain, especially in the morning. One morning the cat followed me and crouched beside me on the rock. Her tail began to twitch as she anticipated the approach of a behemoth coming up the inlet. As the ferry suddenly emerged through the small firs on the point, she retreated under the two pines we call the 'marriage tree' because they are entwined in perpetual embrace. By late morning the breeze freshened to wrinkle the surface of great placid Jervis Inlet after its sunny morning repose. The sun warmed the back of my neck as it finally cleared the mountains immediately behind. I delighted in our fortunate string of summer-like days when the usual April fare is rain, gray-shrouded mountains and an all-permeating dampness.

This inlet was the place of my fathers. I looked at ridge upon unobstructed ridge of green granite-mottled mountains, their shoulders still carrying the vestiges of a winter mantle of snow. If Dad's ashes had not been scattered on Lake Washington, they probably would have been carried here to filter amid the evergreens into the multi-colour moss and silent green water. In the distance, directly across six miles of water, I saw the great hump of mountain, which lay north of a Jurassic-Park-like falls plummeting down from Freil Lake to Harmony Island. There we played, fished, swam and adventured through my own childhood, and my children's childhood.

My uncle was so enchanted by this silent warm-watered recess of Hotham Sound that he bought Harmony Island when I was only ten. Later, when it became a popular boater's anchorage and the Canadian government wanted it for a marine park, he made a trade with them for the ninety-acre parcel across the channel where we began to build our cabins.

When we had almost completed our cabin after working on it over seven summer vacations, Dad showed me a poem he found one day among some old papers. My great uncle, Charles Clarke, wrote it after he came from Iowa in the summer of 1928 for the maiden voyage of the *Nor'wester* with my grandfather and great-grandfather. Charles never got back to the west coast again, but the experience stuck with him and he wrote a poem, a mid-western plains person's reverie of the serene majesty of British Columbia's coastline. I framed it and placed it on the wall.

A CABIN BY THE SEA

When the sun shines on the fir trees, it's there that I would be,
There beside the forest, there beside the sea.

When the sea fog shrouds the landscape and hides the dripping trees,
I'd love to be among them and hear the sounding seas.

I'd love to have a cabin where I could take my ease,

Snug above the rocky beach and safe among the trees.

I'd love to feel the salt spray and walk along the shore
And hear the scuttling shellfish and the ocean's solemn roar.

I'd love, Oh! How I'd love again, to look upon the sea,
To see and feel it all again in quiet reverie.

The sea gull in the sky above, the shell fish on the shore,
Oh! How I'd love the sea again and the ocean's solemn roar.

I'd love to see the sunshine and the water's emerald blue
And see again the rocky cliffs stand out in varied hue.

And then again, I'd love to see the shrouding, blinding fog,
The mists that hang o'er the islands and drip from tree and log.

I'd love again to see those logs which the tide makes rise and fall,
Which line the shore for miles and miles from out the forest tall.

Oh! I'd love to see it all again, the great, mysterious sea,
And gaze o'er its wide, wide waters in solemn reverie.

I'd like to look out Westward, out where the red sun dips
Into the far flung ocean plowed by the stately ships.

I'd love to see the fir trees and hear them softly croon
And watch the big wide ocean 'neath the whiteness of the moon.

Oh! I'd surely love to be there in a cabin by the sea,
Where the song of eternal harmony would come wafting in to me.

Little did he know that his dream of a contemplative moment would become our reality seventy years later. I felt like I had fulfilled a prophecy. I gazed over my shoulder at the rocky beach strewn with oysters and lined with driftwood. I, too, could hear the song of eternal harmony. There above the rocky beach and snug among the trees was our cabin. The evergreens obscured the roof's peak, but the cedar-shingled sides flanked by vertical log posts revealed where the little structure was cemented securely to the granite bedrock. A small deck, which became a dock at high tide, skirted a promontory of rock and the little dining nook faced bravely north, practically standing in the water at high tide. I loved it here and felt as bonded to the rock as the cabin. Like a native I heard the voices of my father and grandfather on the wind and my eyes looked upon the same unchangeable sights they beheld. I wanted to pass this heritage on to my children and grandchildren.

This place also evoked in me a sense of spiritual heritage because it was in this same country I first met Christ. Hotham Sound and our cabin site on Nelson Island were located at the western mouth of Jervis Inlet. Traveling east and north up this inlet for forty miles into the coastal mountains brings one to a small inlet called Princess Louisa which penetrates another four miles east under towering nine thousand foot peaks. It is one of the most beautiful places on earth. At the mouth of Louisa on a small peninsula of land is the youth camp called Malibu where my spiritual journey began thirty-four years before.

Lyza and I decided to make a pilgrimage back to this camp by attending the National Young Life Leadership Conference there in the middle of May. Our elder son, Dave, was now the White Rock/South Surrey Young Life Area director, a staff member in the organization that launched us on the Christian path. We looked forward to the rare opportunity to see him at work and to re-acquaint ourselves with our spiritual roots. We found it amazing that our son ended up working in the same ministry that led us to Christ. What goes around comes around, they say, and we were thrilled to revisit our roots during this sabbatical.

Knowing where you come from helps you understand where you are going. That is why the story of Abraham and his descendants is a necessary consideration for every one of his spiritual descendants. If we understand our spiritual heritage we are equipped with a greater sense of purpose and a desire to pass on this heritage. Abraham's inheritance is *our* inheritance. The lessons God taught his descendants are *our* lessons.

Abraham's story continues in Genesis with Jacob's descendents in Egypt where they lived for four hundred years after being chased out of Canaan by a famine. By the end of those years they were suffering as slaves in Egypt. In Exodus, the second book of the Bible, the story resumes with the birth of Moses and his call from God to take the children of Israel out of Egypt back to Canaan, the land God promised to give Abraham as an inheritance five hundred years before. This journey's events take up the next five books of the Bible: Exodus, Leviticus, Numbers, Deuteronomy, and Joshua. It culminates with the fulfillment of God's promise to give Abraham an inheritance as they conquer and possess the land, filling it with their descendants. The content of those five books is the process by which they gained their inheritance. It's filled with lessons, symbolic events, and metaphors recorded for those who would come after so that we would be able to understand what the inheritance really is. Speaking of the journeys of Israel, Paul the Apostle, in the New Testament book of Corinthians says,

Now these things happened to them as an example, and they were written for our instruction, upon whom the ends of the ages have come. (1 Corinthians 10:11)

We are the people living at the 'ends of the ages' and so these lessons are for us. Abraham's physical descendants eventually lost the land and were dispersed for two thousand years, from 70 AD until 1947. God is not finished fulfilling the promises He made to the Jews, but the fulfillment of these promises is ultimately found in Christ. Abraham's spiritual descendants (or 'seed') include all the sons of faith who have been born of the Spirit of God. The promises of inheritance made to Abraham and his descendants still apply, but their application is for us as well. The land of the inheritance is now the real estate of the soul, not a piece of real estate in the Middle East. Possessing the real estate of the soul involves bringing the peace, joy and righteousness of Christ to reign over all the parts of our inner person. Those born of Christ are the promised seed, or inheritors; the lessons of the Exodus were prepared for us.

The Exodus story begins in Egypt under slavery. To gain our inheritance we must first be delivered from Egypt, the symbolic embodiment of the slavery of sin, the tyranny of Satan and the dominion of death. It took a long time for me to recognize that I was born in Egypt. I thought I was born in the Promised Land. That promised land included Princess Louisa and Jervis Inlet. On my Dad's den wall was a picture of me when I was just two years old, taking a bath in a clam bucket on old Mac's float (he lived at the head of the inlet). My grandfather's name was on a plaque at Chatterbox Falls, commemorating pioneer boaters and the six generations of Clarkes who knew and loved Princess Louisa dating back to my great grandfather in the 1920's. It was one of the playgrounds of my privileged youth.

As we arrived at Malibu to attend the conference during our sabbatical, it looked as spectacular as ever. The pungent aroma of freshly cut cedar planks enveloped me as I sat on a bench overlooking the inlet. This place was definitely a touchstone for us. Here we met Christ, met each other and met the man who invited us to White Rock. I stared up through broken cloud cover at glaciers and snowfields suspended behind towering granite cliffs thrusting to dizzying heights on all sides of the narrow fjord. The sun struck them, creating a dazzling, almost heavenly realm of glorious reflections and bright blue skies. Down below we sat under somber gray overcast, amid the foggy mists, and though we only caught occasional glimpses of that higher sphere, we could always feel its presence.

Malibu always seemed a little like that—one thing happening on the human level where rowdy teenagers were having fun, and another thing happening on a higher spiritual plane. Every week in the summer the *Malibu Princess* unloaded 300 teenagers onto the dock from all over the U.S. and Canada to spend a week having the time of their lives. Young Life served up a mixture of water sports, competitions and entertainment geared to satisfy the fun-loving nature of teenagers, salting in penetrating messages every evening to satisfy their hunger for meaning. The appetite for truth proved as strong as the appetite for fun and many were introduced to a relationship with a personal God. Some people might be critical of Young Life's 'worldly' way of reaching kids, but after spending twenty-eight years in the established church I haven't seen a more effective approach to reaching into the world of unchurched young people. I was one of them, so maybe I am biased, but I still love the mission thirty years later and long to live more on the edge where heaven and earth meet, the way it is at Malibu.

To get people to consider heaven and the kingdom it represents, they have to first recognize the hell and the darkness that is present on earth. Egypt in the Bible context represents this kingdom of darkness. Egypt was a way of life for the Israelites and Moses had trouble getting them to conceive of a better place. At the right time, when their bondage became so cruel their lives weren't worth living anymore, they were ready to hear Moses' message of a promised land. So it is with most of us. It takes a big dose of bondage in our lives for us to see the darkness within and around us. Often human nature is blind to its need for regeneration until suffering awakens us.

When Paul the Apostle prayed that the eyes of our heart would be enlightened, he was not talking about physical eyes but about the spiritual eyes of our hearts. Most of us don't even know that our heart has eyes. Paul prayed for a spirit of wisdom and revelation because it takes divine intervention to penetrate the blindness of the heart. The Israelites were blind. I also was blind in spite of my privileged life, and all of us are blind until God opens our eyes.

Jesus healed a man blind from birth in the gospel account. The story is humorous because of the Pharisees' reaction and the healed man's response to them. The Pharisees refused to believe that the man was healed, angrily interrogating his parents, wanting them to discredit the miracle. They repeatedly questioned the man and when they denounced Jesus as a sinner, he responded, *"Whether he is a sinner, I do not know; one thing I do know, that though I was blind, now I see"* (John 9:25). The Pharisees refused to see an obvious miracle right in front of their eyes, although they were the 'enlightened' religious leaders of their day. Jesus addressed this spiritual blindness by saying,

> *"It is for judgment I came into this world, so that those who do not see may see, and that those who see may become blind." Those of the Pharisees who were with Him heard these things and said to Him, "We are not blind too, are we?' Jesus said to them, "If you were blind, you would have no sin; but since you say 'We see' your sin remains."* (John 9:39-41)

The Pharisees contended, "We see," and so they remained blind. Pride, religious guilt and duty, intellectual self-reliance, unresolved transgression of God's moral law, materialism, and sensual domination continue to blind people's spiritual eyes today. The man blind from birth was healed when he washed in the pool of Siloam after Jesus put mud on his eyes. After his eyes were opened, Jesus found him and said,

> *"Do you believe in the son of Man?" He answered and said, "And who is He, Lord, that I may believe in Him?" Jesus said to him, "You have both seen Him, and He is the One who is talking with you." And he said, "Lord, I believe." And he worshipped Him.* (John 9:35-36)

Imagine this man's wonder as he looked at the face of the one who healed him. Of all the things to see in the world around him, Jesus was the centerpiece, and the guide to all the man would see from that time forward. So we need to see Jesus, our Enlightener, in the center of our field of vision, the only One who can help us see into the meaning of the rest of life.

The Israelite slaves in Egypt needed this enlightenment as well. They had lived four hundred years in Egyptian darkness. When Moses came to set them free he not only had to break Pharaoh's power over them but he also had to open their eyes to see the sources of Egypt's darkness. The purpose of the ten plagues was to expose and judge the false gods of Egypt, letting the Hebrews clearly see those gods for what they were. Jehovah successively demonstrated his power over the fly gods, frog gods, river gods, cow gods, and sun gods. When Moses served notice that God intended to set the people free, the news brought initial joy to the Hebrews, then intense pressure and cruelty from the Egyptians. This pressure became the first of ten testings or temptations designed to prepare the people for their inheritance. At first the Hebrews welcomed Moses, but when Pharaoh would not let them go, they became bitter and spoke against him. Moses' good news became bad news.

Then God went to battle for the Hebrews, to break Pharaoh's stubbornness with ten plagues, the last one being the death of all the firstborn children in Egypt. When the death angel passed over the people, the Hebrews were saved from this plague by applying the blood of a lamb on the doorposts of their house. The death angel passed over them and their lives were preserved. The Passover feast, which the Jewish people still celebrate, comes from this event. Jesus turned the Passover celebration into the Christian celebration of communion on the eve of his crucifixion. John the Baptist said of Jesus, *"Behold the Lamb of God, who takes away the sin of the world"* (John 1:29), making the direct connection that Jesus was the Passover lamb.

The symbolism of this Old Testament story is that we, like the Hebrews, are blinded by the darkness of this 'Egyptian' world system and dependent upon the mercy of God to enlighten us and set us free. The chains of slavery around our necks are the chains of sin. Satan is our taskmaster with a whip in his hand. Only the blood of Jesus, the Passover Lamb, can finally break the slavery of sin and Satan and give us life and hope. Just as the Israelites experienced increased pressure on their lives immediately before their deliverance, many people experience the increased pressure and bondage of this world before Christ sets them free. This pressure is the first of ten tests on the pathway into the inheritance. It could be financial pressure, the pressure of a breakdown of relationship, emotional or psychological pressure, or the pressure and slavery of addictive habits. Most people's path to enlightenment leads through a valley of trouble. God allows trouble and pain in our lives to open our eyes to the ultimate emptiness and corruption of a world system that is separated from God.

My own experience was an anomaly to this pattern as there was no great pressure from the world system pushing me into an encounter with God. As Lyza and I walked the old cedar boardwalks of the camp I was reminded of just what a clueless kid I was when I first came to Malibu at sixteen years old. Watching the tidal current eddy past the dining room and into the narrow passage to the inlet, I thought about my background. I was glad for Young Life's very non-denominational approach to dealing with issues of the Christian faith. I was glad they went after normal everyday kids like myself. Young Life knew its basic mission and stuck to it—the simplicity of relationship with Christ. That was a good thing for me because my spiritual experience was meager; my brief encounters with my mother's Episcopalian roots amounted to an occasional Easter or

Christmas service and one teenage run-in with confirmation. My fondest memories of that experience were the spitball wars in the back of the class and the church-sponsored junior high dances on Friday nights. At the end of the confirmation class I knelt before a conical-capped bishop as he prayed for me. It was all very serious, but I didn't get the point. My eyes definitely were not opened through becoming an official member of the church at confirmation. The strong currents of youth, like the rapids in front of me, carried me right past the bedrock of faith.

As I contemplated my past, my attention was drawn to a tall figure waiting in the line-up for lunch with hands in his pockets, hooded against the rain, looking incongruous both by his height and by the obvious age gap between him and the surrounding college-age crowd. "Now there's an old dog like myself," I thought. Our eyes met and we grinned at each other in mutual recognition of our similar vintage. As the doors opened and the crowd surged into the dining room, we edged toward each other and sat at the same table, discovering over lunch that we were about the same age and had been at Malibu during the sixties and early seventies. Over the next few days we became friends, and spent a lot of our free time together, sharing the same cabin with our sons and eight or nine other young men. Dick was a pilot and traveled around the world, but Christ had definitely become his reference point, too, at Malibu.

"Hey, Dick, you gonna go water skiing?"

The weather was abysmally cold and wet. He sized me up. "Are you?"

"Well, I thought I might if you do."

"Are there gonna be any babes to impress? That's why I always used to do that stuff—to impress the babes."

I observed his thinning hair and took note of my own slightly sagging stomach.

"I don't think it'll be an issue, Dick."

Thirty minutes later we were shivering in the wind and rain on the dock after cajoling each other into this last gasp attempt to recapture our youthful prime. Not many 'babes' were braving the elements as the ski boat slowly hauled Dick out of the numbing water while he screamed at the driver to go faster. He made about two hundred yards when he crashed with a tremendous splash and they had to drag him back into the boat like a salvaged log. Later at dinner, I couldn't resist relating to the cute server with the spiked hair how we, the old dogs, had gone water skiing that afternoon in the rain and how I made it all the way around and even jumped the wake as I came back into the dock.

"Some people couldn't take the cold water and had to be hauled back in the boat."

Dick, pretending he didn't hear any of this, engaged the girl with his eyes and said, "You are just the best waitress we've had and the prettiest. Do you have a boyfriend? Have you ever met my son?"

Dick was fun and he reminded me of my teenage years. Those years were great for me. Far from tasting some of the bitter fruit of Egypt, I was in the lap of some of the most benign circumstances life could offer. My childhood was happy, my parents loving, and the physical gifts of health and natural ability were all in my favor. Yet hearing the simple message each night at Malibu when I was sixteen arrested my attention to the reality of God's love for me, and I just fell in love with Him. The speakers at camp made it plain and simple. Jesus died on a cross for me and God was offering personal relationship through Him. I figured if Jesus was what God was really like, He was worthy of my love. When I prayed a prayer of surrender on a rock overlooking the rapids, I knew something happened.

Looking back thirty-four years later, what a significant encounter it had been. Sin? Bondage? I was not greatly convicted of it then. The darkness of my nature became more evident in the next three years of high school amid the social free-for-all of football, skiing, and girls. I quickly got into weekend drinking and carousing. The only spiritual counselors I knew were Young Life people and they must have doubted my Malibu conversion. My reputation was much more of wild exploits than any Christian virtues. Some distorted evidence of my faith periodically emerged when I, in an inebriated state, expounded Christ's salvation to a fellow imbiber.

Needless to say, such witness carried little effect, but it did reveal the seed of the Holy Spirit planted in me. I was still a citizen of Egypt living off its offerings, unaware as yet of the ultimate emptiness and slavery it inevitably engenders. The time came to call me out. To call me away to a land that God would show me. I had no idea how powerful the force was that had set me free. However, that seed was a time capsule of grace that eventually completed its work.

Lyza, on the other hand, knew she was a refugee from Egypt. The instability of divorce forced her mother with her four children to travel around Washington and British Columbia in search of work as an interior designer. Lyza's mom held it all together and loved her children, but the search for relational and financial stability took its toll on the whole family. By the teenage years, Lyza finally had a steady stepfather and a consistent address so she was in the same school for those crucial years. In her sixteenth year, the vice principal called her to his office one day and informed her that her closest brother, John, after a mysterious disappearance of several weeks, had taken his own life. Nobody was sure what went through his mind or why he did it, but Lyza was crushed. Only eighteen months apart, she and her brother had clung to each other through their topsy-turvy childhood and she was dumbfounded by his choice to end his life.

Weeks after this shattering event, Lyza went to a Young Life weekend camp in Warm Beach, Washington. She was wide open to the message of Christ's love, His forgiveness, and especially His offer to come into her heart and establish relationship with her. To her this was an amazing offer. She never heard anything like it before. No one had told her about Jesus, about why He died on the cross, or that a person could know God personally. Like many people she had only vague concepts of religion and churches and a smattering of Catholicism from her parents' background. The message of Jesus was a message of God taking the initiative to find her. It was so refreshing, made so much sense and was so real that when the offer came from the speaker to 'ask Christ into your heart', she simply had no resistance to it, and found a quiet spot alone in her cabin bunk to pray.

Both Lyza and I knew that life was different after encountering Christ. Once your eyes are opened you can no longer pretend you don't see. Darkness becomes darker and light becomes lighter and even though it took some time for both of us to navigate out of the pitfalls of our diverse backgrounds, a course was set that would lead us into a new way to live and eventually lead us to each other. Having the eyes of the heart opened is a radical event. It is not a religious experience (as the blind man found out in his run-in with the Pharisees), but a relational experience.

The revolutionary nature of it all was certainly evident to Lyza and me in retrospect as we surveyed the thirty-two years following our initial experience at Malibu. Walking back to board the *Malibu Princess* at the close of the conference, the words of Charles Wesley's hymn we sang in those early Young Life days came back to mind.

> *Long my imprisoned spirit lay,*
> *Fast bound in sin and nature's night*
> *Thine eye diffused a quickening ray,*
> *I woke, the dungeon flamed with light.*
> *My chains fell off; my heart was free,*
> *I rose, went forth, and followed thee.*

For us, following Him had meant new associations, meeting each other, a new country to live in and a new family of Christ to live for. The journey back from the conference on the *Malibu Princess* was like stepping into a time warp for us. The old boat still looked the same as when our romance started. Standing in the bow with a cold spring wind in our faces and the peaks of Queen's Reach sliding by, we nudged each other, both looking at the same spot on the deck under the captain's bridge. I nuzzled Lyza's neck. "That's where we were." She gave me the sideways reproach look. "Yeah, and you should be ashamed of yourself." I grinned unapologetically and tried to kiss her again even though we were on a crowded deck. We had spent a good deal of our homeward bound trip on the Princess those many years ago kissing under the captain's bridge, sealing our newfound relationship. It had been a good choice, a good life, and a great adventure. We felt confident that the sabbatical year stretching before us would be the same. We were grateful that a far-flung patch of wilderness called Jervis Inlet was the site of both our natural and spiritual heritage. It was time now to head back to Seattle and the *Fred Free*, the little wooden sailboat we'd go north to Alaska in this summer, and into a new wilderness experience. I hugged Lyza closer and thought of Dick for a moment. "Well, Dick, you may have impressed a few babes in your day, but I got the best 'babe' of the bunch."

Casting Off

The Red Sea, Exodus 14
The Second Temptation – The Power of Evil

The Ten Temptations: 2. The Power of Evil… Pharaoh & Chariots

1. Pressures
of Life

Seven Stages of the Spiritual Journey:

1. The Passover in Egypt	2. Red Sea Crossing	3. Mt. Sinai Visitation
		4. Wilderness

Chapter Three

Balancing my weight, one foot on the newly painted bowsprit and one on its port support cable, I tried to gauge my chances of successfully leaping to the dock heaving up and down a few feet in front of me. Actually it was *me* heaving up and down in the fresh seas rolling into the Mercer Island shoreline in front of my mother's house. I performed this acrobatic ritual every time I disembarked from the sailboat where it lay moored between dock and piling, but this time it was especially tricky, not only because of the wind but also because I held two wet paint brushes in one hand and a half litre of blue paint in the other. An inner voice said, "Don't do it, this is not smart!" but it was overruled by imprudence and I grabbed the jib stay and stepped on the slick bowsprit for the precarious plunge to the dock. Plunge—into the lake, it almost became—as my foot slipped off, my hand raked down the stay and my torso swung crazily over the green waves, held back from an inglorious baptism only by my other thigh and leg tangled in the cables.

The exasperation at feeling the wet stickiness over my left arm cancelled out the pain I felt as I watched with stunned fascination the paint roller slide to the bottom of the lake, leaving little globules of blue paint suspended in its track. As the droplets wiggled their way to the surface and exploded in oily rainbow slicks, I hoisted my bruised appendages over the bowsprit and glared ruefully at the mess I'd made. It wasn't until later I discovered the radical new Picasso design on the deck and cabin. Where the wind had carried them, ocean blue paramecium-like creatures with long whip-like tails now decorated the freshly painted white and gray surfaces.

This kind of thing usually happened when I had only a couple of days to get the work done and was pushed beyond all normal boundaries of time and caution to get the boat fixed up for our few weeks' vacation. What a luxury to have time to just enjoy the process. The simplicity of physical labor, food and rest was a welcome lifestyle change. I spent two weeks poking around in the bowels of the boat doing engine maintenance, painting and caulking. It was important that everything was in good working order, and I did all the jobs I always put off because of tight time schedules. I rewired the lights, the bilge pump and anchor winch, replaced the ancient cable rigging, stay fasteners and the shims around the mast, retied the sails, and replaced the halyard blocks. The little sailboat got a new lease on life. Making it fit to sail and live in was our ticket to independence, reducing our world to twenty-six feet of self-sufficient living space. I loved the freedom. Wherever we dropped anchor was our own backyard, whether in the tiniest cove in the wilderness or amid the high-rises of Vancouver's harbour.

Later, sitting on the old dock with a ham sandwich from Mother's larder, I reminisced about my childhood on this waterfront property. I still knew every rock in the bulkhead, every tree, hump, and hollow in the woods behind. On a whim, I had even driven the old roads that I had walked to school—primary, elementary, and senior high. Sometimes my memories of Mercer Island seemed far removed, like a life on another planet, but it felt right to be here now, eating meals, talking with family, and working with my hands each day. It was good to have time to drop in at my brothers' and sister's houses and join in some of their weekly events. Most of my siblings still lived near each other and our parents, and had maintained a pleasant family intercourse through the years. This rare opportunity for family connection reminded me what our commitment to Christ had cost us. I didn't question or regret our choices, but I knew I had missed out on a lot.

Through the years I felt a little schizophrenic about my double life as the Canadian pastor and the American son, but as I now enjoyed the extended time on Mercer Island with my family, I knew the separate parts of my life were really part of a larger harmonious plan. The shift to marriage, Christian activism, and Canada at twenty years old was very abrupt and had pretty well left this whole life in the dust. Of course, we came home for holidays and short visits, but all too quickly it was back to an entirely different existence. Experiencing this dichotomy was part of what happened to us. Jesus' call to discipleship had been a revolutionary, upending transaction. He said things like,

> *"If anyone wishes to come after Me, he must deny himself, and take up his cross and follow Me. For whoever wishes to save his life shall lose it; but whoever loses his life for My sake will find it. For what will it*

profit a man if he gains the whole world and forfeits his soul?" (Matthew 16:24-26a)

We couldn't just add Christianity on top of everything else in our lives and expect that nothing would change. Our personal encounter with Christ was the beginning of a whole new direction and purpose. *"Therefore if anyone is in Christ, he is a new creature; the old things passed away; behold, new things have come"* (2 Corinthians 5:17). Part of the activation process of 'all things becoming new' was water baptism, the obedience that Jesus clearly commanded. Water baptism was the outward sign, or seal, of the inward regeneration He brought about through a person's declaration of faith. Baptism was the catalyst for separation from the past, and the call to discipleship and service. It was the second major step in the spiritual journey that contributed to the radical changes Lyza and I experienced. It also set us on a path of progressive regeneration where we came to understand that life is a journey with a meaningful destination. God will not allow us to stand still. He moves us toward the inheritance He has prepared. In the Exodus story, the Red Sea is the symbolic equivalent of water baptism. God moved the people quickly from their Passover experience to a Red Sea experience. The account of the process of getting them there is insightful.

> *"Now you shall eat it* [the Passover] *in this manner: with your loins girded, your sandals on your feet, and your staff in your hand; and you shall eat it in haste—it is the Lord's Passover."* (Exodus 12:11)

They couldn't sit around the table too long and neither can we if we want to go forward into God's plans for our lives. God appeared in a pillar of fire by night and a pillar of cloud by day to personally lead them through the suburbs of Egypt to finally camp (between two mountains called Pihahiroth and Migdol) on the shoreline of the Red Sea. Then Pharaoh's heart hardened again and he gathered his legions and came after them to drag them back to Egypt. God led them to a place where they were boxed in, with a sea in front of them, two mountains on either side, and Pharaoh's army on the fourth side. He was forcing a showdown with Egypt.

As Pharaoh drew near, the sons of Israel... cried out to the Lord. Then they said to Moses, "Is it because there were no graves in Egypt that you have taken us away to die in the wilderness? Why have you dealt with us in this way, bringing us out of Egypt?" (Exodus 14:10,11)

You would think after seeing God turn the Nile to blood, smite the Egyptians with hail, frogs, lice, etc., that these people would have a little more insight and a lot more trust. Instead they sang the refrain that came up every time they were tested on the journey to Canaan. "Why, oh why, did God allow this or that to happen? We want to go back to Egypt where we were secure."

This predicament of the Israelites is regularly mirrored in the experience of new Christians. Upon receiving the forgiveness of Christ, initially people often have a blissful kind of spiritual honeymoon in which they glimpse the glorious promises of Christ and taste of His presence in a remarkable way. However, after the honeymoon the bottom can seem to drop out. One morning they wake up not feeling so wonderful anymore. God feels distant and former habits and ways of life become attractive again. Old friends invite them back into the old lifestyle and they are tempted to go back, and sometimes do, which causes them to wonder if their spiritual experiences were just some emotional or religious phase. Their faith is in crisis, they feel hemmed in, and Pharaoh and all his hosts are breathing down their necks.

Before this Red Sea crisis God protected the Israelites from facing the heat of battle. Knowing they were too tender in this new life to face warfare, He piloted them around the rough spots.

Now when Pharaoh had let the people go, God did not lead them by the way of the land of the Philistines, even though it was near; for God said, "The people might change their minds when they see war, and return to Egypt." (Exodus 13:17)

It's amazing how God monitors our development and guards our path, not letting us experience certain testings until we are ready for them. However, now it was time to test them, time to expose them to the real strength of Egypt, and remind them whose power delivered them so they would learn to live out of that resource. The situation was desperate, the people were terrified, and only God's pillar of fire and cloud separated them from the Egyptians.

Then the Egyptians chased after them with all the horses and chariots of Pharaoh, his horsemen and his army, and they overtook them camping by the sea... (Exodus 14:9)

Moses cried out to the Lord and He responded—

Then the Lord said to Moses, "Why are you crying out to Me? Tell the sons of Israel to go forward." (Exodus 14:15)

Forward? Forward meant death by drowning, but in God's economy we are always to move forward, never backward. Forward seemed impossible, and, in fact, God wanted to reveal that truly escaping the power of Egypt *is* impossible for man. They needed to know that only a supernatural intervention could deliver them.

"And as for you, lift up your staff and stretch out your hand over the sea and divide it, and the sons of Israel shall go through the midst of the sea on dry land." (Exodus 14:16)

Many of us have seen Charlton Heston's Hollywood version of what happened next. The Israelites marched down into the sea with great walls of water on either side and emerged on the Sinai Peninsula. Once God removed the protecting pillar of fire, Pharaoh and his minions followed them into the path between the walls of water. Then God pulled the plug and the mighty waters engulfed them. The Israelites, jaws agape, must have had Moses' words ringing in their ears,

"Do not fear! Stand by and see the salvation of the Lord which He will accomplish for you today; for the Egyptians whom you have seen today, you will never see them again forever." (Exodus 14: 13)

Imagine the joy of those Hebrews, oppressed under Pharaoh's whips and terrorized in a system as brutal as early slavery in America. In one stroke, their oppressors were utterly destroyed.

> *The waters returned and covered the chariots and the horsemen, even Pharaoh's entire army that had gone into the sea after them; not even one of them remained."* (Exodus 14:28)

A hush must have fallen over the Israeli camp. As they stared in shock, the roaring waves subsided and perhaps a helmet, a chariot wheel or a whip washed up at their feet. Then the joyous sound of a tambourine broke through the silence as Miriam, Moses' and Aaron's sister, danced jubilantly to its beat and sang prophetically of victory and freedom.

> *"I will sing unto the Lord for He is highly exalted; the horse and its rider He has hurled into the sea."* (Exodus 15:1)

Soon the whole nation roared out hilariously Miriam's song of praise and thanksgiving to God as they realized their enemies were gone. Dead! The same stroke that administered death to the Egyptians administered life and freedom to them.

For Moses and the children of Israel, crossing the Red Sea finally pulled them irrevocably out of the Egyptian system and established them as a separate people. After four hundred years of living as slaves under the Egyptians, they needed to regain their identity as God's people. Pharaoh and his hosts represent the devil and the complicit forces of sinful nature that hold men in the grip of slavery. Nothing can reform Satan or defiled human nature. Victory over the power of sin is only possible through death: first, through the death of Christ, which broke the legal tyranny of sin over mankind; and secondly, through the believer's identification with His death through baptism, which breaks the tyranny of sin over that individual's life. Therefore, the significance of baptism cannot be understated. It is no less than a believer's personal sharing in the death and resurrection of Jesus Christ. It is more than a symbolic ritual; it is a step of obedience that releases power into a person's soul to actualize Christ's victory in his or her life.

Some people commit to Christ but don't get baptized, and often chronically struggle with the old life. They cannot seem to leave it behind. Power is released for them to make the break after they finally submit to the baptism that Christ clearly commands. The empowerment of the Holy Spirit to break sin's hold is baptism's greatest benefit. As the Israelites stood on the shores of Sinai, a great barrier separated them from their past—the Egyptians could not get to them and they could not get to Egypt even if they wanted to. An irrevocable line of demarcation had been drawn.

Unorthodox, creative and fun were words to describe those early days of our baptism into the Christian revolution of the late sixties, an expression of faith commensurate with the times. It didn't occur to me at the time that our activities might be offensive to various established church traditions—our approach to baptism was probably one of the clearest examples of this. My own and Lyza's baptism had been part of the hurly burly days of university life. We spontaneously got baptized with a number of other new campus believers in some church in Bellingham whose name I don't even remember. What I do remember is the close encounters I was having with God, which paralleled what happened to the disciples in the book of Acts. We learned that Christianity was not just propositional but experiential as well. I'm not saying we saw a lot of miracles as they did, but we saw some, and got enough of a taste of the supernatural reality and the presence of God's Spirit to realize this stuff was real.

It's one thing to approach religion as so many different sets of mythologies to be evaluated for their universal and symbolic meanings. It's another to consider that the literal account of the Bible is historical, supernatural, and ongoing in its ramifications. Approached like this, it is nothing short of astonishing, liberating, joyful and terrifying. Some might think me a romantic or a mystic, but my personal experience gave a satisfactory enough empirical base to accept the Bible as truth and reality. Having embraced it as such from the beginning of my Christian walk, I have had cause for nothing but further satisfaction up to the present hour. Anything less would not have interested me and would certainly have not been as much fun.

As far as doing the business of Christianity, we did it as we saw it presented in the New Testament. We didn't ask permission; we just did it. We did the Young Life thing, but I'm afraid we even went a bit beyond Young Life's comfort zone. We went to the high schools and streets and beaches and preached a simple gospel. We established a coffeehouse in an old bus depot, brought in Christian music groups, began Bible studies, and started all night prayer meetings. From that outpost of faith we went out on the street along the waterfront and into the bars, mixed with the rowdies and bikers and told whoever would listen of God's love and grace.

When it came to baptism, we did it as occasion warranted. Philip, the evangelist in Acts, just ran up, jumped into a man's chariot as he was going down the road and explained the scripture to him. Then they stopped at a roadside pond and baptized the man (Acts 8:38). One night in the coffeehouse (more like one o'clock in the morning), a couple of longhaired travelers listened and responded to our witness, praying for Jesus to come into their hearts. We then rose up, walked across the street and waded out into the bay to baptize the two young men. Others were baptized in the local municipal gravel pit, which had filled up with water.

Looking back, I'll be the first to admit some deficiencies existed in our approach, but the immediacy of an encounter with Christ and the necessity of making a break with destructive lifestyles made the reality of separation to God through baptism a potent experience in those days. Our whole lives reflected the truth that life with God and entry into His inheritance was not just business as usual, but was a radical confronting of our motivations for living and a submission to God's will. It was a full immersion, not a religious sprinkling. So, in this sort of mentality, we also left behind our American life and moved to Canada. Now, thirty years later, we were leaving America for Canada again, this time by boat for a very different kind of journey.

As we finished our last preparations for the months afloat and said goodbye to the old surroundings, I knew clearly that Christ never wanted to take away from me all that was good of my past life—He only wanted to sanctify it. So many are afraid that when God confronts the darkness of sin in their lives, it is all about what He will take away from them. Such perceptions of Him are distortions of our own making because we don't really understand His nature. What He takes away is only that which hinders the reign of love in our lives. In my case, physically removing me in my teens from my secure and lovely surroundings was necessary for my spiritual development. I never would have learned to put my security and trust in Him without this separation, but now from this vantage point thirty years later, I could exult in both my natural and spiritual heritage.

So with everything stowed, one morning we cast off our lines and chugged at six knots per hour along Mercer Island's west shore, another pleasant stroll down memory lane for me. Many of the childhood places were still there, the McDonald's house on one side of my folks and the Koons on the other. Tommy Koon, Lindsay McDonald and I were all the same age and used to scamper from one front yard to another and from one kitchen to another, especially in the summer when swimming in the lake was the primary activity. Farther north, the Kenkman's boathouse came into view where we played sponge tag, and then we passed Dickie Burdell's house, the only guy in the neighborhood who could water ski better than me. He could jump the wake of his dad's ski boat and land four feet outside the opposite wake. A mile further down, the relatives' places came into view. Nowadays the old landmarks were being pushed aside by the imposing mega mansions of Seattle's rich and famous. Microsoft executives claimed the choice lots on the lakefront and a former Seattle Seahawk quarterback's house perched like a storybook castle just down from my sister's house on the hill. Bill Gates staked his claim over on the Bellevue side and we could see his huge house blending into the hill as we rounded the end of Mercer Island.

I felt sad that the spiraling property values and taxes that accompanied development precluded any of the children in our family from affording to inherit our old homesteads. None of us had chosen very lucrative professions. My uncle's and my aunt's waterfront properties, where we had just given a ritual blast of the air horn, were under the same pressures. My mother's family, the Vinals, had lived in a tent on their waterfront property in the dirty thirties while Elwin Vinal, my grandfather, built the old family home up on the hill. All three of his daughters ended up living on the lake.

In those early days there was no floating bridge to the Seattle shoreline, just an old ferry called the *Dawn* my dad worked on as a teenager. Those were rustic days when my Grandfather Clarke would strap on his Colt 45's to settle a dispute between farmers on top of the island—a far cry from the effusion of wealth and modern architecture now adorning the lakefront and the skyscrapers on both the Seattle and Bellevue side of Lake Washington. The family homesteads, like the old days they represented, slipped behind our wake. Ultimately, the modern wave of prosperity might sweep them away, but I would never forget the love and character and history forged in those places. It was an internal heritage I carried with me.

We steered underneath the two floating bridges now connecting the Island and Bellevue to Seattle and entered the ships' canal.

The crew—Lyza and me, Ginette, and Boaz—were full of anticipation at the beginning of our voyage. We were headed to the border of Alaska and back, over two thousand miles round trip. Bo already took ownership of the bow, tail wagging, as we passed boats and houses at close quarters through the ships' canal, an umbilical cord of water connecting Lake Washington to Lake Union. We motored on, under bridges, past boat works with names like *Foss* and *Leclerq*, between the huge ocean-going seiners of the Seattle shipyards until Chittendon locks emptied the fresh water into salty Puget Sound.

We jostled into the lock chamber like cattle, fifteen to twenty yachts, sailboats and runabouts. The fresh water world of mallard ducks, green lawns and willow trees slowly disappeared until we sank down in the lock chamber to the saltwater level, leaving the laky smells behind. A crowd of visitors looked down on us from the walkways to witness this baptism out of the innards of the city of Seattle and into the waterways that led to Alaska.

The seagulls, the spawning salmon, and the wonderfully smelly tidal odor waited for the two heavy doors to open and greeted us with cries, splashes and a tangy new world. I strained at the tiller to avoid hitting glossy Chris Crafts in the outflowing current. Navigating the channel, green buoys to the starboard and red buoys to the port, a resident sea lion balanced on a bell buoy to salute our passage. As the mouth of the locks closed behind us, we felt cast adrift like the Israelites must have felt when the waters of the Red Sea closed behind them. They were left to wander in a sea of sand and we to wander upon the inky blue waters of Puget Sound and beyond.

Earthen Vessels

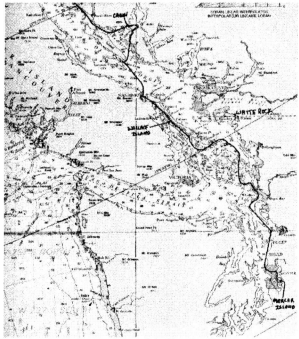

Reproduced with the permission of the Canadian Hydrographic Service

The Bitter Waters of Marah, Exodus 15
The Third Temptation – The Bitter Experiences of Life

The Ten Temptations: **3. The Bitterness of Life (Waters at Marah)**

1. Pressures 2. Power
   of Life   of Evil

Seven Stages of the Spiritual Journey:

1. The Passover in Egypt	2. Red Sea Crossing	3. Mt. Sinai Visitation
		4. Wilderness

Chapter Four

What began as a light headwind now blustered straight down Admiralty Inlet, sending regular dousings of cold spray over our shoulders and heads. Motoring into headwinds often brought the downside of open cockpit boating trickling down my neck and leaking into my shoes. Six or seven hours of such treatment in a heavy brawling sea could severely strain my relationship with *Fred*. Today the choppy seas were unexpected as they often are, but my sense of confidence in the tight little ship was higher than usual because of all our attentive labours. Then the ominous shout came from below.

"It's leaking on the bunks!"

"It can't be. Where?"

"Down the hatch!"

"But the hatch has just been resealed"

"It's pouring down the insides of the hull as well."

Just about anything could be handled on this old wooden sailboat except the dreaded portent of misery—"Water on the bunks!" In the years before we finally resorted to a plywood-fiberglass solution on the front deck, the original yellow cedar planks always leaked no matter how many ways we tried caulking them. We used to lie on our backs in the narrow berths, waiting for the leaks to pop out a seam in the ceiling or run off a joist in a sudden "plop" onto our pillow. Sometimes a leak had the audacity to splatter me between the eyes just as I was dropping off to sleep. The worst were the fifth column drips that held back until the dead of night and then parachuted in to concentrate their forces on the foot of the bed. In the morning I would wake up warm, but wet, like a two-year old in the crib, afraid to move or the cold air would hit.

So at the words, "The bunks are wet," with barely a moment's contemplation, I swung to starboard, making for Edmonds Marina, the nearest respite, now surfing a following sea toward the narrow opening in the breakwater. Later, in the artificial calm of the marina, as I resolutely scanned the channel and willed the wind to subside, I felt a cloud of depression descend on me. The cause of my discouragement was the recognition that after all the effort, the *Fred*

Free was, after all, still *Fred*, a sixty-year old Norwegian pilot sailboat that was going to leak on me. He was a Sherman tank of the seas. Sailboat, maybe, but built more like a tug, with oak ribs bolted to one-and-a-half-inch yellow cedar hull planks reinforced laterally with thick two by sixes. He was only twenty-six feet long without the bowsprit, but fully eight feet wide in his beam. When hauled out of the water the huge five-foot keel made him look like an iceberg with more underneath the water than above. Approached from the stern his wide beam reminded one of a pregnant duck.

Yet he was not altogether without grace. From a distance he looked like a white seagull primly afloat on the sea. At rest, he was steady and a joy to be on when conditions were right. He lived up to his legend of stolid seaworthiness through three generations. It was just that *Fred* was not overly solicitous of his inhabitants' creature comforts. He was prone to dampness, perfumed with diesel fumes, and deadly effective at dispersing cuts and bumps and head lacerations from his beams with protruding bolt ends.

Maybe that's why *Fred* was always a 'he'. Rough and ready, good-natured and amiable, but insensitive, unyielding, and tough on his children, even while coddling them on the bosom of a Gulf Island paradise. *Fred* was my father's boat, and behaved like one of my father's sons. I heard that his name came originally from a L'il Orphan Annie comic strip, but the *Fred Free* always reminded me of my dad.

After two weeks of painting, caulking, polishing, face-lifting, even installing new appurtenances like the brass barometer clock, new light fixtures and even a spice rack, I thought that this time we had really fixed him. I had rewired the whole boat after thirty years of not knowing which wire went to what. This was the ultimate overhaul for *Fred* in preparation for his once-in-a-lifetime trip to Alaska. I should have known better than to think things had changed. *Fred* would probably always leak, but his essential personality never failed to cast a mystic spell on me even after some of our worst falling-outs.

People are like that. In essence they are usually lovable, but also invested with serious defects of character and construction. These defects cause offence to others and open the door to breakdown, pain and bitterness. Even when God reforms people, their personalities stay essentially the same. The temperament, faults and foibles usually remain engrained in their basic construction. That's the agony and ecstasy of life, of marriage, of working and of living with all kinds of people. On the one hand we hope, dream and strive for something better; on the other hand, human weakness in us and around us frustrates those dreams. Nothing ever seems to happen like it is supposed to and we are left with disappointment. Learning to accept this paradox and embrace it as the way God allows life to be helps bring a peace of a different kind. As the Apostle Paul said in the Bible, *"But we have this treasure in earthen vessels, so that the surpassing greatness of the power may be of God and not from ourselves..."* (2 Corinthians 4:7). We are stuck being 'earthen vessels' but also having treasure within.

I knew this trip was bound to be full of setbacks and disappointments, but I still longed to fulfill this cherished dream. I remember several years before gazing longingly up the channels running north between distant misty mountains dreaming I could sail on for hundreds of miles up British Columbia's west coast and into Alaska's inland waterways. The route could take months on *Fred*, including all the side trips into fjords and bays along the way. I knew there was no end of these inland passages. The adventure, the wildlife, the fishing was only a remote wish then. With only three or four weeks of vacation each year, we would never have enough time to do it before the gravitational call of ministry would force us home.

This time it was different. Time stretched before us like the blue horizon, yet cold water had already splashed on our idyllic imaginings and a niggling doubt hovered over us that maybe *Fred* was too old and faulty a craft to handle the challenge. Probably my dreams of this trip were like the vessel conveying us there, full of promise at a distance but fraught with problems up close.

The morning dawned bright and tranquil in Edmonds and we ran with the ebbing tide up the broad waterways of Saratoga Channel past the pulp mills of Everett, through the LaConner Slough and out into the sparkling reaches of Bellingham Bay and the American San Juans. After running all day to the monotonous beat of the Perkins diesel, we followed the late May sun into an anchorage off Clark Island. My spirits were brighter as I patted *Fred* on his stern and said, "Freddie boy, if you're up to it, then I'm up to it. I've got a few creaky joints, too, but what else is life for if we don't chase a few dreams."

As I contemplated the challenge ahead, I knew there would probably be times when rain would fall for days and we would be confined under tarps in a leaky cabin. At least, I thought wryly, our journey through the wilderness of British Columbia's north coast would probably serve as an appropriate backdrop for consideration of Israel's trials during their journey through the wilderness of Sinai.

Abraham's dream to inherit the land of Canaan and fill it with his descendants was destined to include a passage through a desert wilderness. Although Abraham wasn't alive to see it come to pass, Moses led those descendants towards Canaan through the Sinai desert country. In our consideration of the inheritance, this wilderness was a very important stage of the journey. Here was where the Israelites were tested and where, through difficult times, God prepared them to obtain their inheritance. At the end of what became a forty-year ordeal, the purpose was clear.

> *"All the commandments that I am commanding you today you shall be careful to do, that you may live and multiply, and go in and possess the land which the Lord swore to give to your forefathers. You shall remember all the way which the Lord your God has led you in the wilderness these forty years,* **that He might humble you, testing you, to know what was in your heart, whether you would keep His commandments or not.** *He humbled you and let you be hungry, and fed you with manna which you did not know, nor did your fathers know, that He might make you understand that man does not live by bread alone, but man lives by everything that proceeds out of the mouth of the Lord."* (Deuteronomy 8:1-3, emphasis added)

This was suffering with a purpose and design. God led them into the desert. On purpose! He could have taken them an easier way, but He wanted to reveal what was in their hearts and to reveal Himself. The above scripture even says that He (God) let them be hungry. He wanted to raise them to a higher level, to teach them to hunger for His word even more than for bread. Obtaining an inheritance requires training and discipline; it takes time. *"An inheritance gained hurriedly at the beginning, will not be blessed in the end"* (Proverbs 20:21). God's people need to experience God as father, the father who loves His children enough to prepare them for life. *"Thus you are to know in your heart that the Lord your God was disciplining you just as a man disciplines his son"* (Deuteronomy 8:5).

The riches of an inheritance is heady stuff, not easy to handle. We have seen examples of a young person getting too much wealth too easily and how quickly it can lead to his destruction. Wouldn't God be even more careful to prepare spiritual children for eternal riches?

All of us have periods in our lives that we could term a 'wilderness'. A time of dryness, confusion, trials and suffering for extended periods of time. In some ways, life itself is a wilderness from beginning to end, full of temptation and difficulty and sorrow. Yet, if we see a greater purpose behind it all, we have peace. Finding meaning in suffering is one of the most fundamental spiritual challenges of life. Most major religions of the world in one way or another attempt to account for the problem of evil, pain and suffering in the world. At the very heart of Christianity the explanation for pain in the world and the ultimate resolution of suffering is found in the cross that Jesus died upon. The preaching of the cross reconciles us to God and the ongoing application of the truths hidden in that cross progressively reconciles us to the sufferings of life. The secret of victory contained in the cross is hidden within the wilderness journey, to be discerned and revealed with each test as it unfolds. If we grasp that traversing a wilderness is meant to lead to a rich inheritance then trials and sufferings take on a new meaning.

No one wants to suffer just for the sake of suffering, but suffering has a value and even nobility if it has a purpose such as sacrificing one's life to save or help another. Many novels or movie plots give meaning to suffering by playing off this kind of sacrifice, and it resonates with our hearts because it is an eternal theme. God Himself, in Christ, was willing to suffer for a purpose. Having won for us the eternal inheritance of everlasting life it is now important for Him to prepare us for it. God designs the desert experiences in our lives to build His character in us and to perfect His nature of love within us. Trials and suffering are part of that process.

Coming to terms with this concept is a big challenge for all of us because our tendency is to question God's character for allowing life to be this way. We tend to get bitter over life's trials. Experiencing life strengthens and empowers people or it crushes and hardens them. We either get bitter or we get better. People have their own burdens to carry, their own set of circumstances, and it appears that some are handed a much harder set of circumstances than others. But we can only live one life, our own, and make choices for one person, ourselves. Ultimately, we answer to only one Person, God, and comparing our lot to other people only invites further resentment.

God designed the wilderness testings to teach the Israelites very specific things, and all of these lessons have a counterpart in our spiritual pilgrimage today. God sets up the classroom of life and we must pass His tests to go to the next grade. If we flunk a grade, we have to repeat it; we can learn our lessons quickly but we can't skip any grades. The Old Testament story is a metaphor to give us a visual picture of the lessons we will face. Paul clarifies this in the New Testament in his letter to the Corinthian church.

"For I do not want you to be unaware, brethren, that our fathers were all under the cloud and all passed through the sea; and all were baptized into Moses in the cloud and in the sea; and all ate the same spiritual food; and all drank the same spiritual drink, for they were drinking from a spiritual rock which followed them; and the rock was Christ." (I Corinthians 10:1-4)

The rock was Christ? Passing through the sea was baptism? They ate spiritual food and drank spiritual drink? All these allusions are actual events in the wilderness and hold special meaning for each of us in our wilderness experiences in this life. When interpreted and understood, they can illumine our eyes to see God's hand guiding us into our inheritance. *"Now these things happened to them as an example, and they were written for our instruction, upon whom the ends of the ages have come"* (I Corinthians 10:11).

It's incredible that God took the trouble to order the events of a nation's history in order to give us spiritual insight for our lives. God orders history to reveal Himself and this applies not only to Jewish history but all of human history. In the book of Numbers, chapter 14, and verses 22-23, it is interesting to read,

"Surely all the men who have seen My glory and My signs which I performed in Egypt and in the wilderness, yet have put Me to the test these ten times and have not listened to my voice, shall by no means see the land which I swore to their fathers...."

According to this scripture there were ten testings or crisis points in Israel's journey to the Promised Land—ten times when the Israelites went head to head with God over some kind of issue. The verse says that the Israelites were putting God to the test, but God was also testing them. Ten times they were tested and ten times they failed. Each one of these trials has a specific symbolic meaning and an application to our lives. What they went through, we go through in our spiritual journey. If we can understand their testing we can also gain insight into interpreting our trials. The Israelites could have crossed the desert from Egypt to Canaan in about eight days if they traveled straight through, but it took them forty years! And a whole generation died in the desert.

"Today if you hear His voice, do not harden your hearts as when they provoked Me, as in the day of trial in the wilderness, where your fathers tried Me by testing Me...As I swore in My wrath, 'They shall not enter my rest.'" (Hebrews 3:7-9,11)

It's important that we understand and pass the tests of our life because we could experience the same tests again and again, just like the Israelites. Some people spend their whole lives going round and round the same issues. Many of us die never having learned the lessons God tried to teach us.

We have already examined two of the Israelites' testings. One at Passover when the people experienced the increased pressure from Pharaoh before their deliverance and the second at the Red Sea baptism when they were tempted to go back to Egypt. Eight more tests unfold on the wilderness journey before they enter the Promised Land. The next one has to do with disappointments in life.

61

The incessant drone of the jet enveloped me as I gazed down on the vast wilderness of Baffin Island. It was awesome to me that these immense fields of snow could just exist, with nobody living there to witness their wondrous silence. Talk about traveling across a great empty land! I wondered how the Israelites would have fared in that cold desert below or in the even larger wasteland of Greenland, which soon came into view. How far away my brother and sister-in-law really were from us, living as they did in Northern Ireland. I realized what a great gulf separated us; yet a more significant sense of separation weighed on me as the airbus raced me to my destination. It was the sense of separation a man and woman can feel after twenty-five years of marriage.

Lyza's missionary brother and his wife had spent fourteen tough years trying to bring hope and healing in the epicenter of Northern Ireland's bitterness and hatred, and ironically, they were now experiencing in their marriage the same kind of irreconcilable differences that separated the Irish people. I couldn't shake a compelling desire to touch base with these two whom I loved very much. I knew I couldn't probably change the course they were on, but I somehow wanted to see them face-to-face. Could I squeeze in a trip to Ireland during the week *Fred* was getting his final touches done in dry-dock in Nanaimo? Lyza encouraged me to go and so here I was, looking down at these vast tracts of land from 33,000 feet up. Lyza, Ginette, and Bo went back to White Rock to wait out my week in Ireland and get a grandbaby 'fix'.

I struggled with the same feelings of disappointment I knew this couple must feel. It seemed patently unfair to me that the brokenness in their marriage was the reward for a dedicated pair that left home and family, sold their little house to live off its equity, and gave their best years to that tormented hotbed of Northern Ireland's strife. Self-recriminations ran through my mind. What kind of a pastor was I to have partnered with them in their work and not seen what it was coming to? I should have done more. We didn't stay in close enough touch. What good was it to send them? The temptation for discouragement—and yes, bitterness—was there for me, too. It was a painful reminder of what deep heartsickness can be wrung out of you over the long journey. I was also aware of my own helplessness to change this situation. Part of the mystery of human sovereignty that God gave each of us is that each person alone can make the most crucial choices of the heart. Still, I wanted to understand, to share their pain, and maybe sow something good into them.

The third temptation in the wilderness was about these same kinds of struggles. It was about looking forward with hope and trust for one thing, but receiving another. It was about having to trust even when they wondered if God Himself had betrayed them. The story picks up after the great deliverance from Pharaoh in the Red Sea.

Then Moses led Israel from the Red Sea, and they went out into the wilderness of Shur; and they went three days in the wilderness and found no water. When they came to Marah, they could not drink the waters of Marah, for they were bitter; therefore it was named Marah. (Exodus 15:22,23)

Marah is the source of the name Mary, and it means 'bitter'. I always thought the name Mary was a sweet name, especially because it evoked the image of the virgin smiling gently at her Son. But it means bitter. However, she was worthy of the sweet images her memory evokes because of the many good choices she made along her path. Mary had every reason to live up to the bitter meaning of her name. Her first opportunity came as a teenager when the angel revealed she was going to have a baby. As a result of this pregnancy, surely she experienced the wounds of public shame, misunderstanding, censure and rejection. How many would ever believe that *'the Holy Ghost came upon her'*? It took an angel appearing to her future husband to convince him. Her most bitter hour was when she watched the Son for whom she had sacrificed so much be exposed to public shame and hung on a cross. Mary fully tasted the bitter fruits of this life, and yet, her initial response to the angel was the choice she continued to make later in life, *"Behold, the bondslave of the Lord; may it be done to me according to your word,"* (Luke 1:38). Even down through the centuries, we are still inspired by her example of responding to life with grace.

So Moses led the people to the waters of Marah. Imagine what it was like, marching into the scorching Sinai desert for three days with no water. No water for their bleating sheep and goats, but worst of all, no water for their crying children. God's miracle man, Moses, led them straight into a hot and empty wasteland and their mutterings increased with the heat. Then, as they climbed exhaustedly over a hill in the desert, there, lying in a little valley before them, were pools of water. They all scrambled to the shore, plunged their blistered faces into the cool waters, and greedily gulped down great mouthfuls to sooth their parched throats. Suddenly, there was coughing and spluttering. Disgustedly, they spat out the foul water. It was horribly unpalatably bitter.

What kind of cruel trick was this? To get their hopes up only to have them dashed, taken from them, and seemingly by an act of God. One could think God was sadistic, on some kind of power trip. Many feel betrayed by God over the nasty twists and turns and bitter experiences of life. They have personally drunk the waters of Marah. But the story for Israel wasn't over yet…

> *Then he* [Moses] *cried out to the Lord, and the Lord showed him a tree; and he threw it into the waters, and the waters became sweet. There He made for them a statute and regulation, and there He tested them.* (Exodus 15:25)

God showed Moses a tree. Strange! One might first assume that some chemical property in the tree neutralized the bitter water. But scripture is far more incisive than that and is loaded from beginning to end with symbolic incidents that reveal the mystery of Christ. The cross is hidden throughout the Old Testament. In this case, the tree God showed Moses points to the wooden cross that Christ hung upon. *"Cursed is everyone who hangs on a tree"* (Galatians 3:13). When the tree was cast into the water, the water became sweet. The cross is the ultimate resolution of life's bitterness. While He lived, Jesus was guilty of no sin. He was innocent. He blessed and healed people. Yet when He came to the end of His life the same people who were ready to make him king cried out in the Praetorium, "Crucify Him!" Betrayed, rewarded evil for good, abandoned by His closest disciples, mocked and shamed, He was offered vinegar as He hung dying. Vinegar was a bitter drink given as a mild anesthetic to the tormented. He refused it. He chose to fully embrace the pain of the cross, refusing to give in to a bitter spirit. He chose to forgive. *He said, "Father forgive them; for they do not know what they are doing"* (Luke 23:34). His refusal to imbibe the bitterness brought the sweet water of salvation to the world. *"He was crushed for our iniquities; the chastening for our well-being fell upon Him, and by His scourging we are healed"* (Isaiah 53:5).

After the tree healed the waters, and the people drank their fill, God spoke to them, revealing a new part of His covenant with them.

> *And He said, "If you will give earnest heed to the voice of the Lord your God, and do what is right in His sight, and give ear to His commandments, and keep all His statutes, I will put none of the diseases on you which I have put on the Egyptians; for I, the Lord, am your healer."* (Exodus 15:26)

This was the place, in the midst of bitter waters, where God chose to reveal Himself as their Healer. He gave them one of the many names by which He revealed Himself and His character. "I am Jehovah-Ropheka, the Lord that healeth thee."

It is significant that in the context of bitter experiences we come to know God as our healer. Life is designed to reveal God's wisdom and character. What could seem to destroy us can actually become a tool for building and healing us. Our choices determine which. We will not escape the bitter experiences of life, but we can escape the negative effects of those experiences—bitterness. Forgiveness brings healing, but people often find it impossible to let go of bitterness apart from the empowerment of God. It's interesting to note that more and more medical studies link physical ailments to emotional roots. The human body wasn't made to handle the stress of bitterness. Much healing would be released in our bodies simply by getting rid of bitterness.

Every person has his portion of blessings and his share of burdens. Only God measures out the perfect balance for each unique life, but usually He allows a particular sore point to test our faith. With Abraham it was his inability to have a child. With Moses it was his failure in Egypt and his inability to speak. Many people have trials that repeatedly touch a certain kind of vulnerability. Like Hannah, the longing of the barren for a child, or a single person's longing for a mate can gnaw away at the heart. Some are visited with tragedy when least expected, such as a car accident or a wife dying of cancer and are left saying, "Why me?"

I still remember the anguished cry as Lyza sobbed in my arms when our little Stephanie took her last choking breath. That anguished mother's cry pierced me and sensitized me more deeply to human sorrow. Stephanie, our second born, had a serious congenital heart defect. Several times we raced through red lights to the hospital with our hearts in our throats, as she turned blue, unable to breath. They tried heart surgery, and she spent four of her nine months in the intensive care nursery at Vancouver General, but we slowly lost the battle. Why us?

Why not us? Has anyone in this world been exempt from pain? Parents can never forget or replace a child, but life moves on. Time eventually blunts the edge of grief and healing flows from Christ into the wounds. Christ is risen; we will see our Stephanie again. Our son Matthew's birth the next year was deeply comforting and then Julie was born, who became the beloved little girl in our family. Sometimes the bitter passages of life need the broader sweep of time to gain perspective and find the sweetness that God reveals. Whatever our experience—of the sweet or of the bitter—it is the tree of God that brings reconciliation and peace, if we will only yield to its healing virtues.

The trip to Ireland was bittersweet, a dreamlike interlude of five short days in Londonderry. I gave up trying to overcome jet lag and lay awake every night, listening to the inebriated squabbles of some unhappy Irish couple down on the street. They repeated their fight every night in the darkness as if to remind me of the futility of it all. The time spent with my brother and sister-in-law was sweet in friendship and sharing their sorrows, but bitter because their marriage appeared to be dead. I was bleary-eyed from lack of sleep by the end, but satisfied I had made the trip, even though there seemed nothing left for me to do.

Marriage is a huge arena in which the battle against a root of bitterness and hardness of heart rages. No wonder Jesus said to His disciples, *"Because of your hardness of heart Moses permitted you to divorce your wives; but from the beginning it has not been this way"* (Matthew 19:8,9). When He said this, the disciples looked dumbly at Him and said, *"If the relationship of the man with his wife is like this, it is better not to marry."* In other words, they were aware that the terms of marriage seemed impossibly hard.

I remember my wife once reading to me from a magazine article where actor Kevin Costner was quoted as saying, "Marriage is a hard gig." This proved true for him as his marriage broke up some time later. Yes, marriage is a hard gig, but so is the rest of life, and only those who purpose to look deeper will find the grace to pay the price to keep their hearts soft. The stakes are very high when it comes to marriage and family, and the battle against a root of bitterness can last for generations.

As we had sailed on the *Fred* up through the Canadian Gulf Islands on our way to Nanaimo, we made a stop at Wallace Island in Trincomali Channel off the north end of Saltspring Island. *Once Upon an Island*, a classic west coast story, had captured our imaginations two months earlier when I found an old copy in my Uncle George's cabin. As we read about the southern California couple that escaped city life and careers to buy Wallace Island, and homestead on it in 1946, we planned a stop there to see what was left of their dreams. Owning an island would be my idea of the perfect inheritance.

Their tale begins with an idyllic Adam and Eve existence, wandering hand–in-hand through juniper-scented forest glades and frolicking in crystalline emerald bays. The Connovers went back to nature and back to God as they simplified their lifestyle and made plans to build their paradise. Without funds to buy the island, nevertheless they managed to acquire it, but ended up totally impoverished by the end of their first year. The first hard winter almost broke up their marriage, but after hitting rock bottom in every respect, they found provision for their needs—usually at the last minute. They overcame huge obstacles to achieve their dream of living on an island and building a resort. The book ends on a high note with the inspirational feeling that this couple had realized their dreams through perseverance and commitment. The book was written twenty years after their arrival and we hoped that maybe the Connovers would still be there, an old couple sitting stoically by their fire in their cabin in the cove.

As we came to a little bay too shallow for *Fred* to anchor in with his deep keel, we saw the big wood sign on the north point of entry, 'Marine Park'. A government float marked the spot where the Connover's dock would have been and signs identified trails, scenic beaches and points of interest. A little cabin nestled in a hollow overlooking the dock was old and empty. An ancient rose bush grew over the front porch, profusely in bloom, but sprawling and undisciplined, too big for the scale of the little house.

The picture from the book of Jeanne Connover's pretty young face leaning out of the window of the cabin over the flower box was still fresh in our minds. We tried to match the story we had recently read with the tumbledown buildings scattered here and there around the grassy clearing and nestled among the trees. I sized up the lay of the land with the eye of someone who had picked his own cabin site, and wondered what it would have been like in 1946. Certainly a feeling of isolation, still an abundance of fish and a much more untamed Gulf Islands then. I remembered Alan Hedger, (an old friend and pioneer farmer who was born on Saltspring in 1906) telling me how you could walk across the backs of the salmon when they ran through Active Pass. I remembered my dad making friends with the Jacks, a native family that lived in the Pass and caught salmon, and old Dalton Deacon and his family on Mayne Island. Now they were all faded into Gulf Island history along with the Connovers. Wallace was now a marine park, and their cabins a kind of museum piece.

A wistful sorrow brooded over the place as we walked through the memories of the story we'd read and felt a deep disappointment to learn that after twenty-eight years of marriage and living on the island, David and Jeanne Connover separated and eventually divorced. Jeanne took their one son off the island to the suburbs of Victoria for his high school years and never came back. She ended up remarrying and now lived in Arizona, as far away from Gulf Island rain and mists as one could get. David married twice more, first to a younger woman who ran off with the keeper of another nearby island, and then to the wife of the man his second wife ran off with, providing a sordid ending to this tale of romance, commitment and perseverance.

The seeds of their marital conflicts were evident in the book. Jeanne wondered then if David loved the island more than he loved her. The question of being first place in your spouse's life is a common issue in many marriages, one that was familiar territory for Lyza and me as well. Maybe Dave and Jeanne never really sorted out that question in the ensuing years, and unresolved, it nurtured a sense of loneliness that became resentment and finally dissolution twenty-eight years later. David Connover's pictures of Marilyn Monroe were taped to the window of a locked guest cabin. He had made a claim to fame as the photographer who first discovered Norma Jean. These pictures were being sold so the cabins could be restored, preserving their place in island history. It all fell a little flat for me.

"What is valuable in an inheritance?" I pondered. An island? A history? David sold the island in pieces during his final years to support his retirement on Wallace Island where he remained until his death in 1983. The happily-ever-after fairy-tale ending came to a dismal end in the final unwritten chapters. Though they conquered the challenge of taming the island, they could not tame and conquer the strongholds of human nature at the root of their marriage conflict.

Everyone is tested in life at the waters of Marah, but it doesn't have to become our permanent camping place. God supplies something called grace to every person at the very point of hurt or offence to help that person forgive and bear the pain. Fully surrendering the situation to God activates this grace, but holding the hurt within grows bitter roots. Such is the witness about Jacob's brother Esau who lost the inheritance promised to Abraham's children.

> *"See to it that no one comes short of the grace of God; that no root of bitterness springing up causes trouble, and by it many be defiled; that there be no immoral or godless person like Esau, who sold his own birthright for a single meal."* (Hebrews 12:15,16)

The implication of this verse is that Esau forfeited his inheritance by allowing a root of bitterness to defile his life. He felt cheated by his brother Jacob and never got over it. Many people never get past Marah because they feel that life—and hence, God—has cheated them by handing them deficiency or tragedy.

Walking off the ferry to Nanaimo with our bags on our backs and Bo on a leash, it was only a short hike from the ferry terminal to the shipyard where *Fred* had been hauled, repainted, and refitted with a depth finder, a GPS, and a VHF radio in our absence. Such electronics were great leaps of progress for our unsophisticated old boat. For sixty years our family navigated the coast inside Vancouver Island with only a compass, calipers and chart, sounding unfamiliar bays with a lead line or a fish pole. The coast was so familiar we did most of our navigation native-style by gauging tide, wind and shoreline distances. To push one button and know your depth, and another to know your latitude, longitude, and speed, was amazing wizardry, but of much comfort when considering the unfamiliar waters of the north coast. We spent an extra day taking a crash course for using the VHF radio, passing the test under a volunteer auxiliary coast guard man's supervision, while sitting in *Fred's* cockpit with a spring sun warming our necks. At last, more equipped than we'd ever been in our lives, we nosed our way out of the marina, wove our way through the boat traffic of Nanaimo harbour and into the great expanse of the Gulf of Georgia. In spite of the new equipment, I knew *Fred* was still *Fred*, an earthen vessel, and like my earthen brother and sister in Ireland, we would have our trials with him along the way. I would pray for reconciliation for my brother and sister, but whatever happened, we would still love both of them and continue on.

Our trusty sea dog got more nervous as the swells of the strait pitched us about. Labs are partial to water, but when he signed on for this voyage, he was not really aware of the perils at sea. You could see he was attempting to process the limited deck space and the mysterious upheavals in his doggy brain. It shouldn't have surprised me, though, when a high-pitched shriek jerked my head up from the chart I was studying. "Dog overboard!" Ginette frantically gesticulated as the dog's head receded in the wake.

"Quick, Daddy, do something!"

As I hauled the boat around to rescue him, Ginette said, "Dad, he just sat down into midair."

"What do you mean?"

"I saw him do it. He walked to the end of the deck, turned around, and just sat down overboard."

I shook my head and laughed at the thought of his woeful backflip overboard and at Ginette's bemused grin now that she realized it was funny. Lyza was on deck now.

"What happened?"

"Bo sat overboard." Ginette giggled.

I could see the castaway one hundred feet astern, now paddling doggedly, looking chagrined. Retrieving a dog overboard involves dragging him by his collar over the rubber sides of the yellow and black inflatable boat we call *Crayon*, and then instantly jumping to the narrow bow to escape the inevitable shaking shower. We wait while he looks around with an embarrassed grin, tongue hanging out, looking apologetic, then we transfer him to the sailboat by heaving his bottom up. Once back on board he makes the rounds, greeting everybody one at a time with his tail wagging, looking foolish. There is never an ounce of blame or recrimination in such happenings; he's just relieved to be safe aboard again and exhibits a readiness to let bygones be bygones.

I say 'such happenings' because this was not the only time. A couple of days later he flew off sideways when we unexpectedly took a large cruiser wake crossbeam. After a couple of face plants in the surf off the front of *Crayon* while zipping ashore, we started a ship's betting pool to guess how many times he would tumble before the summer was over. No matter how many times it turned out to be, I knew it wouldn't alter his affable spirit and enthusiasm for boat life. He may have fallen victim to the vagaries of the sea a few times, but develop a root of bitterness about it? Never!

Beyond the Comfort Zone

Hunger in the Wilderness of Sin, Exodus 16
The Fourth Temptation – The Removal of our Security and Provision

The Ten Temptations: **4. Hunger (Manna in the Wilderness of Sin)**

1. Pressures 2. Power 3. Bitterness
   of Life   of Evil   of Life

Seven Stages of the Spiritual Journey:

1. The Passover in Egypt	2. Red Sea Crossing	3. Mt. Sinai Visitation
		4. Wilderness

Chapter Five

Many sailors confess to a certain love-hate relationship with their passion. Someone said, "Sailboating was like standing in the shower with all your rain gear on and stuffing hundred dollar bills down the drain." Most smaller sailboats have an open cockpit and the boat is steered by means of a tiller or wheel so the pilot can keep an eye on his sails and the nuances of the wind. The glory of this arrangement is the exhilaration you feel when the sun is shining, a fresh breeze is at your back and you are sailing down some channel surrounded on every side by green mountains, the bright blue of the sea and sky, and brilliant white clouds drifting on the horizon. Those times addict you to sea life.

More often than not, however, this firsthand relationship with the elements amounts to a front row seat for misery. It is exposure to scudding clouds, mists, wind and rain that penetrates your warmest outdoor wear and chills you to the bone. It means having nowhere to go when the wind suddenly turns contrary and the next harbour is miles away. At such times you hunker down with your numb hand clenched to the tiller and endure the pummeling of freezing gusts of wind, cold spray and sheets of water splashing in your face while you plough into trough after trough. Forging on stoically after a few hours of this, rigor mortis sets in and you sit like a stone sentry as water trickles down your chin through the inside of your parka to pool in your shoes. You vow to yourself to abandon this stupid way of vacationing once and for all and long for a lounge chair in Palm Beach.

Perversely, the next day your oaths evaporate with the morning mist in some quiet harbour where the sun is warming your back and winking merrily over a green silent mountain. Your dark brooding passes and the fickle life of open cockpit sailing possesses you once more. Some, like the fifty-something man and his wife we met on the pier at Minstrel Island, finally make the break and buy a powerboat. "We just got beat up too many times," he said. "We couldn't do it anymore." I studied his slightly wrinkled, bronzed face and his wife's worn appearance and thought, "I'm fifty this year."

I glanced down at *Fred* tethered to the float in his gleaming bright new paint and polished brass and considered. Would there ever be a parting of company? I knew what the man was talking about, for I had considered a divorce from *Fred* just the day before when we rounded Chatham Point into Johnston Strait where the wind and tide were running strongly in opposite directions. What followed was a pitching wet roll in the soup for about an hour as we managed to wet the bunks once again. After that we gave up our confidence in the ability of the front deck and hatch to keep the water out and vowed to stuff all bedding into garbage bags when it looked like the sea was up.

Powerboat people don't have these trials. They may get thrown around a bit in the seas, but they are enclosed in a warm cabin behind the wheel. They get where they are going fast, live in more spacious living quarters, and enjoy the luxury of refrigerators, generators, and all the 'mod cons'.

It took us a week to get from the Gulf of Georgia to Owen Bay, the furthest point north of our former journeys. We stopped at our cabin site on Nelson Island to spend a couple of days with our children. Bidding them farewell, we ran up Malaspina Strait to Lund and on through Desolation Sound and Hole in the Wall to Owen Bay.

Then the real adventure began. Johnstone Straits, the main waterway north between Vancouver Island and the mainland, was a wind tunnel, particularly for the northwest summer winds. The current in places ran five to six knots so we approached it with trepidation. My heart beat in time with the puttering diesel as I pushed and pulled the tiller against the tidal eddies and upwellings of Okisollo Channel at six in the morning. We were heading for the upper rapids where the channel narrowed and the current increased even more. Hoping to catch the early slack tide, I decided to follow a large troller through a more dangerous but shorter route, figuring he would know how to avoid Seal Rocks in the middle of the upper rapids. The anxious exhilaration of following him thirty feet from the shore amid churning white water only increased as the passage poured us out into the main body of Johnstone Strait. There we rounded prominent points every few miles, sliding sideways with the increasing ebb tide until passing Chatham Point around breakfast time.

The rest of the crew soon awoke to a melee of warring wind, tide, and whitecaps and more water on the bunks. The abrupt change when rounding a point never ceases to amaze me. Like the surprises of life itself, you can be sailing along in smooth seas and suddenly be caught off guard. My moods varied with the sea through the eight-hour journey, alternating between fear at navigating Race Passage where the agitated water raged, to confidence and delight to find we could handle whatever came. I took great pride in learning to set waypoints with the GPS along the way. It was a comfort that these points, set as we went north, would be there in case of fog or bad weather on the way back.

By late afternoon we escaped the straits into Port Harvey and passed on through Chatham Channel, past Minstrel Island to a safe anchorage. The next day we sailed down Knight Inlet, which emptied into Queen Charlotte Strait through a plethora of islets where we finally anchored. A tiny unnamed island was all that separated us from the great swells rolling off the foot of the strait.

The notorious north coast fog paid us its first visit in the morning and we stayed put until we were reasonably certain it had lifted for the day. Little islands appeared and disappeared in gray shrouds, warning me not to be hasty in trusting the coast was clear. Wispy ribbons of mist wound through nearby trees, its vestiges becoming long green strands of lichen trailing down over branches into the thick undergrowth. "It must rain here a lot," I thought. It reminded me of the vegetation in the Olympic Peninsula rainforest, only more windblown. It was not a comforting consideration to add to my list of disconcerting revelations about this country.

I wished I had not decided to write about Israel's wilderness wanderings during this leg of our sabbatical. It seemed too prophetic. I swatted a horsefly with my manuscript, leaving a dark smudge. The day slowly lightened up and blue sky appeared, but a bank of fog still hung its fuzzy paws over the forested point to the south, probably just waiting to pounce on my back if I tried to escape down the channel to Echo Bay.

Ever since I was a young man, I had gazed with wondering desire at the charts of this particular area. The maze of little islands seemed to my mind a multiplied million of the rocky islands off the south coast. I pictured windblown islets surrounded by pristine waters teeming with fish and riddled with little coves to anchor in. The 'windblown' was right and the multitude of coves was right, but instead of the Gulf Island flora we found a very different kind of vegetation.

The water was clear blue and cold, but the shallow, sandy bottom did not foster the abundance of fish we expected. The islands were smooth sandstone covered to the tide line with an impenetrable growth of salal, which precluded hiking or even going ashore. The wind had stripped bare many of the stunted cedars' tops, creating a spiny, prickly appearance and increasing the inhospitable feel.

After fishing for a considerable time and coming up with only three little rock cod for dinner, a disappointment crept over me like the overcast pressing the horizon. This was not what I expected. The dusky harbours, the murky, sandy waters in the bays and the refrigerated atmosphere were strange and different. I wondered, was the rest of our journey going to be like this? If so, why were we heading 500 miles further into this forbidding north country? Would we find provision? …Have enough warmth and shelter against the cold? …Be able to handle it?

Apparently the Israelites struggled with the same kind of feelings as they journeyed into the unfamiliar Sinai Desert—especially when they began to think about food.

The whole congregation of the sons of Israel grumbled against Moses and Aaron in the wilderness. The sons of Israel said to them, "Would that we had died by the Lord's hand in the land of Egypt, when we sat by the pots of meat, when we ate bread to the full; for you have brought us out into this wilderness to kill this whole assembly with hunger." (Exodus 16:2,3)

Hunger was the fourth temptation to be faced on the inheritance journey. The big lonely desert was unfamiliar and barren. How would they survive? Egypt was no piece of cake, but at least it was familiar and they knew where their meals were coming from.

Security is a huge thing for most of us. People can live in the most horrible circumstances and the most abusive relationships, yet still cling to them for no other reason than the misery they know is better than the uncertainty they don't know. If we can maintain some semblance of security and familiarity, we can feel like we're in control, even if we are not. That is why we resist the unknown, even when it may hold great promise.

When God comes into our lives He is not content to leave us alone. He wants to bring us out of our constrained little world into His. God's intention is not only to remove us from the bondage of Egypt, but also to progressively remove Egypt's bondage out of us. His intention is to remove our securities based on self-preservation and cause us to rest our security entirely on Him. He does this by teaching us to build our confidence upon His promises and rest our security in His faithful character. To do this He moves us beyond our comfort zone.

> *"He humbled you and let you be hungry... that He might make you understand that man does not live by bread alone, but man lives by everything that proceeds out of the mouth of the Lord."* (Deuteronomy 8:3)

What could produce more insecurity than the prospect of starvation? In the fourth testing God goes for the jugular—will the people rely solely on Him for their sustenance? Talk about being vulnerable. Not many issues threaten our existence like removing the food supply.

> *Then the Lord said to Moses, "Behold, I will rain bread from heaven for you; and the people shall go out and gather a day's portion every day, that I may test them, whether or not they will walk in My instruction."* (Exodus 16:4)

God actually made bread materialize out of heaven with the morning dew. The people were to take a daily portion of this bread from heaven called manna. We know from the New Testament what this manna really meant to signify, for Jesus said,

79

"Your fathers ate the manna in the wilderness, and they died. This is the bread which comes down out of heaven, so that one may eat of it and not die. I am the living bread that came down out of heaven; if anyone eats of this bread, he shall live forever; and the bread also which I will give for the life of the world is My flesh." (John 6:49-51)

Jesus is the bread; Jesus is the manna. These people were acting out a story to teach us spiritual lessons about Christ being our daily bread and our daily security. It is a story about learning dependence on God and His word. Manna was a 'fine, flake-like thing' that appeared like frost on the ground when the dew evaporated each morning. This was 'angels' food' and the people gathered it up and ate it. It was so unfamiliar that their exclamation, "What is it?" became its actual name, 'manna' which means, 'What is it?' They were instructed to gather a portion each day not reserving any for the next day or it would spoil. When the sun grew hot it would melt and disappear.

So, in our spiritual journey God provides a portion of His living word each day. If we don't gather it, it melts away in the heat of the day and we lose it. We need to hear from God each day as much as we need to eat our daily meals. Jesus said to the devil, when tempted to turn the stones into bread after fasting for forty days, *"Man shall not live on bread alone, but on every word that proceeds out of the mouth of God"* (Matthew 4:4). The hunger of our spiritual man for truth and communication with God is our deepest need.

God is committed to looking after our physical needs. Jesus said, *"Look at the birds of the air, that they do not sow, nor reap, nor gather into barns, and yet your heavenly father feeds them. Are you not worth much more than they?"* (Matthew 6:26). If God is committed to meeting our basic physical needs then we are free to make a priority of seeking our spiritual needs to be met. Our security base can then rest in Him, not upon the unreliable securities of money, land, employment, or a full freezer. Having an inheritance on earth, no matter how great, will never bring the security that an inheritance in God brings. Hearing and obeying His voice is the only real security that leads to the only real inheritance.

If the Israelites did not learn to hear and obey God's voice, they would never be able to conquer Canaan Land. This is why the manna lesson had so many specific instructions. If we ever want to move beyond our comfort zone into new dimensions spiritually, physically, or emotionally, we must pass the test of learning to truly rely upon the Power that is greater than ourselves. On our little sailboat we were moving way beyond our comfort zone just as the Hebrews were way beyond theirs, but it was years earlier that Lyza and I were foundationally schooled in the 'manna' lesson. Most often it is in the realm of physical provision that we really learn the spiritual lessons.

Coming from a background of material and emotional security, provision was something I took for granted, unlike my wife who knew something of insecurity and hardship from her background. Dad was always good for a few bucks if I needed it, even though I did learn to work and hold jobs as a teenager. However, if I got in a tight squeeze, I always knew there would be a provision. Then came our great leap into marriage and our move to Canada. We had crossed the Red Sea and Dad's ultimatum, "If you do this, son, you are on your own. I won't help you," cast us emphatically into dependency upon our heavenly Father…

Lyza was six months pregnant with our firstborn, Dave, and reaching up onto the shelf of the bedroom closet of our beach cottage for an eight-ounce box of chocolates. Walking into the bedroom, I caught her in the act.

"What are you doing?" I asked suspiciously.

She looked a little sheepish, but determined. "I've got to have at least one little chocolate."

"You can't take those. Those are the Christmas presents for the mentally handicapped people. You wouldn't take candy from a disabled person, would you?"

Our little band of followers had donated these gifts as a thank you for using their premises for our coffeehouse. Today Lyza would probably have told me to drop on my self-righteous head, but back then she was a little less confident to stand up to me so she put the chocolate dejectedly back up on the shelf. I felt sorry for her and a little guilty because I couldn't afford to buy her chocolates. We sat down and prayed together, "Lord, maybe chocolates aren't in the 'need' category, but Lyza sure wants them, so we just commit this

craving to you. Could you please take care of it somehow?" We had already been learning that God provides, but learning that 'man doesn't live by bread alone' took some time for the guy born with a silver spoon in his mouth.

The summer in the tent had passed and we were now living with our friend Dwight in his dilapidated cottage on the same lot where the tent had been pitched. Dwight Tachiyama was learning his own faith lessons by coming with us to Canada to preach the gospel. (He must have learned some of those lessons because he and his wife, Dianne, are still with us—close friends and faithful elders in our church) Provision during this time became a daily dependence, hand-to-mouth existence as we prayed for everything from rent, to food, to gas and college tuition. We were in Canada on a visitors' status and were not allowed to work for remuneration. The reality of being alone in the cold world was beginning to sink in. The test was on. Could we really trust our heavenly Father for our basic needs? There was nowhere else to go. The next day after the 'stealing chocolates' incident, there was a knock at the door.

"Who is at the door?" Lyza called from the kitchen.

I looked up from the old couch.

"It's our landlady, Mrs. Roden."

"It's not rent time. I wonder why she's here?"

I didn't know, but as I opened the door a smiling Mrs. Roden held a large, brightly wrapped package. With a quick "Merry Christmas," she thrust the package into my arms, and left. Lyza came out to see what was going on and helped me tear off the wrapping. Underneath the torn wrap was the warm yellow-brown color of Samplers Chocolates. Not just an ordinary box, but a monster-sized one, three layers deep. "It must be three pounds!" Lyza exclaimed. Tears appeared in her eyes. "God did this. He does care about everything. He really does."

I was thinking more self-righteous thoughts about God proving you shouldn't steal from the mentally handicapped, but all Lyza saw was the goodness of a heavenly Father who not only provided our needs but delighted in demonstrating His abundance by supplying our wants. When those Israelites grumbled for meat, God not only gave them manna—he rained down quails upon them so they covered the camp. When we let go of our tight grip on our bread, we release God's hand to provide His way. Lyza let go of eight ounces. God rained three pounds on her.

The one hundred dollar rent was a monthly pressure in those days. We made a pact with each other not to talk to anybody but the Lord about our financial needs, but one hundred dollars was a lot of money for us in 1971. We just prayed and waited to see what would happen, and for almost a year somehow the rent always showed up. It came from all sorts of sources, different every time. One time, I heard a noise on the front porch and looked up just in time to see a head of black hair disappear down the stairs. By the time I got to the door, the person had already hopped into a car, but I caught a glimpse of her as she sped off. Looking down at my feet I saw the envelope. Carefully unsealing it, I slid out the bills, five Canadian twenties. This girl only knew us casually and lived in Vancouver, almost an hour away. She had no way of knowing how much our rent was or that we needed it a day before it was due. Ravens brought Elijah his dinner. God sent a raven-haired emissary with our rent.

The first two years of our marriage were manna years financially. So many little miracles and answers to prayer happened that it would take too much time to recount them all, but we never forgot the lesson that the Lord was Jehovah Jireh, the Lord our Provider, who sees the need before we get there. God first revealed this name to Abraham when He provided a sacrificial ram caught in a thicket to be offered instead of his own son, Isaac. The ram foreshadowed Christ, the sacrificial lamb provided for us. Redemption is the greatest need we all have, and God saw and provided for it from the beginning of time. To forever confirm that foundational provision, Jehovah Jireh continues to supply for the entire scope of our needs.

As we trusted God to feed us in those days, we also established the coffeehouse ministry, which required a building, tables, and all sorts of paraphernalia. Miraculously, the Lord provided the use of a building free of charge, BC Telephone cable spools for tables, and money for heat and light from people in the community often at unexpected times. One night a big Norwegian builder we hardly knew dropped by the coffeehouse and called me out of a prayer meeting. He wrote out a check for two hundred dollars because 'God told him to'. The next day Lyza's and my quarterly college tuition was due. The amount, eighty-seven dollars each, was all that Western Washington University cost in those days. Later that Norwegian, Ralph Mothe and his wife, Bjorg, became elders in our church.

Part of our manna test in those days was obedience, just as the children of Israel had to learn. The Lord directed them not to gather manna on the Sabbath day, but instead to gather enough for two days the day before. Usually, if they kept the manna more than one day it rotted, but not on the Sabbath. We also learned how to gather manna in the right time and way. One month the manna didn't seem to be falling very heavily for us. In fact, the cupboards were bare, the heating oil tank was empty, and our house was cold. We thought maybe we were carrying this faith thing too far, yet at this point we didn't have much choice since we still couldn't work in Canada until we graduated from university and could then apply for landed immigrant status.

I remember the morning when, feeling at a low ebb of faith, I hurriedly jogged down the front steps, thinking, "Maybe there will be something in the mailbox today!" As I rummaged disappointedly through the junk mail, I didn't realize that God was engineering yet another lesson about trust, obedience and provision. My eyes fell upon a green-colored pamphlet with an interesting title, considering our circumstances. It said, "Bountiful Blessings Financially!"

"Oh great," I thought, "Some book on how to make a million. I'd settle for a ham sandwich at the moment." Looking closer, I realized it was a Christian teaching booklet and the main subject was tithing and offerings. Not having any background in this sort of thing, Lyza and I were intrigued enough to read through it together. The gist of it was that the Bible teaches the principle of tithing, giving back to God the first ten percent of all we get. The booklet said this honors God in our lives and puts us in a position of vulnerability in His care for Him to meet our needs. We read through all the scriptures, agreed with the points made in the booklet and grasped the challenge of it. Besides, as the saying goes: "When you ain't got nothin', you got nothin' to lose." The principle seemed to apply whether one had little or much so we decided to try it.

We prayed, and said, "Okay God, we get the message. Instead of giving us breakfast this week you gave us your word in the mailbox.

Man doesn't live by bread alone but by every word from your mouth. From now on, any money you give us, from whatever source, we will give ten percent of it to you." The next money that came our way was just ten dollars. With no food at home and no oil in the tank we walked purposefully into a Baptist church and dropped two dollars in the offering plate (an extra dollar for the missionaries). From then on, we always had more than enough and the first ten percent always went to God. The Lord took the guy with the silver spoon in his mouth down to the bottom to indelibly imprint the manna lesson on him. We have lived by these guiding principles ever since.

"He... let you be hungry... that He might make you understand that man does not live by bread alone, but man lives by everything that comes out of the mouth of the Lord." (Deuteronomy 8:3)

What caused us to strike out for Alaska was not the destination, but the experience of getting there. We knew hardships awaited us along the way as well as wonderful experiences, but no matter what happened each day, our every need would be supplied. Our ministry journey was the same. Thirty years after those formative experiences of provision we could testify that Jehovah Jireh had traveled the whole distance with us, ready with a word in season, an enablement in every extremity, an insight for every perplexity, a supply for every need. We may not have reached any pinnacle of success, but we would never have traded the last thirty years of walking with God. He still gives us manna each day for the journey and we are content.

Life is a journey the Creator has set us upon, and the destination is secondary to the process of getting there. People like to strive for the goals of security, recognition, knowledge or material prosperity. Christians like to focus on the destination of heaven ("pie in the sky after you die"), and even though it's good to be able to look forward to a worthwhile and happy end, the true substance of life happens along the way. One thing that two years of living by faith—depending on manna—taught us was that we can live freely in the present because the future is already provided for. Daily manna, daily provision and daily experience of the security of God's presence are an end in themselves. Learning to live on manna from heaven means that every external circumstance of our life fits into an overall framework of seeing life from God's point of view. It gives a confidence in His sovereignty and the perspective that He is orchestrating all of the details of life to teach us wisdom. Internalizing that wisdom truly becomes the bread of life.

So, in spite of the disconcerting revelations about this inhospitable country we kept our northward heading, skirting the mouth of Kingcome Inlet up Sutil Channel to the beginning of Queen Charlotte Strait. This relatively protected route took us past little outposts of civilization before braving the big jump into the rough waters of the strait that led to the open ocean.

The little floating villages of Echo Bay and Sullivan Bay clung to granite cliffs and abutted the impenetrable forests, servicing the sports fishermen and occasional boaters passing through. These were little manna stops for us where all the essentials could be found at a price. We loaded up on diesel, ice, propane and food, not sure what other provision we would find between there and Bella Bella, the halfway point of our journey north. We would trust to providence for sunshine, fish and clams, confident that leaning on God's loving care would work as well on the north coast as it had for thirty years in White Rock. We were in good Hands.

So You Wanna Go Back to Egypt?

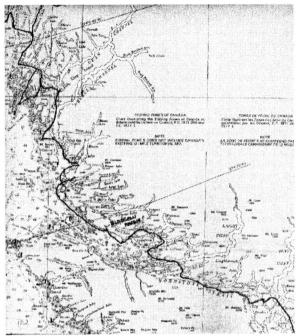

Reproduced with the permission of the Canadian Hydrographic Service

Water From the Rock in the Desert of Rephidim, Exodus 17
The Fifth Temptation – The Removal of God's Conscious Presence

The Ten Temptations: **5. Thirst (Water from the Rock at Rephidim)**

1. Pressures 2. Power 3. Bitterness 4. Hunger
   of Life   of Evil   of Life

Seven Stages of the Spiritual Journey:

1. The Passover in Egypt	2. Red Sea Crossing	3. Mt. Sinai Visitation
		4. Wilderness

Chapter Six

Water was the last thing we had to worry about where we were going. There was water, water, everywhere, and all you wanted to drink. It flowed down the mountains in trickles, streams, rivers, and torrents, draining huge watersheds, diluting the surface of inlets with fresh water, dumping such volume that the flood tide could run in reverse after a heavy rain. Water poured over smooth five-thousand-foot granite faces, forking and branching its way down in silvery rivulets emerging from the forest as a river to cascade over a cliff, a mighty waterfall pounding straight into the sea. It poured from the sky on our heads and filled the horizons every day. Our boat had a sixty-gallon water tank, which we filled in port, but if it ran out along the way we could easily fill it by siphoning water with a hose from any number of streams falling from sheer rocks into deep water.

Our wilderness was a wet one, but the Hebrews' wilderness was hot, sandy, and dry. The test was bound to come sooner or later with eight hundred thousand people. How would God sustain them all with fresh water? *"Then all the congregation of the sons of Israel journeyed by stages from the wilderness of Sin, according to the command of the Lord, and camped at Rephidim, and there was no water for the people to drink."* (Exodus 17:1)

This fifth test, like the third test, was also about water. This time they were not dealing with the bitterness issue, but with the issue of God's conscious presence in our lives. Water, among other things, is a symbol of the soul-refreshing presence of God's Spirit. The psalmist David expresses the cravings of the thirsty soul in Psalm 42:1, *"As the deer pants for the water brooks, so my soul pants for You, O God. My soul thirsts for God, for the living God; When shall I come and appear before God?"*

Although we may be aware that God is there somewhere, it is personal contact with His Spirit that brings the presence of God into our very being. After we have initially experienced His presence in some measure, there come times of testing when God's conscious presence is removed or He seems to have departed from us. Our souls become troubled and begin to wither. We experience a spiritual desert. Most people experience a spiritual dryness at one time or another and may be tempted to feel God has deserted them.

The Israelites knew God's presence was with them. They had seen mighty miracles when God brought them out of Egypt, such as the dividing the Red Sea and the destruction of their enemies. God continually assured them of His presence with the pillar of cloud by day and the pillar of fire by night, called His 'Shekinah Glory'. When God appeared to Moses, the Shekinah Glory appeared to the people. When they needed protection from Pharaoh, the Shekinah Glory stood between them and his armies. When they went through the desert the cloud shaded them in the day and the pillar of fire warmed them at night. When the glory cloud moved, the people moved. When it stopped, the people stopped. When they stayed in one place and camped (sometimes for weeks or months at a time), it was because the cloud of God's presence was camping.

This Shekinah Glory of God's presence is reflected symbolically in the New Testament by the tongues of fire appearing over the disciples' heads on the day of Pentecost. The glory of God was now to dwell in men. In the Old Testament, this glory cloud usually appeared in association with the people's meeting place with God, whether it was Moses' tabernacle in the desert or Solomon's temple in Jerusalem. With the coming of the Holy Spirit after Jesus' resurrection, the temple of God's dwelling was, and still is, the temple of people's bodies. This is a major shift from an external focus of worship to an internal one. God now dwells in living people, in their hearts, not in buildings.

Jesus expressed this shift perfectly when He went to the streets with the amazing offer of such close fellowship with God. When He encountered the woman at Jacob's well, she deflected his personal questions (how many husbands she had) to engage Him in religious questions.

> *"Our fathers worshiped in this mountain, and you people say that in Jerusalem is the place where men out to worship. Jesus said to her, "Woman, believe Me, an hour is coming when …the true worshipers shall worship the Father in spirit and truth…God is spirit; and those who worship Him must worship in spirit and truth."* (John 4:23)

In other words, which religious denomination you belong to or where you worship is irrelevant. The relevant issue is whether we have the impediments of sin removed and are truly reconciled to God so that His Spirit can dwell in us. When the woman honestly faced her past, she recognized the man she was talking to was the keeper of Jacob's well, the Keeper of living water. Jesus said to her, *"If you knew the gift of God, and who it is who says to you 'Give Me a drink,' you would have asked Him and He would have given you living water"* (John 4:10).

The 'living water' was the presence of God and the woman's desire for intimacy shifted from relationships with men to fellowship with God. A few days after His encounter with the woman, Jesus stood in the cold stone Jewish temple and offered the water of God's presence to everyone, crying out: *"If anyone is thirsty, let him come to Me and drink. He who believes in Me, as the Scripture said, 'From his innermost being will flow rivers of living water...'"* (John 7:37-38). God's intention has always been to bring His presence into the hearts of men as Jesus declared, and it was all foreshadowed in the Exodus story.

The first thing the people did when they had no water to drink was to turn on their leader, Moses, once again. *"Therefore the people quarreled with Moses and said, 'Give us water that we may drink.' And Moses said to them, 'Why do you quarrel with me? Why do you test the Lord?"* (Exodus 17:2).

People have a propensity for staying one step removed from God. Rather than deal with Him directly, the tendency is to rely on somebody else to be the mediator. As a pastor, I continually ask people, "Did you pray about it? What is God saying to you?" So many times I get a blank look or an evasive answer. Perhaps we are afraid to talk to God firsthand? Or are we too lazy? Leaders can never take the place of God's own presence in our lives. *"But the people thirsted there for water; and they grumbled against Moses and said, 'Why, now, have you brought us up from Egypt, to kill us and our children and our livestock with thirst?"* (Exodus 17:3).

The people's conflict was not really with Moses anyway. It obviously wasn't Moses who brought them out of Egypt—as if he could dry up the Red Sea! The people were afraid that the desert heat was going to kill them; however, God was about to reveal something new about Himself in the process of meeting their need.

It was being killed by rain that I was worried about. Why did I ever think we could tackle the north coast in the *Fred Free*? I wouldn't want to go back to Egypt, but how about the familiar south coast? A cold breeze blew through the boom crutch reminding me that, as well as the omnipresent rain, the nor' westerly winds were waiting for me outside the mouth of this tiny inlet we were in. All that separated us from the insistent pelting six inches above our heads was the lightweight blue tarp stretched over the boom. We wondered if this plastic blue sky was the only one we would get in this country.

It wouldn't have been so bad if *Fred* were a proper host and at least kept the elements at bay, but his shelter was incontinent like the old man he was. The leaks weren't apparent at first and didn't appear at all in a passing shower, but when the rain poured down all night, *Fred* reached saturation point and dripped through the little paper towel diapers we taped over the most conspicuous leaks. The inexorable rain came down the mast, over the sail cover, onto the decks and seeped along hidden seams to splat on my head while trying to cook lunch. Something had to change or we were going to become pickled in our own juices ...and probably kill each other.

Feeling judgmental of those Hebrews? I knew how they felt. Nothing is more miserable than camping experiences gone awry and that's what they were doing. Camping. Living in tents. At the mercy of God and surrounded by inhospitable desert. No grocery stores, hardware stores, and certainly no Starbuck's for a warm java on a cold night. I could relate. The nearest outpost of supplies, Namu, according to *Charlie's Charts*, was a ghost town due to the collapse of the salmon fishery.

Of course it wasn't all bad (there were some moments of bliss) but at these miserable junctures they were easy to forget. *Fred* and I maintained our connubial bond, though it was often strained. My other connubial partner was amazing, keeping up a good attitude even though she had to put on her raincoat to go into the closet-sized bathroom. That same closet had the effrontery to fill my Henri Lloyd parka hood with a cup of water the night before.

By the next day Lyza's amazing attitude severely deteriorated and she threatened mutiny on the *Freddie*. Ginny had to give her a straight talking to just before bed. "Now, Mommy, I just can't have any more talk about jumping ship. It makes me unhappy and, besides, we have to stick together." Ginette remained effervescent almost all the time and only really complained when we dropped the twenty-pound seatback on her ankle while trying to make up her bed.

I remembered the envious looks and facetious, "Oh, poor you!" when people heard we would spend the summer cruising the Inside Passage. Now, a cruise ship (most people's conception of cruising) and *Fred* are as poles apart as a berth on the Titanic and a summer in the fo'csle of John Daly's fishing boat. 'Luxury' on the *Fred* was sitting at anchor in our new fold-up chairs squeezed together on the back deck, coffee in hand, watching the sun go down while keeping the dog from sitting on our laps.

After escaping the little rain soaked inlet we came to a protected bay, where a couple stopped by on *Sedna,* their trim thirty-five-foot fiberglass sailboat, to answer some questions I had asked them earlier when I stopped by their boat that morning. At that time they were sitting opposite each other in their spacious cockpit, neatly dressed in blue Dockers shorts and pressed polo shirts. I glimpsed through the doorway to see the varnished woods, well-appointed interior, and electrical conveniences. Everything appeared so neat, clean and orderly, but most of all I just knew that when it rained... it was dry in there! Now they floated past us, turning their boat on a dime. They waved good-bye and gazed curiously on the 'ghost of boating past' with towels and underwear dangling from the rigging and the quaint people straddling their large dog to wave back at them.

They probably appreciated the classic little number *Fred* was, especially with his new paint job, but they had no conception of what it meant on our boat for my wife to ask me to grab her a can of dog food. On their boat, the husband would nip to a rear locker, grab a can, and give it to his wife. Earlier that morning, after first overcoming the immediate tiredness I felt at her request, I first lifted three clothes bags obscuring the red and white plastic ice cooler that for lack of space was placed in front of the can locker. After wrestling the cooler to a different angle, I straddled it on my stomach, and deftly ducked my head under the folding table flap. Rummaging among the various cans, I scraped my finger on a screw while trying to keep the big cans on the bottom and the little tomato cans on top so they wouldn't roll in the bilge (last spring I found a three-year-old can of creamed corn embalmed in diesel bilge water).

Finally, I spied the dog food cans as I jumbled the coke cans to the stern to reach them. The light aluminum punctured on something sharp, and sticky foam shot me straight in the eyes. Desperately throttling the can, applying thumb pressure to the hole, I struggled to my feet and shoved it out the porthole onto the deck where the waiting dog excitedly licked at it. Returning to the locker on my stomach, I finally secured his real sustenance, which in exhaustion I finally handed to my wife who asked how it got so sticky. As the good people from Prince Rupert sailed out of sight, I wondered what *Fred* might be worth on the classic boat market.

In the middle of a journey, when things go bad, we are most prone to question our original inspiration. We ask ourselves, did God really tell us to do this? It's not hard to understand why the Israelites were struggling at this point with no water in sight. "If God called us out here, why is there no water and where is God? Has He abandoned us?" We have the same questions when bad things happen. In this case the Lord wanted to show them a miracle.

> *So Moses cried out to the Lord, saying, "What shall I do to this people? A little more and they will stone me." Then the Lord said to Moses, "Pass before the people and take with you some of the elders of Israel; and take in your hand your staff with which you struck the Nile, and go. Behold I will stand before you there on the rock at Horeb; and you shall strike the rock, and water will come out of it, that the people may drink." And Moses did so in the sight of the elders of Israel.* (Exodus 17:4-6)

These were strange goings-on. Could there be a less likely source of water than a rock sitting in a desert? The symbolic interpretation of this event is illuminated in the New Testament. *"...and all drank the same spiritual drink, for they were drinking from a spiritual rock which followed them; and the rock was Christ"* (1 Corinthians 10:4).

The rock was Christ! Moses hit an actual boulder with his staff and a stream of water gushed out, but somehow Christ was there and even followed them along the way, sustaining the people with water in the desert. Jesus declared that He is the source of living water in the gospel of John:

"Now on the last day, the great day of the feast, Jesus stood and cried out, saying, 'If anyone is thirsty, let him come to Me and drink. He who believes in Me, as the Scripture said, 'From his innermost being will flow rivers of living water.' But this He spoke of the Spirit, whom those who believed in Him were to receive..." (John 7:37-39).

Moses struck the rock and the water came out. God struck Jesus, the Rock, on the cross for our sins and by that act the water of the Spirit was released for all who believed. When Jesus died on the cross and cried out, *"My God, why have You forsaken me?"* he was suffering the removal of God's presence—His own desert experience. God the Father had to turn His face away from Jesus because at that moment he was fully identifying with our sin. He was executed for sin in our place. Striking the rock in the desert foreshadowed this event but it also teaches us that Christ is fully identifying with us and will fellowship with us in the desert experiences of our lives. The water of His presence flows especially in the desert. If we stop resenting suffering and embrace it, we open ourselves to experience a new identification with Christ. Ironically, it is in our sufferings that we most often question God's presence and harden up against Him, thereby cutting off the very fellowship we need. This is what Israel did.

He named the place Massah and Meribah because of the quarrel of the sons of Israel, and because they tested the Lord, saying, "Is the Lord among us, or not?" (Exodus 17:7)

Is the Lord among us or not? We question whether God is for us or whether He is condemning us for our shortcomings, and sometimes, under intense pressure, we even question whether He exists. We forget in the darkness the words He said to us in the light. All believers go through this test and God expects us to trust in Him even when it appears He is not there. Like Peter, who lost faith and began to sink because he focused on the raging waves, the Lord will walk to us on the water of our storms to reach out a saving hand, all the while asking us, "Where is your faith?"

Once God has demonstrated His power and presence in our lives, we are expected to continue to believe even when it seems like

He has left us. For Him to be unfaithful to His presence in our lives is for Him to be unfaithful to Christ, to the cross, to His very self. Jesus Himself said, *"I will never leave you or forsake you."* Going through times of spiritual dryness brings us closer to God in the long run because in the end we understand that God is faithful and was there even when we didn't perceive Him. By this we learn to trust. No one can learn this for us; we all have to learn to trust God's presence and care by ourselves. Sometimes God accomplishes this by removing all our human support systems so that in our loneliness we will apprehend our dependence on Him.

Our children, too, have to learn to transfer dependence on their parents' presence to dependence on God's presence. This, too, usually happens in a desert. Our daughter, Julie, when she was only sixteen, was an exchange student to Ireland for a semester. I remember my fatherly concerns as I watched my little bird bravely walk all alone down the long corridor to the airport gate. At the end of the hall, after one tear-filled look back at the huddle of family and friends, she turned the corner out of our sight. I admired my gutsy daughter but I felt apprehension for her, going for the first time so far away from home. As I walked my tearful wife back to the car, I thought about how mixed my emotions were.

At first her phone calls were full of bubbly enthusiasm for everything: the art classes, the accents, (which she soon could mimic perfectly), her cousins, the field trip to France. Every experience was, "Awesome!" But as the months passed, homesickness set in and threatened to derail her. The phone calls home became tearful and it got so bad at one point that we offered to send her a plane ticket home. She seriously considered giving up and coming home, but then something just galvanized inside her. She decided she wanted to stay even if she was lonely for her family. She didn't want to waste the opportunity, but chose to embrace the homesickness as part and parcel of the whole experience. As she accepted the loneliness from God, a marvelous transformation happened—she felt closer to Him than ever before—and that trip became a spiritual landmark in her life, a place where she met with God in the midst of a desert place.

What do You think, Lord? Should we go for it or not? I threw up a quickie prayer as we journeyed down Wells Channel in the bright sunshine. The tide carried us down from Sullivan's Bay, and the breeze was almost balmy. Nervous about this country and its capricious weather, I thought, "Let's make hay while the sun shines." According to the chart, Blunden Harbour was just nine knots up Queen Charlotte Strait. A quick afternoon run and we'd be further up the dreaded ocean-exposed coastline.

Why don't you just enjoy the sunshine at that little cove back there?

Was that just me, or was it good advice from above? The voice wasn't thunderous, it was more like the still, small voice that Elijah heard, and it was easy to pass off while evaluating my options. I dismissed it as a vagrant thought and pressed on ahead. Lyza gave me a sideways shot of concern with her eyes as the light breeze stiffened out in the channel mouth. I attempted to reassure her.

"The marine forecast said the winds weren't that bad and would lighten towards evening. Besides, it's only nine knots and we can tough it out if it's a bit breezy."

A bit 'breezy' turned increasingly belligerent as we cleared the last protecting headland and started to feel the onslaught of Queen Charlotte. "There's one of those stupid powerboats", I muttered to myself enviously as it charged up from my stern and bullied its way through the rising seas. As usual, the pilot was snug behind the Polaroid windows of the bridge, probably nursing a gin and tonic while surveying a dry chart spread out on a specially designed teak table. Our front hatch was already fastened securely when the U.L.W.I.S. (unusually large wave of inordinate strength) appeared. I recognized this one could be trouble when it was still thirty feet off.

Fred's bowsprit rose and heaved sideways on the precursor to the big boy, then dove into the intervening trough. Then the crest of the breaker crashed like surf over the bow and catapulted over the front hatch, smacking against the front cabin and shattering buckets of cold water over the cockpit. Bo and I were rudely jolted out of any remaining complacency as *Fred* shed cascades of water over the deck and out the scuppers.

I sheepishly peeked below and tried to make out the words working their way out of Lyza's mouth. She was as mad as a wet hen. Déjà vu about the bunks, but this time, water dashed right on her face, the bedding and the book she was reading, as she had been trying to ignore the growing tumult outside. My earlier assurances that we didn't need to throw the bedding into plastic garbage bags were now another reason to mistrust the captain's judgment. We could only power down after the rudeness of the rogue wave and come to terms with dozens of other 'rogues' looming on the horizon. We were too far out now to turn back; besides it would add insult to injury to retreat from this blow and have to risk it another day.

"Let's just go for it. We're in it now and it can't be that bad," spake the brave captain.

It *was* that bad as an hour-and-a-half run turned into a three and a half-hour ordeal, bucking tide and a headwind and doing only three knots to lessen the impact. The sea was bright blue under a sunny sky, which at least lightened the mood. A gray sea and sky doubles the anxiety. According to John Raban, in *Passage to Juneau*, "... a sailboat's movements in the water include six degrees of freedom: pitch, roll, sway, heave, surge, and yaw." His comment about his own boat was, "... Its freedom to roll and sway was mercifully inhibited, but it was taking every other liberty on the menu." *Fred* took *every* liberty on the menu. He pitched, rolled, swayed, heaved, surged, and yawed, sometimes forcing me to brace both Lyza and Ginny in their seat as they held Boaz back from jumping overboard. It felt like we all just might tumble out into the dark blue abyss. Suddenly a burgundy stain heaving with the waves appeared like a carpet directly in front of us.

A kelp patch! That meant less than thirty feet of water. I thought we had cleared that group of rocks on the chart. My shallowly rooted pride in my seamanship was shaken. Radically altering course forced me to run sideways to the waves, called a 'beam sea', which exacerbated the roll of the ship. Driftwood logs bobbed up and down in the tumultuous seas as I craned my neck to catch a glimpse of what might lie in the trough behind each wave welling up in front.

By the time we crawled into the cover of the Raynor group of islands, we were thoroughly disenchanted with afternoon sprints up the coast. Our last navigational challenge was threading our way through a maze of shoals in the fading light of day. As we neared our haven, fog rushed in like an occupying army to capture and secure each islet and rock. We evaded disaster by carefully lining up island point to island point and felt along with the depth finder like a blind man with a walking cane. As we slipped into Blunden Harbour, the wind was still whistling at our back, but the fog mysteriously ceased its advance and camped around our refuge, just daring us to venture into the strait again. As we let down the anchor we were soaked and dispirited. As our kids would say, "We got the snot beat out of us," causing us to rename the place Bludgeon Harbour (no offense to Edward R. Blunden, the master's assistant on the R.N. survey vessel *Beaver* for whom it was originally named). The trauma lingered over us as if we'd gone through some kind of physical abuse. At the same time we felt grateful to have made it without mishap.

Going through this ordeal reminded me of so many times in the past when we responded to decisions in life by impulse and knee jerk reaction, half-listening to God and ended up in a storm struggling with the fickleness of human nature or our own weaknesses. Sometimes we stuck our necks out to help others, only to end up feeling sore, bruised, and not sure whether the pillar of cloud led us into the rough seas or whether we ran ahead on our own. There was safety in walking with God, listening, waiting, and going when He went, stopping when He stopped.

Ginette was now a veteran of Clarke family horror stories at sea, a rite of passage for each of our children. We also managed to indelibly imprint in the dog a nervous trembling disorder that manifested from then on every time his *Fred* 'world' even slightly heaved under him. He would quiver around the boat, finally straddling the tiller, gazing astern as though deliverance might come from afar. Eventually he would lie flat on that tiny patch of deck with his nose smushed into the point of the stern, blocking the swing of the tiller and making himself a nuisance to the captain.

This was our first introduction to Queen Charlotte, may she rest in peace. She must have been some queen for Captain Van to name these bodies of water after her. My bet is that she was a capricious, mean-tempered soul!

The next morning the day dawned serene. Mercifully, sun, as a pillar of fire, visited us by day, and *Fred* became a Chinese junk, with our bed sheets and clothing billowing in the breeze. Nothing dried thoroughly in this country where the northwest wind was inherently laden with moisture. Relatively comfortable again by nightfall, it dawned on us that we had gained no time on our journey north by making our precipitous dash the day before. We would have easily made this leg the next day in a calm morning run.

How much needless hassle do we experience for not learning to listen and wait for God's presence to guide us? Even so, He is still with us in the middle of the storm. At least we had learned not to trust sunny north coast afternoons.

"Is God among us or not?" the Israelites challenged in their thirst. *"Would that we had died in Egypt by the Lord's hand."* Probably I was never tempted as much as I was in Bludgeon Harbour to consider our wilderness wandering to Alaska a folly. Looking glumly out of the harbour mouth at the brisk seas running south, the thought of forty to fifty more miles up the strait around Cape Caution into open-ocean Queen Charlotte Sound was very intimidating. The few boats in the harbour with us looked bigger, stronger, and better equipped for these waters. Maybe *Fred* was just too old and leaky. Maybe I was foolish to take Lyza and Ginette up here. I didn't tell them my self-doubts—the captain has to look as if he is confident.

The next morning at 6:00 AM it was all I could do to stick my nose out into that strait again. However, overnight the water had completely changed its demeanor and was now a flat calm. The chart showed two bays we could use as 'escape hatches' if it got rough later in the day, but it never did. By noon, we were abreast of Cape Caution in large ocean swells that broke with crashes on jagged rocks along the rugged shoreline. Though the winds were mild, the ocean swells were new to us and quite unnerving as *Fred* bobbed up little hills and down into the valleys in which the horizon disappeared. Veering east around Egg Island we surfed them into a new world of ocean-washed shores where rocks on the chart became clearly identified by crashing plumes of spray cast up by the rollers even in the calm weather. Four hours later we pulled into Millbrook Cove on Smith Sound as dry as we started out and relieved to have made the passage. Enchanted by the unique touch of the ocean upon beaches, sea life, flora and fauna, my fears and doubts were transformed into a great exhilaration for the adventure we were on. On the other side of Cape Caution it was a whole new experience, filled with abundance and wildness. What a loss it would have been to turn back.

Days later, while motoring up Hakai Passage north of Calvert Island, Lyza read to me from *Charlie's Charts - North to Alaska*, our guide book up the Inside Passage. Charlie put some sage advice in his introductory chapter that had escaped our previous notice.

> As a long time sailor, it is painful for me to admit that perhaps the best type of boat for this trip is a trawler type vessel capable of at least 8 knots and with an inside steering station. This is not to say a sailing vessel cannot be used... But the prevailing winds over most of this area are such that one should expect to motor for most of the trip while heading north... The ship must be capable of being lived aboard and of facing weather and sea conditions that worsen rapidly... The area lies within the migratory low-pressure system belt around the world. Thus it lacks a settled, continuously sunny cruising season. The annual movement of summer's North Pacific High and the winter's Aleutian low cause variations in the pattern of the weather but do not completely deter the passage of the low pressure systems in summer, providing for frequently cloudy skies often laced with rain.

After reading this, Lyza stared at me significantly as we surfed the moderate rollers up Hakai on a remarkably sunny day and said, "I don't think I really realized this before we came up here."

"I told you my uncle said the weather wasn't any good north of Vancouver Island," I replied.

"Well, that never really registered. I pictured it like cruising down south. I'm not sure I would have come if I had known what this guy said. He's an old salt."

I looked with mock offence at my first mate's 'betrayal' and started singing a line from an old Keith Green song, "So you wanna go back to Egypt where it's warm and secure?"

Been to the Mountaintop

Spirit and Truth at Sinai, Exodus 19

The Ten Temptations:

Spirit and Truth at Sinai

1. Pressures 2. Power 3. Bitterness   4. Hunger   5. Thirst
of Life   of Evil   of Life

Seven Stages of the Spiritual Journey:

1. The Passover in Egypt	2. Red Sea Crossing	3. Mt. Sinai Visitation
		4. Wilderness

Chapter Seven

Mountains—that's what most of British Columbia is. A huge province encompassing 366,255 square miles from the 49th parallel to the 60th parallel and most of it is mountains. Our route wove through channels, passages, sounds and inlets, all surrounded by the peaks and ridges of the magnificent coastal range. We had made our way into River's Inlet, the famous salmon fishing grounds, and spent the day probing into the recesses of Penrose Island, finally stumbling upon a small bay tucked behind an islet, which turned out to be a popular stopping point for travelers. It felt like a tropical paradise apart from the icy water. White shell beaches rimmed the bay, turning the sea turquoise green when the tide was on them. Long low rock shelves framed the beaches and made sharp protrusions into the surf, harbouring hundreds of pools packed with huge ocean mussels and teeming with tidal life. Leaning against a beach log, I scanned the horizon. I couldn't stop exulting over the place.

The distant ridge sloping to a sharp triangular point in the open seas was Calvert Island braving an expansive Pacific Ocean and stretching far off north into Fitzhugh Sound. It was like a Texada Island of the north for me, reminiscent of the great island that trundles north from the Gulf of Georgia, eerily transposed upon this wild domain. Earlier in the day I easily caught dinner off pristine reefs as ocean rollers lifted me gently up and down under an orange and pink sunset. At my back were huge conifers, many broken in two halfway up their solid trunks, probably snapped like matchsticks in previous winters' gales. I drew in a great draught of evergreen air and exhaled it slowly through my nostrils. My frayed emotions and pent up frustrations exhaled with the carbon dioxide into a limitless atmosphere where the obligations of my life felt truly laid aside. I was standing on a mountaintop and new vistas opened in front of me.

"And it doesn't really matter what happens to me now... 'cause I've been to the mountaintop... and I don't mind." So said Martin Luther King Jr. in a famous speech shortly before he was shot. Apparently he reached a certain place in his experience where the vision of hope and the clarity of his mission were indelibly imprinted within. He knew where he came from, where he was going, and what his purpose was. He had a mountaintop experience and it put him to rest. No one could take from him what he had.

Everybody needs a few mountaintop experiences in their lives. It's true that a good part of our existence consists of doggedly persevering through the valleys of humdrum experience, but once in a while we need to climb up on some peak and gaze over the hills and river valleys, see the big picture, and understand the lay of the land. Most people don't live on top of mountains—they live in the valleys—but we should at least visit the mountains.

In the realm of spiritual experience, God's design is that we visit some spiritual mountaintops. Of course we don't live for experiences, but by faith. Nevertheless, every person I know in the Bible, in history, or living today who lives a life of dedicated faith has had a significant experience or two along the way. These experiences ground and seal faith, indelibly imprint the truth in our minds and mobilize us for action in God's kingdom.

On their journey, the Israelites visited a mountain shortly after the fifth test at the waters of Rephidim. It was called Mt. Sinai.

When they set out from Rephidim, they came to the wilderness of Sinai and camped in the wilderness; and there Israel camped in front of the mountain. Moses went up to God, and the Lord called to him from the mountain, saying, "Thus you shall say to the house of Jacob and tell the sons of Israel... (Exodus 19:2,3)

What he would say, among many other things, was the Ten Commandments. This was to be the pivotal encounter of Israel with God where He would establish the great covenant around which the entire Old Testament revolves. This encounter was more than some casual transaction in which God gave them some rules to live by and sent them on their way. It was an awesome experience of the very presence of Almighty God. It was a literal mountaintop experience.

And Moses brought the people out of the camp to meet God, and they stood at the foot of the mountain. Now Mount Sinai was all in smoke because the Lord descended upon it in fire; and its smoke ascended like the smoke of a furnace, and the whole mountain quaked violently. When the sound of the trumpet grew louder and louder Moses spoke and God answered him with thunder. (Exodus 19:17,18)

This was no mild exposure to God. It blew their socks off! God stepped onto the scene. If we are going to go anywhere with God we must experience Him. He is not merely a proposition to be thought about. It takes life-changing experience to alter our course.

Moses had been to this mountain before. He had been minding his own timid business tending Jethro's sheep when on this same mountain he had encountered a bush that burned with a fire and yet was not consumed. Moses would never have left his sheep and gone back to Egypt to start this whole journey if he had not had this radical encounter with God. Now he was back again at the same mountain with all the people so they could have their own radical encounter, their own experience of His fire, His power, His presence.

God's purpose is to ignite us with a fire that will burn in us but not destroy us. Of course, everyone is different and some people's experiences will be much more extreme than other people's will be, but everyone must have an experience of his or her own. This is what the initiation rites of the Passover (salvation), the Red Sea (baptism), and Mount Sinai (receiving the Holy Spirit) are about. When Peter the Apostle preached the first sermon on the day the Church was born, the day of Pentecost, three thousand people stood spellbound at what they'd seen and heard and said to him, *"What must we do?"*

He told them, *"Repent, and each of you be baptized in the name of Jesus Christ for the forgiveness of your sins; and you will receive the gift of the Holy Spirit"* (Acts 2:38). These are God's terms. We will not experience Him on our terms. It must be on His.

Just as the Passover and the Red Sea have their counterpart in the New Testament experience, so does Mt. Sinai. The mountaintop experience of Mt. Sinai parallels the mountaintop experience of the day of Pentecost. At Mt. Sinai the people were gathered around for the inauguration of the old covenant and God came down with the fire of His presence and gave them His law. At Pentecost the people were gathered around for the inauguration of the new covenant and God came down in the Holy Spirit and fire and wrote the law of grace into their hearts. They both were occasions where the manifest presence of God came down to confirm His covenant.

> *When the day of Pentecost had come, they were all together in one place. And suddenly there came from heaven a noise like a violent rushing wind, and it filled the whole house where they were sitting. And there appeared to them tongues as of fire distributing themselves, and they rested on each one of them. And they were all filled with the Holy Spirit and began to speak with other tongues, as the Spirit was giving them utterance.* (Acts 2:1-4)

Each man became a Mt. Sinai with fire over his head. The presence of God came upon them as a violent wind, and each one's mouth proclaimed a message. Jesus warned them this would happen after His resurrection. He said, *"For John baptized with water, but you will be baptized with the Holy Spirit not many days from now"* (Acts 1:5).

The word baptism used here is the same Greek word, 'baptizo', used in reference to water baptism. It means to immerse, to completely dunk. God's presence is carried by and manifested in our lives by the person of the Holy Spirit. A baptism in the Holy Spirit is an immersion in the Holy Spirit. In the Christian life, if you're in for a penny, you might as well be in for a pound, as the old saying goes.

Part of God's plan for our journey into the inheritance includes Mt. Sinai experiences. The new covenant Mt. Sinai experience is like the old covenant experience, a time to get the message and receive the commandments of God, this time not on tablets of stone, but on the tablets of our hearts. One can attempt to keep an external observance of the Ten Commandments and still not embrace them in the heart. Jesus' enemies were the religious people who kept the letter of the law, but who did not love God with all their hearts and their neighbors as themselves. They crucified the Son of God. The New Testament revelation says of the people of God,

> *"You are our letter, written in our hearts, known and read by all men; being manifested that you are a letter of Christ, cared for by us, written not with ink but with the Spirit of the living God, not on tablets of stone, but on tablets of human hearts."* (2 Corinthians 3:2,3. Also see Hebrews 8:8-12)

God descended upon us in order to emblazon with His own finger the law of love into the very core of our being. There is a need to penetrate the veil over our minds and the hardness of our hearts to bring an inner enlightenment and transformation. That's why we must pray for a spirit of wisdom and revelation in the knowledge of God.

Such an encounter was definitely necessary for me. It was early in my college years and I was on a mountain of sorts (actually a small hill) up behind the campus buildings of Western Washington State University. The year was 1969 and the time was one o'clock in the morning.

It was nine o'clock in the morning when the disciples were gathered in an upper room in Jerusalem and suddenly the Spirit came upon them. Time is significant. God is not bound to slow, gradual change or evolutionary timetables. He acts definitely, suddenly stepping into our time and space, sometimes with judgment, sometimes with blessing. Rather than an impersonal force that could not act, the Holy Spirit came as a *Person* at an appointed time.

I had been studying late into the night, but mulling over in my mind the words I had been hearing from friends all that week. 'Jesus people' had begun invading the college campus, former hippies and drug users testifying to Jesus, conversion, and experiences of supernatural phenomena. A hippie I was not, but intrigued with their radical message and lifestyle I was, especially since hearing an amazing report from Lyza, my girlfriend then, who was at that time finishing her senior year of high school in Kirkland, Washington. She had gone with a friend down to the Ballard district of Seattle to a small Episcopal mission church called St. Luke's where the rector, Father Dennis Bennett, was promulgating an experience he called the baptism in the Holy Spirit. From what I had experienced growing up in the Episcopal Church, it seemed an incongruous place for such radical teachings. Mind you, it wasn't radical to me because I didn't know enough of any Christian teaching to discern what was on the edge or what was normal. Lyza shared with me that she had 'spoken in tongues' as a result of this exposure and that she was reveling in a new awareness of God's presence in her life. My other friends on campus had similar experiences after visiting a Jesus people community living at a place called Laramont in the suburbs of Bellingham. They gave me a very elemental explanation and instruction from a few New Testament passages and said, "You just ask to be baptized in the Spirit in the same way you asked Christ into your life."

While trying to study, the strange stirrings of spiritual desire kept intruding themselves upon my scholarly pursuit. "Why not?" I kept thinking to myself. "Why couldn't it all be true? Those incredible descriptions of the life of the believers in the book of Acts... how could all their straightforward accounts of miracles and adventures be interpreted in some symbolic way? It doesn't make sense. And if those things really happened to all of them, why couldn't they still happen now?" I suppose it was impulsive to drop my pen, leave my books and get in the elevator that took me down from my sixth floor dormitory. Walking around on the dark path in the woods behind campus, I found what I thought was a secluded spot and sat down in the leaves to pray.

"Jesus, I guess You know me by now and I think I am starting get to know You, but I sure would like to know You better. I've heard that You have promised to baptize people in the Holy Spirit. God, I know I'm not serving You very well and I know there is a lot of messing around in my life, but I really want to surrender myself to You. I really want to know Your life and power. Jesus, I ask You to baptize me in the Holy Spirit."

I waited for a while. My friends had told me to just ask like that, believe that He would do it and start speaking with my mouth, but not in English. Just 'whatever'. I was just beginning to feel something might happen when two people came walking up the path in the darkness talking together. Self-conscious, I quickly got up and pretended I was just standing around. I thought maybe the golden moment was lost, especially since I had been so embarrassed, but thankfully God is not so easily put off.

"Jesus, I'm back again and I meant what I said the first time. Will You baptize me with the Holy Spirit?"

I began to speak some nonsense phrases, feeling very foolish and glad I was alone in the dark woods. As I continued I became aware of a feeling of lightness in my head and a kind of quickening heartbeat. The phrases began to link together and take on a life of their own. My mind did not comprehend as I listened to myself with increasing wonder. A warm rush, a sensation of power and presence seemed to well up from my feet and legs and a pent-up stream of words burst out of my mouth. It was an overwhelming experience, enough to unmistakably imprint upon me the reality of Christ and His ability to divinely intervene in my life. The speaking in tongues part was amazing, but the more significant aspect of the experience was the resulting hunger and passion I had to read and know God's word.

In retrospect, there is no doubt in my mind that this encounter, this mountaintop experience, is what radicalized my faith and put me into overdrive spiritually. That is the purpose of mountaintops, to arrest us and to mobilize us. The twelve disciples had spent three solid years with Jesus, but they were useless when it came to upholding the testimony of their faith in the world. In Gethsemane they all ran away under pressure. Jesus, after His resurrection, gave them the Holy Spirit and told them,

> *"But you will receive power when the Holy Spirit has come upon you; and you shall be My witnesses both in Jerusalem, and in all Judea and Samaria, and even to the remotest part of the earth."* (Acts 1:8)

Without the Holy Spirit there is no Christianity, no conversion, no separation from sin, no power, no witness. From the time of my confession of Christ at Malibu, I had the Holy Spirit in me, but I needed a baptism in that Spirit to be the catalyst into usefulness. The most obvious difference after this experience (beside blabbing around in tongues when I was by myself) was a voracious appetite for the scripture. Literally, the Spirit was taking the written words and inscribing them upon my heart. The other difference was a passion to witness to the reality of Christ and the gospel. The previously described choices to move to Canada, live by faith, etc., all came as a result of this foundational experience. Whether a person speaks in tongues or not is of secondary importance to having a significant encounter with the Holy Spirit. Somewhere along our path we must make the connections with God's Person that we need to make.

> *"For you have not come to a mountain that may be touched and to a blazing fire, and to darkness and gloom and a whirlwind...*[Sinai] *But*

111

you have come to Mount Zion and to the city of the living God, the heavenly Jerusalem, and to myriads of angels, to the general assembly and the church of the firstborn who are enrolled in heaven, and to God, the Judge of all, and to the spirits of the righteous made perfect, and to Jesus the mediator of a new covenant..." (Hebrews 12:18,22-24)

Distractions

Golden Calf Idolatry at Sinai, Exodus 32
The Sixth Temptation - Idolatry

The Ten Temptations: **6. Counterfeit Gods (Idolatry: The Golden Calf)**

1. Pressures   2. Power   3. Bitterness   4. Hunger   5. Thirst
   of Life   of Evil   of Life

Seven Stages of the Spiritual Journey:

1. The Passover in Egypt	2. Red Sea Crossing	3. Mt. Sinai Visitation
		4. Wilderness

Chapter Eight

My favorite writing spot was a retractable chair in the cockpit with my feet propped on the cabin stairway. Most of the time it was comfortable. I would take in the scenery while sipping a coffee, and homey dinner smells would waft up from below. Sometimes it was a trial, especially when attacked by horseflies or mosquitoes or when contending with water drips under the tarp in bad weather. Once in a while I wondered whether taking the time to write was worth it. Maybe I should just relax and relish the time off. Two things kept me writing. One was I enjoyed it; the other was that even if these stories never reached a wider audience, I wanted my children and grandchildren to know what God did in our lives.

I wish I knew more about the lives of my forebears. Writing down thoughts and experiences builds bridges between the generations. God encourages, in fact, commands us to pass the baton to the next generation. David took this responsibility seriously and hundreds of years after the Exodus wrote Psalm 78.

"Listen, O my people, to my instruction; incline your ears to the words of my mouth. I will open my mouth in a parable; I will utter dark sayings of old... We will not conceal them from their children, but tell to the generation to come the praises of the Lord..."
(Psalm 78:1-4)

The 'dark sayings of old' and the 'parable' refer to the Exodus story. *"I will open my mouth,"* the psalmist says. *"We will not conceal them from their children."* Children in our culture generally are missing a sense of roots and generational continuity. Between lack of communication, the breakdown of families, and the omnipresence of TV and Internet, children live in the immediate experiences of the moment. Not only are they ignorant of the Bible stories needed to understand much of Western culture's history and literature, they are ignorant of their own family histories as well. Living life successfully requires a preparation of heart and a framework to interpret what happens to us. Our history must be invested with a set of core values and the seminal stories that give those values power. These are what

115

we pass on to our children and others. This is what defines us as a people.

> *"For He established a testimony in Jacob, and appointed a law in Israel, which He commanded to our fathers. That they should teach them to their children; that the generation to come might know, even the children yet to be born, that they may arise and tell them to their children, that they should put their confidence in God, and not forget the works of God, but keep His commandments, and not be like their fathers, a stubborn and rebellious generation, a generation that did not prepare its heart, and whose spirit was not faithful to God."*
> (Psalm 78:5-8)

One day on our trip up the coast, in Codville Lagoon, we came upon an old friend who was a touchstone of my family roots. Ellen and I grew up together; her mom was my aunt's partner in the Sunnybeam Nursery School of which we were both alumni. In the summers she and her family sometimes joined our family on the *Nor'wester*, where she first caught the sailing bug. I hadn't seen Ellen in thirty years.

Mother had given me a note she'd received from her in the spring as we were preparing for our trip. Ellen and her husband, who were both teachers in Alaska, were bringing their boat south to leave in LaConner, Washington, for the winter. "Keep an eye out for them," Mom said. "It would be fun if you met up with them."

I thought, "Right, Mom. Do you know what the odds are of our paths crossing in the myriad channels of the north coast, especially coming from opposite directions?"

We had just spent one of the few hot summer days swimming in Codville, in the cold salt chuck and in a beautiful lake at the head of the lagoon. Motoring *Crayon* the mile back across the bay in the late afternoon, we reached *Fred* to find a note from Ellen, of all people. She had recognized our unique boat on the way in and they were anchored around the point in the next bay. We spent the next morning reminiscing over a huckleberry coffeecake and marveling at this amazing chance meeting. Later, I had even more reason to call it divine providence. Ellen gave us an extra tarp in response to my 'leaking cabin' stories, which proved to be a virtual lifesaver a week later.

"What kind of church do you pastor?"

"Well, it's kind of an inter-denominational church with people of all sorts of backgrounds. Some of them were teens in the late sixties and early seventies who were part of our coffeehouse ministry on the beach."

"Are they still there? I mean, are they still going on?"

Sitting across from Ellen in her and husband Doug's sailboat, the *Marathon,* I was a little surprised at the questions. Ellen looked the part of the sixties generation herself. Now in her late forties, she still wore shoulder-length hair, though streaks of gray ran through it. Her pretty countenance and engaging smile hadn't changed and her figure was still trim like the boat she captained.

"Is your church like a charismatic-type church?" She said with some knowledge—she was trying to relate. "We had a charismatic church like that in Alaska and a lot of the people are not there anymore. They ended up getting divorced or getting back into drugs and stuff."

My response was outwardly off the cuff. "Well, that happens a lot I guess. People need to deal with their issues whether they are Christians or not." It was just a passing comment in the midst of our enjoyable interchange, but the grief I carried over failed Christians could even find me in Codville Lagoon, a hundred and fifty miles north of Vancouver Island. Sailing the next day across Fisher Channel into Lama Passage where we would get some sorely needed provisions at Bella Bella, I thought again about Ellen's observations of the Christians in her little town.

"The sons of Ephraim were archers equipped with bows, yet they turned back in the day of battle. They did not keep the covenant of God, and refused to walk in His law; and they forgot His deeds, and His miracles that He had shown them."
(Psalm 78:8-11)

Probably the most painful part of ministry life for me was watching people come to a genuine Spirit-filled faith and then somehow fall or slip away through the years. Sometimes we saw tremendous grace at work in lives where faith and right choices were exercised, but we also saw the wasted potential and destruction that resulted from wrong choices. These people were like our own spiritual children and we deeply felt the grief over them. On the other hand, nothing brings greater joy than watching someone discover for the first time God's forgiveness, His love and His presence. If only they could hold on through the process to the full end of their faith.

> *"He wrought wonders before their fathers in the land of Egypt, in the field of Zoan. He divided the sea and caused them to pass through, and He made the waters stand up like a heap. Then He led them with the cloud by day and all the night with a light of fire. He split the rocks in the wilderness and gave them abundant drink like the ocean depths. He brought forth streams also from the rock and caused waters to run down like rivers. Yet they still continued to sin against Him, to rebel against the Most High in the desert. and in their heart they put God to the test by asking food according to their desire. Then they spoke against God; they said, 'Can God prepare a table in the wilderness? Behold, He struck the rock so that waters gushed out, and streams were overflowing; Can He give bread also? Will He provide meat for His people?' How often they rebelled against Him in the wilderness and grieved Him in the desert! Again and again they tempted God, and pained the Holy One of Israel."* (Psalm 78:9-20, 40-41)

The journey of life can be hard. I suppose we don't often consider that it might be hard on God. But the psalmist, who recorded the testings in the wilderness, also revealed a God who was pained and grieved. The words He used when He gave them the law at Sinai is the language of relationship.

> *"You yourselves have seen what I did to the Egyptians, and how I bore you on eagles' wings, and brought you to Myself. Now then, if you will indeed obey My voice and keep My covenant, then you shall be My own possession among all the peoples, for all the earth is Mine; and you shall be to Me a kingdom of priests and a holy nation."* (Exodus 19:4-6)

It says He brought them to Himself. The spiritual journey is a journey into God's heart. The tests only strip away what hinders us from really knowing Him. Yet the psalm records that every time a cloud appears on these people's horizon, they rail against God. God tried to raise them steadily to a higher plane of living in trust, but they fluctuated wildly from mountaintop elation to pits of despair, from exalting God's greatness to doubting His existence.

Our journey kept having its fluctuations as well. Every day brought the unpredictable. Leaving the fellowship of the *Marathon* and the security of Codville Lagoon, we crossed Fisher Channel to Lama Passage. Threatening banks of billowing gray clouds engulfed the morning sunlight and the southeasterly wind freshened as we crossed. We hoisted the staysail, which smoothed our passage across the foamy whitecaps. Instead of plowing into the seas, we heeled over enough to ride high on the gray backs of the waves, deflecting the crests and keeping us ahead of the spray. We gained Lama passage in two hours. It was always a relief to escape large exposed bodies of water into protected channels.

The wind lessened, but the rain increased so we had a dismal entry into the village of Bella Bella after all. The prospect of fresh provisions, showers and a laundromat were compensation for the four-hour passage. The young native received compensation of another kind when he rang up our outrageously large bill in the band store. "Come back again soon," he said, grinning first at the till and then at me.

Lyza found her phone card in her purse and her children at home so she made the most of the opportunity to touch base with her loved ones. Gregarious by nature, I often wondered if she found the boat companionship a bit sparse, but she never complained. My only clue was the telephone lines burning up at these rare intervals.

I went to the tiny airport to fetch a new Perkins starting motor. *Fred's* starter first malfunctioned back in the Gulf Islands, causing our hearts to leap to our throats every time we pushed the starting button in some isolated place. I had the obscure part flown up as insurance against ignition failure in even more remote areas. Licking our financial wounds, we ran a mile across the bay to the Shearwater Resort, with its restaurant and bar, laundromat, and marine hardware store, all catering to the luxury yachts moored at the dock.

Tying the *Fred Free* at the end of a long float lined on both sides with fancy boats, I sauntered nonchalantly down the boardwalk, trying to fit in, with my Greek fisherman's hat at a jaunty angle and my white beard looking salty. As we ordered some great Chinese food at the large restaurant, the jarring contrast of this little colony of wealth in its wilderness setting hit home.

Beaming insistently down from above were TV screen images. Of all things, we were assaulted with a professional wrestling match. A livid face accented with bleach blond crew cut and black moustache worked his jaw at his opponent, mouthing profanity and fake rage while ten muscle-bound men strained to hold him back. The other contestant, boasting a light blue suit and attended by six dancing women in skimpy silver chemises, taunted the first guy while the jeering throngs in the arena egged them on. I turned to look at the placid bay and endless green forest just outside the window. A couple of seabirds paddled by. I turned back to the battling titans and shook my head. After weeks of immersion in wilderness beauty and solitude, the scene on TV was so bizarre I felt like they were aliens from another planet engaging in some primitive mating ritual. I resented their intrusion—I wanted to flee back to nature. Nature is a sanctifier. It is God's most elemental baptism in His creative self. The word 'sanctify' in a spiritual sense means 'to be set apart for a holy purpose'. It usually involves a cleansing, a separation, a dedication to God. Nature separates us from distracting influences.

Fred's open cockpit was definitely an immersion in the outdoor world. After days of drifting down inlets, hearing only the sounds of nature and beholding the ever-changing moods of sky and land, we became part of the elemental world, attuned to the voices of creation. We forgot the insistent clamor and distortions of the media culture; our world was reduced to our boat, our traveling companions and the everlasting wilderness.

While not wanting to idealize nature, a good dose of it brings into sharp relief the asinine drivel that fills hours on the TV screen. Enough of this brain rot, and we have trouble distinguishing the worthy from the worthless and the valuable from the vile. Worse, our own lifestyle begins to reflect the values we regularly imbibe. "What is real is outside the window," I told myself, and tried to ignore the wrestling match.

Israel also came up with some bizarre behavior at the same time they were having God's special visitation at Sinai. Moses came down from the mountaintop with the Ten Commandments in hand to find the people bowing down and worshiping a golden calf they had created. They were testing God again, or should we say God was testing them. Idolatry was the sixth temptation in the wilderness.

Bowing down to a golden calf is not something most of us could relate to as a temptation. What motivated these Israelites to tear off their jewelry, melt it down, fashion a cow, and call it their god who delivered them from Egypt? We don't know too many people with some object of veneration in a grotto behind their house. Yet one of those eternal commandments given to Moses on Sinai was, 'You shall not make for yourself an idol.' Ironically, while God spelled this taboo out for Moses, the people down below were in the process of fashioning just such an idol. With their leader away for a protracted time period, they got restless and needed something to focus on.

Intensely focusing our life and energy on any one thing is a form of worship. When that thing pre-empts or overshadows the Creator's central place of worship, it becomes an idol. On that basis it is safe to say our lives are riddled with idolatry. Man was made to focus his praise and adoration on his Creator, receiving his life from God and giving it back again. This is worship. A complete circle. Remove the Creator and man will find another place for his life energy to flow. Just like a river, worship can't stand still—it must have an outlet.

I wondered about the time, energy, money and adulation flowing into that wrestling scene on TV. I've been told professional wrestling has more viewers than any other sport on television. Maybe these Israelites were not so different from us after all. Why does such nonsense hold a certain fascination anyway?

Idolatry is a pitfall even to the one who knows and loves God. Consider the irony of Moses on the mountain with God and Aaron down below with the people.

"You shall have no other gods before me." (Exodus 20:3)

Moses was sequestered with God on the mountain getting his instructions. Meanwhile, the people were down below saying, *"... as for this Moses, the man who brought us up from the land of Egypt, we do not know what has become of him"* (Exodus 32:1).

> *"You shall not make for yourself an idol, or any likeness of what is in heaven above or on the earth beneath or in the water under the earth."* (Exodus 20:4)

God's finger continued carving the stone tablets. Moses thought about all those carved images of frogs, half-man and half-animals in Egypt, while the people said to Aaron down below, *"Come, make us a god who will go before us…"* (Exodus 32:1).

Aaron thought, "Next they'll turn on me and I'll get blamed for bringing them out of Egypt. Better a cow than me".

God continued, *"You shall not worship them or serve them; for I, the Lord your God, am a jealous God…"* (Exodus 20:5).

"Uh-oh," Moses is thinking, "I wonder what Aaron and the people are up to down the hill."

> *Aaron said to them, "Tear off the gold rings which are in the ears of your wives…" He took this from their hand, and fashioned it with a graving tool and made it into a molten calf…* (Exodus 32:2,4)

His later explanation under Moses' questioning was, *" I said to them, 'Whoever has any gold, let them tear it off.' So they gave it to me, and I threw it into the fire, and out came this calf"* (Exodus 32:24).

Not only was Aaron guilty of creating this abomination, but he also had the audacity to feign innocence about it. How did this golden calf get here? "I don't know, it just jumped out of the fire." Idols don't just happen—we create the things that separate us from God. Aaron has a little perjury problem here.

> [And God said,] *"You shall not take the name of the Lord your God in vain, for the Lord will not leave him unpunished who takes His name in vain."* (Exodus 20:7)

Upon closer inspection, Moses realized that God was actually writing with His finger in stone. He's very personal about this. The first four commandments are all about Him. You shall have no other gods. Don't take His name in vain. You shall not fashion an idol. Remember the Sabbath to keep it holy. They are all vertical commandments. They are really all about idolatry. The other six are about man's treatment of man: lying, stealing, adultery, and things like that. By the order of the commandments, it is clear that loving God is a priority over loving man.

Aaron was down below breaking the first three:

Now when Aaron saw this, [meaning the calf] *he built an altar before it; and Aaron made a proclamation and said, "Tomorrow shall be a feast to the Lord." So the next day they rose early and offered burnt offerings; and brought peace offerings; and the people sat down to eat and to drink, and rose up to 'play'."* (Exodus 32:5,6) [According to the commentary, the word play suggests sex play.]

*Then the Lord spoke to Moses, "Go down at once, for **your** people, whom **you** brought up from the land of Egypt, have corrupted themselves.* (Exodus 32:7, emphasis added)

*Then Moses entreated the Lord his God, and said, "O Lord, why doth Your anger burn against **Your** people whom **You** have brought out from the land of Egypt with great power and with a mighty hand?"* (Exodus 32:11, emphasis added) [There is some discrepancy here about who is being referred to as having brought them out of Egypt, Moses or God.]

Moses reminded God about His reputation with the Egyptians (what will they think if You kill your people out here?). After talking God out of His anger, Moses went down to see for himself and blew his stack, breaking the tablets with the Ten Commandments at the foot of the mountain. In a rage at what was going on, he pulverized the golden calf, scattered it over the water, stuffed people's faces in it and made them drink it. Better to face Moses' wrath than God's. Ultimately it took divine retribution and some capital punishment to get things under control but the heart problem behind idolatry is not solved by such measures. It is significant that the test of idolatry happened simultaneously with the revelation of God's presence on

Sinai. The heart that loves an idol is antithetical to the heart that loves the presence of God. James described this conflict in terms of adultery. *"You adulteresses, do you not know that friendship with the world is hostility toward God?"* (James 4:4) Or as John says, *"If anyone loves the world, the love of the Father is not in him"* (1 John 2:15b).

We cannot love God and an idol simultaneously. The 'world' does not mean the created world we live in but the distorted temptations of lust, power, and materialism in that world—the distractions. Israel committed spiritual adultery in the desert and this transgression provoked a serious possibility of a parting of ways. We discover that God is considering a 'separation' as they prepare to leave Sinai to continue their journey. He says to them, *"Go up to a land flowing with milk and honey; for I will not go up in your midst, because you are an obstinate people, lest I destroy you on the way"* (Exodus 33:3).

As we read on, God tells Moses to go on up into Canaan and He will send an angel before them to wipe out their enemies. An angel is powerful enough to destroy their enemies but an angel is not God. Moses, the man who talks to God face to face, immediately recognizes the difference. He will not settle for the power of God without the person of God.

> *"If Your presence does not go with us, do not lead us up from here. For how then can it be known that I have found favor in Your sight, I and Your people? Is it not by Your going with us, so that we, I and Your people, may be distinguished from all the other people who are upon the face of the earth?"* (Exodus 33:15,16)

Moses took a stand for himself and the people, saying in effect, "Angels are not enough! Power is not enough! The land flowing with milk and honey is not enough! We want You, God." God's offer to send an angel is a continuation of the idolatry test. Sometimes He will give people what they want even though it is not what they need as a subtle judgment upon their own wrong choices. The psalm at the beginning of this chapter records this sad recourse of God after He expended every effort to change the Israelites' hearts, *"And He gave them their request; but sent leanness into their soul"* (Psalm 106:15, KJV).

The price for clinging to the idols of our life is a poverty of soul, a diminishing of the riches of the inheritance within us. Moses avoided separation from God by pressing in to know Him and His glory. He interceded for the people and God relented. *"And He said, 'My presence shall go with you, and I will give you rest'"* (Exodus 33: 14).

The only way to ultimately pass the test of idolatry is to make a priority of God's presence in our lives. The prevailing conception about what is supposed to distinguish Christian people from others is that they are more holy than the rest, or at least they think they are. The truth is, there is often not much difference. Some non-believers seem to live a lot more righteously than some believers do. Though righteous living is a natural fruit of the tree, the distinguishing mark of the early believers was that they had been with Jesus and that His Spirit continued to be with them after the resurrection. As Moses discerned, it is God's presence that is the distinguishing mark. His presence, like nature, sanctifies us, and righteous living results because our hearts no longer yearn for the cheap substitution of idols.

Idolatry has so many possible applications that only a sensitivity to God can even reveal them to us. From the more obvious idols such as wealth or power to the more subtle ones such as co-dependencies or workaholism, they all have the same effect, to keep us one step removed from Him. To walk with God, as the disciples learned with Jesus, is unsettling. Jesus was constantly disturbing false securities and established worldviews, especially religious ones. Religion can be man's attempt to tame God and make Him predictable. If we can just secure ourselves with a creed, an unchanging code of behavior, a routine liturgy and manageable commitment, then we can keep God in His proper domain and get on with life in ours. Relationship with God is more demanding and uncovers the more subtle compromises we make.

Remembering the sorrow I felt when Ellen reminded me of friends no longer walking with God, I knew that the test of idolatry was one big reason. Some had turned aside because of unrelinquished sins and some over disappointments, but whatever they stumbled over they all had one thing in common. They no longer enjoyed His presence. Somewhere along the path their hearts had chosen the security and predictability of their own works over the loving but unsettling presence of God. The inner journey with God was put on hold, yet I knew it could be renewed as soon as they were ready to leave their false security behind.

Walking back down to the floats with fresh laundry over my shoulder after a good meal at the restaurant, I took another look at the rows of pleasure boats and thought of those decadent old men with their $200,000 floating motor homes sitting in their plush interiors and the boring dryness of their staterooms. "Who needs it?!" I scoffed, "when you have cozy little *Freddy* to grow mildew in." Then an idea hit me. I could use these rich yachters as an example of idolatrous living, an illustration of the sixth temptation. I tossed analogies around in my mind as I swung up on the deck catching my foot on a stay, almost dumping the laundry overboard. By the time I squeezed myself through the tiny triangular opening of the tarp tent, I had the old idolaters compared to bloated salmon coming back to spawn after years of gobbling up smaller fish in the oceans of materialism, pride and power. They were waiting out their final days at Shearwater before judgment fell.

I tried the idea out on Lyza. She gave me a derisive pitying look from the cramped bunks. "Give me some of that idolatrous living anytime." Obviously she didn't appreciate the analogy or the higher ascetic aspects of cruising with *Fred*. As I untied the ropes to cast us off into the next leg of the journey, I thought of the phony little lines inscribed horizontally in the monstrous fiberglass hulls of these great yachts. They were put there to imitate the look of a classic wood boat. Setting my course away from all the wealth and comfort, squinting through the misty rain, I said to myself, "See, they're just *Fred* wanna-bes anyway."

A Place for His Presence

The Tabernacle, Exodus 25

The Tabernacle

1. Pressures 2. Power 3. Bitterness 4. Hunger 5. Thirst   6. Idolatry
   of Life   of Evil   of Life

Seven Stages of the Spiritual Journey:

1. The Passover in Egypt	2. Red Sea Crossing	3. Mt. Sinai Visitation
		4. Wilderness

Chapter Nine

We had ventured out into scary territory crossing open ocean to Goose Island, a low-lying sea-swept isle six miles away from the protection of the mainland. From its western shore, the next stop was Japan. On its eastern side we found insecure anchorage in a sandy bay surrounded with rocky outcroppings interspersed with drift-strewn beaches. The roar of the ocean breakers through the trees reminded us we were far from the safety of mainland channels. It was not a place to hang around too long, and not a place to establish anything of permanence. At the first VHF report of wind picking up we would scurry back to shelter.

Piling ourselves into *Crayon*, we charged ashore to explore the wildness of the place. Soon Ginette conscripted Lyza and me into building a sandcastle, with the bulk of the digging falling to me and the decorative touches being Lyza's forte. Even kids like to build things, especially sandcastles. You get to a beach ready to relax and they want you to grub around in the sand digging moats, heaping up walls and making turrets out of buckets and cups. They have an inherent desire to create something and then fill it with imaginary people, weaving a story using sticks and shells and seaweed.

Boaz, of course, went clear out of his mind; I think God made sandy beaches especially for kids and dogs. The dog even got into 'scoot bum' mode. ('Scoot bum' is when Bo becomes so overcome with canine exuberance that he tucks his rear end underneath, pumps his hind legs like a hare, and runs tight circles around his loved ones, sending a sandy rooster tail in every direction). In this case, he also pulled his lips back over his teeth in a silly mad-dog grin and kept this up—grabbing at sticks, seaweed, anything—until he crashed through the sandcastle and raised a howl of protest. Somewhat chagrined, he went off to roll in a washed-up dead seagull, and finished off his shenanigans by gripping a lingcod carcass in his teeth and flailing it around in circles. All in all, it was dog heaven.

By evening we were back on the boat rocking to sleep in the rollers, pleasantly exhausted from our exertions. Breakers in the darkness of night surged with the high tide into the bay, making our refuge feel even less safe. By the next morning our sandcastle was

129

only a slight horseshoe dent in the sand. Attempting to build anything of value in the face of the destructive forces at work in the natural world is a work of faith. Yet there is something in our makeup that wants to build something that will last, and God encourages that constructive urge.

It was during Israel's sojourn amid insecure desert lodgings that God gave Moses instructions about building a sanctuary:

Then the Lord spoke to Moses, saying, "Tell the sons of Israel to raise a contribution for Me; from every man whose heart moves him you shall raise My contribution... Let them construct a sanctuary for Me, that I may dwell among them." (Exodus 25:1-2, 8)

It was a strange time to talk about a construction project when their lifestyle was nomadic, but the timing was just right in terms of the spiritual pilgrimage that Israel was illustrating. The conversation between God and Moses on Sinai was about more than the Ten Commandments. He gave Moses all the detailed legal code for the new nation (later recorded in Leviticus), which became the foundation of law for all western society. On Sinai guidelines were given for social order, health, justice, agriculture, and a system of sacrificial worship. It was quite a bit of information.

The final topic God brought up was the matter of building a house for His presence to dwell in. Although this may seem strange, there was logic to this instruction to build in light of the steps leading up to it. First, they were to recognize that the water (God's Presence) came from the Rock (Christ) at Rephidim, and then they were to fully experience His presence at Sinai while rejecting its counterfeit, idolatry. Now they were to build a sanctuary for that Presence to dwell in. The people were being methodically prepared to be bearers of God's presence. The purpose of building a sanctuary was to bring focus and expression to this primary goal.

If you think about it, it's preposterous—as if people could make a place for the Creator of the universe to live in! In fact, later on when David got the inspiration to build a house for God, the Lord says to Him, *"Heaven is my throne, and the earth is my footstool. Where then is a house you could build for me?..."* *"Behold, heaven and the highest heaven cannot contain You..."* (Isaiah 66:1,2; 1 Kings 8:27).

Ludicrous as it may seem, the idea of building a house for God to dwell in runs through the Bible. It starts with Moses' tabernacle, or tent, which metamorphosed into the more permanent temple of Solomon, built in Jerusalem, which stood for hundreds of years. Jesus then introduced the radical conceptual shift in understanding God's house, recognizing the Church as His temple. Standing outside the temple building in Jerusalem, He said to the Jews when they asked for a sign to prove who He was: *"Destroy this temple, and in three days I will raise it up."* (John 2:19).

The Jews thought He was crazy, thinking He meant the temple building, which took forty-six years to build. However, the scripture goes on to record: *"But He was speaking of the temple of His body. So when He was raised from the dead, His disciples remembered..."* (John 2:21,22).

He was serving notice that the new temple of God was to be a human body, not a physical building. The resurrection raised the initial temple, Christ's body, by the power of the Holy Spirit. When the same Holy Spirit was released into the bodies of the believers, they singly and corporately became the temple, the dwelling place of God. Jesus said, *"For where two or three have gathered together in my name, I am there in their midst"* (Matthew 18:20). This is a remarkable paradigm shift. God's house—the place of His presence—from then on would be in a community of people. The community of people may erect a building to gather in, but the Church is the people, not the mortar and bricks. This new spiritual temple is clearly described in New Testament passages.

"...you also, as living stones, are being built up as a spiritual house for a holy priesthood, to offer up spiritual sacrifices...." (1 Peter 2:5)

"...in whom the whole building, being fitted together, is growing into a holy temple in the Lord; in whom you also are being built together into a dwelling of God in the Spirit." (Ephesians 2:21-22)

As the Church we are called away from the idolatry of self-worship to service and love for God and interdependence with others. God's call to Moses, *"Let them build Me a sanctuary",* is a timeless call sounding down through the ages to this present day. To enter into the inheritance is not just an individual quest. The transformation of character that is the substance of that inheritance requires a surrender and dedication to the house of God. The instruction to build God a house to dwell in is strategically placed at this point in the inheritance journey to call the people higher, to something bigger than themselves.

They are called to community. In the corporate body the presence of God would dwell in a manner that could not be experienced in the individual body alone. The awesome manifestation of God's presence at Sinai in fire and smoke was now to be translated into and through the creative expression of a community of people. So, individual spiritual experience today finds ultimate meaning and expression in the context of the Church.

Back in the early days of beach ministry, I never really thought God was into building things. I figured the problem with Christianity started with organized religion. We weren't part of any church institution and proud of it. I thought personal belief, experience and action were paramount. However, I should have known better, for in spite of our freewheeling approach, we did secure a building to meet in and we did gather a 'flock'.

The desire to congregate and then meet the needs of that congregation is both a natural and a supernatural drive. My initial avoidance and independence from the organized church was due to ignorance and youthful pride. In the end we are all just humans needing the same remedies for our isolated condition.

Church was not man's idea; it was God's. God said to Moses, *"Let them construct a sanctuary for Me"* (Exodus 25:8), and Jesus said, *"I will build My church"* (Matthew 16:18). It's one thing to be involved in radical introductions to faith and exciting works of the Holy Spirit; it's another thing to get down to the business of living a new life. In our little 'church' on the beach we began to experience the heartache of people we really cared for falling away, floundering in brokenness and leaving our little flock. We didn't know what to do. Some deaths particularly shook us, of young men and women whom God had touched and who then took destructive paths. We began to see the seriousness of life's choices and feel our need for support and further training.

At that time God spoke very definitely to us as He did to the Israelites just after their experience on Sinai. It was time to move on.

I was sitting in the tree house I built in a maple just off the front porch of our beach house. As I was going over in my mind the names of young people who had fallen into trouble, I felt heartsick. Why did everything seem to be so hard? For every new person who met Christ, someone else slipped away. The burden of it was heavy and I needed guidance. I opened my Bible and it fell upon a very obscure little passage in the prophets:

"You have sown much, but harvest little; you eat, but there is not enough to be satisfied; you drink, but there is not enough to become drunk; you put on clothing, but no one is warm enough; and he who earns, earns wages to put into a purse with holes." (Haggai 1:6)

When a passage resonates with your inward struggle, it hits you between the eyes and penetrates to your heart. That passage described exactly how I felt. Diminishing returns. I looked for much and was disappointed with what came back. We poured in heart and soul, only to reap disappointment.

"Why?" declares the Lord of hosts, "Because of My house which lies desolate, while each of you runs to his own house. Therefore, because of you the sky has withheld its dew and the earth has withheld its produce." (Haggai 1:9,10)

Those few verses skewered me. I didn't know it then, but I was getting a lifetime mission statement. Build the house of God! Leave your own independent pursuit, building your own thing, and put the building of God's house first in your heart. It couldn't have been clearer. Later on, the nature of the mission crystallized as I learned what it meant. I came across other verses that caused me to strongly identify with the passion of David over God's house.

Remember, O Lord, on David's behalf, all his affliction; how he swore to the Lord, and vowed to the Mighty One of Jacob, "Surely I will not enter my house, nor lie on my bed; I will not give sleep to my eyes, or slumber to my eyelids; until I find a place for the Lord, a dwelling place for the Mighty One of Jacob." (Psalm 132:1-5)

Being dedicated to God's house is being dedicated to making a place for His presence in your life and in the life of a congregation. God's response to David's heart-cry comes later in the same psalm:

"For the Lord has chosen Zion; He has desired it for His habitation. This is My resting place forever; here I will dwell, for I have desired it." (Psalm 132:13-14)

In the beginning of our ministry God met with us where we were; He met with us on the college campus and went with us to the schools of White Rock where the kids were. God left His own turf to come to ours. Jesus went to the streets of Palestine, not just the synagogues. Nevertheless, He sought us out to bring us home, to be part of a building, a dwelling place for God on earth. Jesus surely made His presence known in our little street fellowship, but His house, we were to learn, is more completely expressed in a local church, a committed gathering of believers in a given locality.

We had much to learn, but the promise in the book of Haggai was that God would bless us if we put His house first. We gathered those who were willing to come and planted our feet in a little White Rock church where cute little grandmas hugged our necks, prayed on us, and served up Sunday dinners after church. The little church, called the Evangelistic Tabernacle at the time, (which we quickly nicknamed 'the Tab' for short) was amazingly receptive to us. It was a stretch, since they were decidedly Pentecostal in their traditions, but their acceptance and warmth put us at ease. They looked past the long hair and other accoutrements of the counter-culture and were blessed by the evidence that God was moving among the unchurched youth in the community. The pastoral couple, Verne and Marge Wilson, epitomized the church's wisdom and welcome. Verne previously coming down to our coffeehouse had first opened the door for us to make cautious forays into their services. The transition was not always easy.

The young man with thick curly hair to his shoulders looked a lot like Absalom, David's son, might have looked. He walked down the aisle of the church in jeans and the red plaid shirt so many White Rock youth wore in those days. A good musician, a former experimenter with drugs, he was considered 'cool' by most of his contemporaries. I was surprised to see him going forward and glanced back, with eyebrows raised, at the row of young cohorts behind me. Kerbey had on his overalls with no shirt underneath; his bare feet rested on the backrest of the pew in front of him. We grinned uneasily at each other, "What's he going to say?"

Clark leaned lackadaisically over the small pulpit and took in the people with his dreamy gaze. Clark always looked and acted a little like he was stoned even if he wasn't. It was part of his persona. He spoke about finding faith in Christ and he was sharing along pretty comfortably until he got on the subject of the fancy cars in the parking lot.

"I don't know how you can be believers in Christ and drive around those Cadillacs in the parking lot. Jesus didn't own anything…"

Even the row of characters behind me was looking embarrassed. "He just insulted these people," I whispered to Lyza. "I can't believe he just said that."

Episodes like that made us feel it would only be a matter of time before we burned our bridges, but the bridges remained intact. A book could be written about the wild and woolly stories of the amalgamation of sixties youth culture and the Evangelistic Tabernacle. They had enough maturity and love to domesticate us and we had the exuberance and zeal to stir them up—a symbiotic arrangement. Jesus brought us to a house that had not forgotten its mission. *"Go out into the highways and along the hedges, and compel them to come in, so that my house may be filled."* (Luke 14:23).

We became part of the house and helped fill it up. There I discovered my pastoral calling and there I learned the purpose of God's kingdom and the secrets of His inheritance. I never planned to be part of a church and I certainly never planned to be a pastor. I was just drawn in, conscripted by the love of Christ and the excitement of preaching good news to those who hadn't heard it. I don't think the Apostle Peter ever planned to be a pastor either.

I wish I could say that the backslidings stopped when we got into a church, but the rigors of the spiritual path continued to sift. We had joined a great church, one that was willing to risk, experiment, and grow. Thirty years later I can still say that the leaders and the people of this church have been an inspiration to me to seek genuine Christianity in the real world.

Probably most notable among many unique qualities this church exemplifies is a commitment to the oneness of all believers. At the time we came into this little congregation with our motley crew of young people, others were gathering to this fellowship under the banner of worship, unity and the reality of the Holy Spirit. We became a non-denominational church with members from many different backgrounds—Lutheran, Baptist, Catholic, Anglican, Presbyterian, Pentecostal, and many from no church background at all. These members all reinforced that today is not a day of narrow creeds or emphasizing one particular truth to the exclusion of others. It's a day of humility—a desire to have unity in the essentials of Christian faith and diversity in non-essentials. A day to love one another and fulfill Jesus' high priestly prayer before His crucifixion: *"...that they may all be one; even as You, Father, are in Me, and I in You, that they also may be in Us; that the world may believe that You sent Me."* (John 17:21).

The greatest historical reproach to the Christian faith and subsequently the greatest stumbling block to the faith of many has been its fractiousness. That is why a crucial step of the spiritual pilgrimage into the inheritance is a call to build a house for God. We can't solve the great problems of Christian disunity, but we can personally learn unity by joining other believers in community. In pursuit of interdependent living and with a certain spiritual idealism, we tried several different living experiments over the years. One of the earliest was the church farm...

"The cows got the bloat. The cow's got the bloat. Hey, ho, the derry-O, the cow's got the bloat."

"He's awful happy," I thought, watching Peter come through the kitchen door at 7:00 AM. "What did he say?" I looked across the table at two other young men living with us on the church farm.

"He said the cow's got the bloat!"

I stared at them, trying to gauge the import of what I'd just heard. The import, I discovered shortly, was that our milk cow, Henrietta, broke through the barn door during the night and got into the grain bin. Later as the vet tried piercing the cow's beach-balloon stomach to release the air, Peter looked more sober as he realized the seriousness of the situation. He hadn't really been making light of this latest disaster in our farming enterprise; he was just trying to exercise the principle we taught him about rejoicing in everything.

Peter had a lot bigger things to exercise this principle over than cows. He had escaped from a life of drugs, which had landed him in Oakalla prison at a very young age. There he met Christ in solitary confinement. After his release he had a chance to be discipled into a new life by living on our church farm. That afternoon, during a house prayer meeting, I glanced out the window and winced at the sight of Les Seatter on his backhoe, dragging the cow feet up across the field to a premature grave. "That's the third cow we've killed," I thought miserably.

We had four or five young men and three young women who volunteered to go through the discipling process, with Lyza and me living with them as 'house parents'. On the sidelines were spectators and advice-givers from the church community who tried to nurture this experiment in communal living. We had the farmers teach us how to milk cows and butcher pigs, complete with earthy humour (you tie the intestines up and bite the end off with your teeth).

One disciple, Ray, started us out in the pig business when he came home from the animal auction with a surprise. Nonchalantly he invited us to take a look in the back of the truck. There was a 500-pound pregnant sow filling the entire truck bed. Although we encouraged enterprise, we didn't really have any pig facilities, which was confirmed later in the day when, glancing out the window again, (I hated looking out that window), I saw mama pig chugging full speed across the back acres, busting through fences like a small locomotive. An entourage of our young men ran desperately after her, trying to get a rope around her neckless bulk. As often was the case on our farm, the creative ideas outstripped the means and wisdom to carry them out and a two-by-four nailed across the pig stall proved an insufficient restraint.

Some insufficient restraints surfaced in the discipling process as well as we struggled with entrenched personal problems and destructive lifestyle behavior in these young believers' lives. Lyza and I, only in our early twenties ourselves, were overwhelmed within a year. By the time we retired our farm project three years and three sets of burnt-out 'house parents' later, we chalked it up as a memorable chapter, although in terms of animal husbandry it was a disaster.

After that we tried other communal living experiments, including doubling up with other young couples in the same accommodations to save money so we could buy houses. Apparently the Chinese character for 'confusion' is two women in one kitchen, which made me feel Confucius knew a thing or two. After those short-lived scenarios, some of us eventually bought into a cluster of homes in adjacent subdivisions, which we dubbed 'Christian Corner' and 'Lower Christian Corner'. Our children became like brothers and sisters, shifting from house to house as a gang, checking out where the best snacks were offered any given day. That experience was more successful, although it probably didn't live up to our ideal of community togetherness either.

Still, it had many high points. We still talk about the snowy day when two pick-up trucks slid into our neighborhood with an army of dads and kids from 'Lower Christian Corner' (the group of families who bought duplexes in the street below us) armed to the teeth with snowballs and garbage can lids. We fought valiantly from the rooftops until the inevitable hard snowball in a kid's face brought the battle to an ignominious end.

After years of shared experiences, a deep bond of affection and a sense of being in it together for better or worse still undergirds our church family. As a church community we started a school, which became a hallmark of our church fellowship, beginning with three students meeting in a Sunday school room and growing to over 300 students from kindergarten to grade 12. Again, the underlying motivation was, "How can we live consistently together with Christ and each other and be discipled into a community of truth and love?" Educating our children could not be passed off to others. The community of Christ was meant to affect the totality of our life.

So the exhortations of the prophet Haggai did me good, moving us from the coffeehouse to God's house, enriching us with years of experience in the fellowship of believers. Although it has not been easy, I believe God has ultimately been glorified as He promised.

Thus says the Lord of hosts, "Consider your ways! Go up to the mountains, bring wood and rebuild the temple, that I may be pleased with it and be glorified," (Haggai 1:7,8)

In some mysterious way God is glorified as we focus on the task of building Him a house. Not only does it benefit us by leading us away from our selfish idolatries, it benefits God Himself. He has a personal stake in it all—He is looking for a place on the earth to reveal Himself.

All of us need a place to call home—a place that is ours where we can put our feet up, feel comfortable and enjoy our family. Even God desires this, it seems. The amazing reality is that God actually wants to live with us. I began to understand this better when I built the cabin on Nelson Island. There is no place on earth I love more or feel more at home. I remember lying on my stomach in the loft one time, gazing down on the cozy domestic scene with various family members stretched out on green futons, the smell of spicy spaghetti sauce in the air, and the fire crackling in the wood stove. My eyes traced over the large stones of hearth and wall and I remembered the enjoyment Lyza and I had one summer picking out the colorful rocks from the beach, and fitting them carefully together with mortar.

Almost everything in the cabin was made of wood—cedar, pine, hemlock, fir and even arbutus. Tight cedar shakes clothed all the outside walls. The little cabin felt more like an outgrowth of the forest itself than a creation of man, nestled underneath and dwarfed by the seventy-foot cedars and firs surrounding it on three sides. We designed the floor plan to wrap around the trees, and to climb the rough slope of ground instead of cutting into it. The plans were hastily drawn on a single sheet of lined paper and it was more intuition than blueprints that guided its construction. No bulldozers or even power tools were used except a chainsaw to cut, limb, and shape the trees and saw lumber to frame the spaces. For better and worse, it was my place and when I sat in it I knew and loved every board and log.

Looking down from the loft out the kitchen window, I noticed the north footing, cemented to a large boulder supporting the dining nook that hung over the water at high tide. There in the footing were my initials, and those of my two sons, scrawled in the concrete when we poured it. As I saw those permanent reminders, I realized why I loved the little cabin. I was its creator and was involved from its inception to its completion. It was an expression of my own creative ability. I realized this must be the very same delight the Creator God takes in the house He builds. He knows and has personally handled every living stone that is built into its walls. He personally chose and cut the rough-hewn timbers He built into the foundation. We are those rough timbers and jagged stones. Maybe we originally appeared unfit for use, but He patiently shaped and skillfully built us together through the years. God is tenderly preparing the house where He lives. I can imagine Him sitting by the fire, putting up His feet, looking around with pride at all the individual parts He personally assembled to make up the whole and saying of His Church, *"This is my resting place forever; Here I will dwell, for I have desired it"* (Psalm 132:14).

One Child at a Time

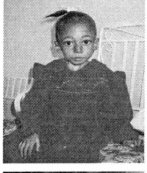

Strange Fire—Leviticus 10
The Seventh Temptation—Counterfeit Service

The Ten Temptations: **7. Counterfeit Service (Strange Fire)**

1. Pressures 2. Power 3. Bitterness 4. Hunger 5. Thirst   6. Idolatry
   of Life   of Evil   of Life

Seven Stages of the Spiritual Journey:

1. The Passover in Egypt	2. Red Sea Crossing	3. Mt. Sinai Visitation
		4. Wilderness

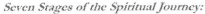

Chapter Ten

Bella Bella marked the journey's halfway point through the north coast to the Alaskan border. From there we headed out Seaforth Channel into Millbank Sound and up to Reid Passage from where we would penetrate deep northeast into the Fjordland recreational area. The next part of the trip was the most isolated stretch, traveling up long lonely passages to Prince Rupert and then back down along an even less traveled route some call the 'Outside Inside Passage', which is more open to the ocean. The weather was the most crucial variable, determining whether this leg would be glorious or miserable.

The next morning dim light revealed only vague outlines of land shapes so muffled in fog and drizzly mist that I could barely see across narrow Reid Passage. Percival Narrows was out there somewhere with its five-knot tide ebbing out of Mathieson Channel into a rock-strewn waterway stretching for two miles.

The weather channel gave me no encouragement either, but I donned my rain gear and hoisted anchor as the visibility reduced to a quarter mile. Groping like a blind man from tree to tree in a forest, I felt my way from islet to point to rock, straining to match the circles and numbers on my chart to the dark shapes looming out of the gloom. We finally reached the Narrows before slack and the little Perkins ran hard against the ebbing stream to gain the broader channel. The crew slept on in their bunks as I drifted on in the surreal dreamscape of gray water and mist through the morning hours, ascertaining my position only by hugging the shoreline. "Clouds and rain often obscure the scenery, but if you can outlast the weather, it is indeed worth the wait," *Charlie's Charts* encouragingly informed me.

Talking to God I said, *Lord, You know it would be a shame to come all the way up here and not see anything. After all, You made all this scenery. Don't You want to show it off a bit? How about a deal? If You just clear things up, I'll make it my business to praise You at the top of my lungs.*

Clearing Oscar Passage, I felt some heat through the overcast canopy and little steamy wisps began to drift up from the sail cover. Ragged strips of dark green shoreline appeared a mile or two away on either side of the channel, and visibility lengthened until off in the distance an olive green humpy point brightened to yellow-green from a direct hit of sunshine. By the end of the thirty-six-mile run, blue patches outnumbered the cloud patches until, turning into Kynoch Inlet, veils were lifted from the mountainscapes one by one.

I could not keep my hands off the camera, as each peak appeared grander than the one before. I fancied God took pleasure in answering my request, like a magician flourishing his cape to reveal each new marvel. I thought I heard Him whispering in my ear, *"Take a look at that. What do you think of that snowfield suspended over the valley? How do you like the sculpted lines of that cliff face set off against those color variations? Wait until you see what's around the next corner."* As we moved down Kynoch it was uncanny how the clouds parted ahead of us and closed behind us, with the blue sky remaining directly overhead.

Kynoch Inlet seemed transplanted from some corner of heaven just to give us a glimpse of what awaits us there. That's probably why it's hidden halfway up British Columbia's north coast and tucked into the mountains so far out of the way that only the really enterprising would discover it. This is also probably why ninety percent of the time it's shrouded with cloud and socked in with rain. Even people who painstakingly wend their way to this ethereal realm often only see a dreary shoreline skirted with brown rockweed. Thomas Manby, Captain Vancouver's botanist aboard the *Discovery*, when exploring these many inlets, described them as follows: "The last week had given the Blue Devils to everybody on board. The sun during the whole time had not once beamed on us his cheery ray. No view offered, to gratify the imagination, a dull insipid green colours the lofty mountains that everywhere surround us, where presumptuous heads arrest the progress of the journeying clouds, creating a weighty atmosphere and perpetual rain."

Captain Vancouver himself said of this country: "... as desolate inhospitable a country as the most melancholy creature could be desirous of inhabiting. The eagle, the crow, and raven, that occasionally had borne us company in our lonely researches, visited not these dreary shores."

The curtains were drawn closed for Captain Vancouver but they were thrown open for us the next morning revealing a scene of such beauty we were dumbfounded. Behind Culpepper Lagoon where we anchored near dark the night before was a backdrop of six-thousand-foot pinnacles (still capped with snowfields in July!), which gave way to a series of lower peaks down to the valley floor. The lagoon nestled at the base like some secret Shangri-La full of mystery, beckoning further exploration. The surrounding mountains were draped with silky silver scarves of mist and a mammoth granite wall loomed across the bay, plunging to the glassy sea floor.

The head of the inlet was grizzly habitat. The park ranger from the only other boat anchored there said they range along the river grass, which looked like a shimmering field of grain, ready for harvest. Golden rockweed gilded the shoreline and set off the flat, mile-wide valley floor from its angular surroundings. The bears never showed up, but they were there in my imagination, great shaggy brown hulks with fullback shoulders, shambling along the shore, guardians of their solitary domain. Later in the morning the calm broke as a lively breeze rolled down the inlet, driving the surface mist before it like a ghostly herd of bison across the steaming sand flats into the forest.

The sun shone the whole day so we saw the hidden valley in its full glory. The dismal beginning of yesterday morning contrasted sharply with the bright conclusion of the run. Often our pathways in life begin in difficulty but take a turn for the better, and sometimes when they begin well, they take a turn for the worse. We're never sure what is around the corner, but we can be sure God is there waiting to surprise us with joy and instruct us in our trials.

The next trial in Israel's pathway was a jarring incident just when everyone thought things were going along nicely. It was a hard test to understand, but it had a deep significance. This seventh temptation happened as Aaron's sons exercised their priestly ministry. Moses brought the people to Sinai and they experienced the revelation of God's law and His presence. Then the people were tempted with idolatry, the antithesis of God's presence. They were instructed to build God a house, a place where they could cultivate God's presence. After that, they were instructed about the priesthood and its duties, which were designed to mediate God's presence. It was all about God's presence. In the midst of this priestly instruction the seventh test came about as Nadab and Abihu, Aaron's sons, offered 'strange fire' to the Lord.

The test was about maintaining discernment between what is of God and what is of man, an important distinction for them then as well as for us now. Much of what originates from man gets attributed to God and much of what originates from God gets passed off as something that man came up with. Nadab and Abihu, the sons of Aaron the high priest, came up with their own bright idea.

> *Now Nadab and Abihu, the sons of Aaron, took their respective firepans, and after putting fire in them, placed incense on it and offered strange fire before the Lord, which He had not commanded them.* (Leviticus 10:1)

The important phrase is *"...which He had not commanded them."* Nadab and Abihu were not involved in rebellion—they simply added their own touches to the priestly service and tried to help God out. In God's original instructions for sacrifice, the fire to burn incense was to come from the brazen altar where blood sacrifice was made. The fire burning in this brazen altar originally came from God Himself when the first sacrifice was offered on it. Fire signifies consecration and zeal. It was God's zeal that initiated spiritual consecration and service.

The 'strange fire' Nadab and Abihu offered on the altar of incense was fire they started themselves, not taken from the brazen altar. 'Strange fire' means, symbolically, spiritual zeal that does not originate with God. It is human effort and energy attempting to accomplish what only God can do.

The brazen altar was the place of blood sacrifice. Animals were slain, their blood poured out and unused parts were consumed by fire. This represented the cross where Christ was the blood sacrifice and His life was totally consumed in the fire of God's zeal to bring us back to Himself. This passion of God burns forever through Christ's one sacrifice and is eternally available to men. That is the symbolic meaning of the fire on the altar that never went out.

> *"The fire on the altar shall be kept burning on it. It shall not go out, but the priest shall burn wood on it every morning; and he shall lay out the burnt offering on it, and offer up in smoke the fat portions of the*

peace offerings on it. Fire shall be kept burning continually on the altar; it is not to go out." (Leviticus 6:12,13)

Jesus told His disciples they would be baptized with the Holy Spirit and fire. The Holy Spirit carried the fire emanating from the cross and ignited the altar of incense, which was the altar of spiritual service within the disciples' hearts, purifying them and filling them with zeal to fulfill their mission. They lit the then known world on fire with the message of the gospel.

Nadab and Abihu, as priests, were to mediate things of God, not try to produce them. They were to feed the fire and keep it going, but it was God's fire, not their own. We don't know where they got their strange fire—whether they rubbed two sticks together or used a flick of a Bic—but whatever the source, it was not God, and His fire swallowed up their fire and them as well.

And fire came out from the presence of the Lord and consumed them and they died before the Lord. Then Moses said to Aaron, "It is what the Lord spoke, saying 'By those who come near Me I will be treated as holy, and before all the people I will be honored.'" (Leviticus 10:2,3)

God consumed Nadab and Abihu. These two died for breaking a spiritual picture and pattern. They died for others to learn a powerful lesson. No one can add or take away from the finished work that God did in Christ; we can only be consumed by it, caught up in it, and work with it. There isn't a sense of anger or retribution in the deaths of these priests, but rather a sense of holiness. They died before the Lord that the people might see God for who He is.

So how does all this translate to the spiritual pilgrimage? God doesn't need our help to accomplish His work. I've produced some strange fire in my time. If God still handled it like He did back then, you'd find me and a lot of my works smoldering in the ash heap. I've tried to convert people God wasn't working on, I've preached sermons He didn't anoint and organized campaigns He didn't order. God's fire didn't consume all my dead works; most of them just fizzled out. Consuming fire might have been more exciting.

Jesus said, *"I am the vine, you are the branches…apart from Me you can do nothing"* (John 15:5). Branches that don't abide in the vine just wither and are eventually burned up. Much that is done in Christendom is 'strange fire' if we would but recognize it. Often people become worn to a frazzle flogging programs that have outlived their usefulness. Others spend their days attempting to make the church 'successful' with their own bright ideas. The church is a supernatural institution. It can only grow and be sustained by supernatural means. Those supernatural means are birthed through the prayer and intercession of believers whose basis for answers is the power of the living God.

Another illustration of this same principle was given in the form of an instruction to Moses about the behavior of priests after the death of Aaron's sons.

> *"Do not drink wine or strong drink, neither you nor your sons with you, when you come into the tent of meeting, so that you may not die— it is a perpetual statute throughout your generations—and so as to make a distinction between the holy and the profane, and between the unclean and the clean…"* (Leviticus 10:9, 10)

This is not a total prohibition against alcohol since it only applied to the times of their priestly service. It is aiming at the deeper issue of strange fire by this reference to strange firewater. Alcohol is a manmade means of producing joy. As such, it is a cheap counterfeit of the joy of the Holy Spirit. When the disciples were filled with the Holy Spirit on the day of Pentecost, they were so overwhelmed with the joy of God's presence that the bystanders could only relate it to one thing. Peter, in answer to the critics, stood up and said, *"For these men are not drunk, as you suppose, for it is only the third hour of the day; but this is what was spoken of through the prophet Joel…that I will pour forth of My spirit upon all mankind"* (Acts 2:15-17).

What the observers thought was drunkenness was really the fire of the Holy Spirit upon people. This was the fire that fell from heaven upon the early Church to confirm that the sacrifice of Christ was complete and acceptable to God. When that fire fell on those ragtag followers of Jesus the world was changed.

When the actions we take clearly have the stamp of being God's idea, they have a lasting quality and a tendency to surprise us with their uniqueness and joy. It was certainly that way for Lyza and me regarding many significant events of our lives. Our adoption of Ginette was a foremost example.

Something was irritating our nightly read in the bunk, a favorite pastime before falling asleep. Sounds of frustration—thrashings, rustlings, very audible sighs and exasperated grunts emanated from the closet where Ginette's head and shoulders were buried. Her assignment was to wrap the foot of her bed, sleeping bag and all, in a garbage bag to protect from possible leaks. Ginny decided she could not do this chore by herself and let us know by making a lot of racket. After tripping over each other all day, we relished our moments of 'solitude' in bed and neither Lyza nor I were in any mood to get back out of bed at this point to help her. Besides, she was making a big scene when she was perfectly capable of doing the task. The last thing I saw as we switched off the light was Ginette sitting in the sawed-out opening of the closet like a little gnome in the mouth of a cave. On her face was a look of protest and reproach, the whites of her big brown eyes luminous in the dark against her black face.

The next morning everything appeared normal with the bedcovers spread out into the closet. *"I guess she finally worked it out,"* I thought to myself. Squeezing out of my bunk, I leaned over and pulled back the blanket to give her a little kiss. I just about kissed two little black feet! Peering into the musty closet, I saw her head buried among the hanging coats, and I laughed out loud. I couldn't help but draw a parallel with the stubborn Israelites I was currently writing about.

"You're gonna make me go in that closet to make my bed? You're gonna make me grow up? I'll show you. I'll just stick my head in the closet. That'll show you!" Kooky cartoon images of Israelites upside down with their heads in the sand kept me laughing most of the morning. Actually, such resistant behavior was rare from Ginette. She fit in so well with boat life and Clarke life in general, we knew God had handpicked her for our family.

"You can go to Haiti if you promise not to come back with a baby under each arm," was my response to Lyza's desire to go on behalf of our church to check out the Foundation for the Children of Haiti, a humanitarian work we were interested in supporting. Such a far-flung trip was unusual for her, but she went with her friend, Sandra, who had adopted four Haitian children after her three sons were grown. The Foundation was an organization run by Gladys Sylvestre, a young, beautiful Mother-Theresa-type whose mission was to save as many of Haiti's at-risk children as she could, one child at a time. Gladys' work was a small oasis of care, order and cleanliness in a place of overwhelming need and grueling poverty. While in the capital city of Port au Prince, Gladys took a group of six, including Sandra and Lyza, on a tour of the public hospital. She paused at one of the beds in the midst of a cavernous room filled with sick children.

"This child is in the last stages of malnutrition," Gladys commented matter-of-factly, "She probably has only a couple of weeks to live." She smiled with compassion at the child who looked back at her with the old-lady face of emaciation. Lyza lifted her eyes to take in the whole ward of children and a wave of helplessness engulfed her. How could anyone even make a dent in all this need? Shifting back to the little girl in front of her, she was struck by the huge, sad eyes.

"May I have a drink?" the little girl whispered in Creole to Gladys. As Gladys searched for some juice to give her, Lyza was struck by Jesus' words, *"And whoever in the name of a disciple gives to one of these little ones even a cup of cold water to drink, truly I say to you he shall not lose his reward"* (Matthew 10:42).

Gladys gently sat her up and held the straw to her cracked lips.

"Could you change my dress please?" was the next question, and the group began to realize this little one had a persistent grip on life and reached out for a good thing when she saw it in front of her. Once she was more comfortable in dry clothes, she was apparently concerned to look her best and asked if Gladys would comb her hair. Actually, most of her hair had fallen out from malnutrition, but Gladys lovingly braided the small tuft of hair that remained. Once these more basic concerns were addressed, as if asserting her humanity was intact, the little girl turned to her recreational needs and held out to the group her only toy—a flabby, dirty balloon.

Lyza and the others stood immobilized by this simple request. What germs might the bedraggled balloon harbour? Nobody moved for an awkward moment—then Gladys, having long ago left behind concerns for her own welfare, took the balloon, walked across the room, rinsed it off under the cold water tap and wiped it dry on her own stylish dress. She blew in the air, tied the balloon, and presented it to the little girl.

As the dying child smiled wanly and whispered, "Merci," Lyza first noticed the tears running down her own face. 'Making a difference one child at a time', Gladys' motto, had just been graphically demonstrated to her and became a kind of epiphany for Lyza. She really understood, maybe for the first time, the power of such a simple gesture of love. Jesus said, *"To the extent that you did it to one of these brothers of Mine, even the least of them, you did it to Me"* (Matthew 25:40). At that moment she determined to at least help this little girl live if anything humanly possible could be done to save her.

Often the approach to meeting needs in third world situations is to organize programs, raise lots of money, and send in the army. A program may be useful, but no human administration can manufacture love. Administration may connect the right people to the right need and supply material goods, but only the fire of God's love kindled in each heart will touch another heart, one person at a time.

Lyza came back from that trip forever changed and although we didn't know it at the time, our family's life was about to be forever altered also. Gladys used her agency's funds as well as donated money from the group to get Ginette into a private hospital where tests discovered she had an operable condition, an abdominal abscess. Once she underwent surgery to remove it, Ginette absolutely bounced back to health. The before and after pictures posted on our fridge were remarkable—could that bright-eyed, fuzzy-haired beauty actually be the same child? A year passed and we received occasional updated pictures, which revealed an increasingly robust, impish little girl. We felt gratified knowing we had helped one child survive.

Then the phone call came. Ginette's mother had put her up for adoption knowing she couldn't provide adequately for her needs. It was an ultimate mother's sacrifice. When Lyza heard the news, it was as if she had gotten a call from the doctor's office informing her she was pregnant. From that moment she was a mother again in her heart. Of course she asked me to pray about it before we made a final decision, but she already knew what the answer would be. We also asked each of our children to think and pray about it without conferring with their siblings. We decided it had to be a unanimous decision for us to proceed with a step that would so dramatically impact our whole family. Lyza and I were delighted when, a week later, we heard back from all three a resounding affirmative. In fact, all of them even used the same words to express their conclusions. "God has given us so much, how could we not share our blessings with Ginette?"

We began adoption proceedings immediately and the process took five months to complete. During this time I felt an assurance that this was a genuine part of God's plan for our lives, not just a good idea. Before Ginny came into the picture, I was actually not too keen on the idea of adoption. I had seen many problems arise in adopting families and besides, it was a foreign concept in my upbringing. There had never been an adoption in the Clarke clan. I still had some concerns about whether I could love an adopted child as much as my birth children—until I saw the video. A friend went to Haiti during our waiting period and brought back videos of little Ginette. With a bright red hibiscus flower in her hair and wearing the cute pink dress we sent her, the little four-year-old looked straight up into the camera and said softly in English. "I love you, Mama, I love you, Papa." It was a done deal; I was a father again.

Flopping in my deck chair after tying the tarp down because of a rain shower, I felt I was being watched. Sure enough, up under the boom cover two Barbies impassively stared at me, scarves on their heads and dressed in the latest fashions designed by Ginette Laroche. An infestation of Barbies had broken out on board—Barbies on the bedclothes, Barbies in the drawers, Barbies sleeping among the bread bags, Barbies sitting primly on top of the spice rack. Ginette, mastermind of these appearances, could turn the whole cockpit into an elaborate Barbie world complete with intricate dialogue and her own designer dresses, exquisitely fashioned from cloth napkins and doilies. Her adaptability was nothing short of incredible.

We could not have had a more compatible shipmate than Ginette. Maybe it was because we took her on the *Fred Free* within two weeks of her arrival from Haiti. Barely speaking English yet, she would wave from the *Fred*'s cockpit at the wealthy yacht owners cruising by and yell, "Hi People!" in her funny Creole-accented voice. Translated from City Soleil, the worst slum in the western hemisphere, to the vacationlands of the wealthy, she landed with both feet, ready for action. No trauma or great emotional adjustment, just an indefatigable enthusiasm for life. "This kid came to play," my dad always used to say of such exuberant people. The *Fred* suited her perfectly; she loved close quarters. She played happily on the long trek north, entertaining herself in her fantasy lands, and she used reams of paper drawing fashions on models, every one unique and individually named. So much potential, so much creativity, such a precious little life. To think it all could have been extinguished with no one to notice, no one to care.

I don't really know how to reconcile all the pain and suffering in the world, and I'm sure I don't know what to do about it. I don't know the solution for the problems of Haiti, but I know one Haitian who will be part of the solution, not part of the problem. We have a profound sense that Ginette's story is God's story and her adoption into our family was one of the works God planned for us to do from the foundations of the world. Ginette was born into our family like people are born again into God's family—from above, out of the passion of God, the fire of God, not from a presumptuous idea sourced in human zeal. As we purpose to be guided by the Holy Spirit in the choices we make, He will protect us from the destruction of strange fire. We can rest assured that He goes before us as we move toward His eternal goals for our lives.

Treasures in the Desert

The Wilderness

The Wilderness

The Ten Temptations:

1. Pressures 2. Power 3. Bitterness 4. Hunger 5. Thirst   6. Idolatry   7. Counterfeit
   of Life   of Evil   of Life   Service

Seven Stages of the Spiritual Journey:

1. The Passover in Egypt	2. Red Sea Crossing	3. Mt. Sinai Visitation
		4. Wilderness

Chapter Eleven

The last half of July into the first half of August was a time of isolation and wonder. We were cocooned away in our little floating world in the vastness of the north country at the mercy of the elements, reliant upon our own resourcefulness, and vulnerable to the Almighty. Our passage was glorious, and although our experiences were dampened at times, especially in inclement weather, we found hidden, even in the worst circumstances, treasures we never would have found otherwise—a sudden unveiling of a mountain or valley, a foraging bear, a fish caught just in time to meet our need.

The two straight days of sun in Kynoch were an anomaly and we received them as a gift. The regular weather pattern descended upon us the following week. As we motored back out the inlet past a snow cave with a cascading stream flowing through it, the overcast began to thicken. Sheer cliffs soared three hundred feet above and plunged four hundred feet deep into the water where two feet from these rock walls we pulled up a yellow-eyed red snapper, his stomach and eyes bulging from the change in pressure. At the roaring falls, we shot videos of *Fred*'s bowsprit nosed right into the spuming spray where it thundered into the inlet.

We pressed into the innermost recesses of the mountains to a reach called Mussel Inlet. In all likelihood the scenery matched Kynoch, but ponderous white cumulus clouds decapitated the highest peaks and gray fog poured into the high valleys, cutting off the spectacular view. Uncomfortable gusts of wind raised whitecaps, pressing us into the farthest end of a long channel where Poison Cove, an oval of dark water, remained hidden until the last moment behind a mossy rock bluff. The lack of sun in the cove and the descending rain made the overhanging cliffs ominous and the river flowing into the bay seemed dark and foreboding. It didn't help to know that its name came from the poisoning of Captain Vancouver's shore crew. One man died and several got very sick from the PSP organism (red tide) in the mussels they ate. Pondering that event two hundred and seven years later made it easier to understand the sinister feeling this land evoked in those sailors at the ends of the earth in this dark cove after weeks of surveying these desolate inlets.

I could relate to the feeling of loneliness and insignificance. We were dwarfed by the surroundings in a tiny sailboat clinging to the river shelf, the anchor barely holding in sixty feet of water that abruptly became fifteen feet further in and two hundred feet just a little further out, and we wondered whether we would be aground in the morning or drifting down the inlet with one hundred and fifty feet of rope hanging uselessly in the deep.

Yet even here treasures awaited discovery. Taking Boaz ashore in the tender, I motored through grasses at the head of the cove into a wide channel with a strong flow of water. Pressing farther up the mildly flowing river of dark emerald blue it became too shallow after only four hundred yards' penetration into the forest where a rushing cataract spilled among boulders into a pool. I picked up a lightweight rod and cast a red and silver spinner into the current's back eddy. Immediately I felt the urgent tug of a good sized cutthroat and my latent trout obsession kept me drifting and casting down the channel for the next two hours. Racing proudly back with my prizes, which included a beautiful pink-spotted Dolly Varden, I realized my initial feelings about Poison Cove being creepy were changing. After all, this unlikely spot was where I found silver and leopard-skinned treasures.

The next seven days were 'dirty thirties', what I called the thirty-mile runs in lousy weather. It began raining that night in Mussel Inlet and kept raining as we left our anchorage early the next morning and point after point went by in Sheep Passage. It rained in Carter Bay, named after the man who died at Poison Cove. It rained down thirty miles of Graham Reach and along twenty miles of Fraser Reach. In Grenville Channel it rained at Lowe Inlet for thirty-six hours straight without even a five-minute break. It drizzled, poured, soaker-hosed, misted, and then it rained so hard the surface of the sea bubbled to a hard boil. It pelted the tarp, dropping from the boom and trickling through my rain gear. Each morning I could hardly bring myself to face it again. As it tapped at me on the glass porthole above my bunk I would roll over in the warm damp bedding, steeling myself to don my still wet rain gear and stand for five more hours in the cockpit with the whole of British Columbia's great outdoors pouring down on me. Lyza plied me with hot soup and tea from below as I endured a fire hose spray from port side, or a bucket deluge from the starboard.

I was beginning to think open cockpit communion with the environment was greatly overrated. Oh, for an enclosed cabin with an oil stove! The Israelites in their wilderness must have experienced the same feelings of awesome aloneness, vulnerability and longing. Huge areas of the earth's surface are wilderness—empty of all human habitation where only God and his creatures live. He designs wildernesses to challenge man and create both an awareness of Himself and a dependence on His providence. The wilderness is where man faces the greatest physical challenges, but there are also spiritual wildernesses where people face challenges of another kind—places of isolation, distress, breakdown of relationship or spiritual dryness where God is also found in a special way. In such places we can feel alone and disoriented, but as in nature, these places have the potential of bringing us closer to God if we can discern Him there. Exposure to a wilderness defines our weaknesses, teaches us to pray, develops new inner strengths, and unveils treasures of the spirit.

We were never quite at ease up north. There were unfamiliar anchorages and unpredictable currents. Whether an inlet was flooding or ebbing could depend on the state of the rivers flowing into it. The weather changed from hour to hour. Even a sunny day could end with a cold mist by afternoon as the ocean air hit the warmer land. Twenty-five foot tides could totally transform the place we anchored in the evening before, revealing rocks and reefs we thought were elsewhere. Vulnerability was definitely the best word to describe it and yet there was also a sharper awareness of everything: God, warmth and food, simple pleasures, daily chores and the plain satisfaction of existence. Hardships were what made the experience memorable and produced the best stories. In our family reminiscences of vacations, endless days in the sunshine without a cloud in the sky are absorbed into a vague pleasant memory without points of distinction. Bring up a disaster—a camping trip where a branch fell through the tent, or the storm that tipped over the rowboat— and animated conversation extends far into the night.

Great mountains and scooped-out valleys of solid granite slid past me in McKay Passage like huge stage props or magnificent pictures in a book. It felt as if I could reach out and turn the page, leafing through the landscapes like glossy photos in a magazine. I would hang my arm over the boom and lean against the support crosspiece with my foot on the tiller, standing high in the back like an oarsman in a Venetian canal. North of McKay, Grenville Channel appeared, a straight forty-mile run between precipitous mountains. Under the overcast it felt like a long dark tunnel. Every ten or twelve miles small balloon-like inlets would open up to the east and offer anchorage in little wild worlds of their own. In the midst of this long soggy trek these special havens made it all worthwhile.

One such place was Lowe Inlet, a refuge we sought out on the fifth day of rain. We anchored in a river mouth and huddled down under our tarps to dry out and warm up, feeling a little ripped off at traveling through all this country and not being able to view it properly. We had only a few square yards of dry living space, but were grateful for Ellen's tarp, which now made our main cabin relatively leak proof.

We fell asleep to the sound of the rain and woke up the next day to the same. This was getting really old! At eleven, the downpour actually abated for an hour and we peeled back the tarps, emerging like creatures from our secret den. Before us was a scene right out of National Geographic. The river, swollen with the incessant rain, poured in a huge torrent over a thirty-foot falls. The solid wall of water, transparent through to the granite rock face behind, did not rush and chatter but tore a hole in the inlet and produced a sheet of pressure-powered mist that shot horizontally out into the bay. The strength of its flow forced the two boats anchored at its mouth to splay out on their anchor chains, their noses straining to the river's mouth like spawning salmon. A school of sockeye churned, tumbled and leaped in the turbulence surrounding our boats, sensing their moment had come. Four or five seals leisurely cruised among the easy pickings, stopping periodically to gaze at us intruders with their bullet-hole eyes.

Ginette suddenly shrieked and animatedly pointed to the beach where a large black bear ambled toward the river a hundred feet from us. We clambered into the small boat and followed the bear up the stream to the maw of the cataract where he climbed into the spume and entertained us with unsuccessful attempts to catch his dinner, periodically shaking the water off his head like a giant dog. We snapped pictures like goofy tourists, but the most vivid images linger in our collective memory.

As if the sight of it all was not enough, I picked up my pole, and tossed a weighted lure into the midst of the sockeye. Within seconds I latched onto an eleven-pound fish, our first coveted salmon of the trip. We feasted that night on the rich orange meat as we cocooned from the darkness in the glow of the cabin lights. Lyza actually surprised me by saying over dinner, "It was worth all this rain just to have seen what we saw today." That thrilling hour in Lowe Inlet epitomized why we had come north.

The rain resumed nonstop for the next three days, accompanying us all the way to Prince Rupert. Prince Rupert, notorious for its chronically fog-bound harbour and its ill weather (nine feet of rain per year, one local told me), was awash in sunlight when we finally dragged ourselves into its fishy-smelling docks. We spent hours at the laundromat, washing and, more importantly, drying everything we owned. We felt a little culture shocked among the stoplights, Dairy Queens, and multi-storied apartments, all incongruously clustered at the base of a mountain that looked just like those we had traveled through. We stayed one night in a local hotel whose kind proprietor allowed us to include Boaz. Turning on a TV assured us civilization was right where we had left it, the world running to wrack and ruin as usual without even noticing our absence. Three days, a dozen taxicab rides, and a lot less money later, we headed out under another rare blue sky.

As we left Prince Rupert, we had a bit of conflict over which way to go. Surprisingly, Lyza wanted to make the 40-mile run to the American border so we could at least say we made it to Alaska. I was more interested in saving time to explore the wilder outside passage on the way back down, and I didn't relish the possible wear and tear of crossing capricious Dixon Entrance. Since I did most of the steering, I got my way and we headed down Ogden Channel toward the ocean.

Morning fog drifting out of the Skeena river channel caused gill-netters to eerily appear and disappear, so we fled westward toward clearer prospects. Auklets fished the tidelines where river and bay waters met. An occasional salmon broke water. By the time we made it to Gasboat Passage, shortly before noon, the water sparkled bright blue to match the sky. The inland sea of Porcher Island bulged to within a half a mile from open ocean, enabling us to hear the ocean breakers crashing on the beach at night while we anchored safely on the other side of the narrow strip of land separating the open ocean from the inland sea. This was the isolated fantasy world I had imagined the winter before while poring over the chart and marveling at this sea within a sea.

We spent two days without seeing another soul, not even a native from the Kitkatla village at the bay's entry. A high-pressure ridge settled over the Queen Charlottes just west of us, giving us sunny days, but a northwesterly gale force wind blew over the low elevation of land that separated us from the ocean. As late afternoon fog crept in, we lit a huge fire on the shale beach to ward off the chill and brighten our spirits. We burned our fingers on the hot tin foil encasing the remains of our salmon and dug in communally with beach chopsticks, imagining the Kitkatla building fires on this beach for hundreds of years. All night our little duck, *Fred*, clung nervously to the edge of the apron of land in the lee of the shore with the gale gusting, and the seas building a hundred feet beyond him to roll out of the ten mile inlet.

The morning sun popped back up in the east, seeming pleased to have slipped from the western fog's grasp the night before and ready to burn a path in front of us southward. Relieved we had not dragged anchor in the night, the prospect of sailing the windswept sea beckoned. *Fred*'s sailing apparatus is old and cumbersome, of the same vintage as himself, so hauling up the canvas on its heavy gaff rig boom is always a major effort, but worthwhile if the wind stays strong and steady. 'Freddy's Law' usually dictates that as soon as you go through all the effort to get him in sail, the wind dies and you bring them all down again—but not this time. With the rackety engine finally silenced, we sailed before the hard-driving wind for twenty-five miles to Captain Cove. Azure waves capped with white foam rushed along with us and the only sound besides wind and sea were *Fred*'s happy flaps, creaks and splashes as he surged and surfed among the waves. Chugging doggedly along like a tugboat was not his first love. His smoothest graces and best profile were revealed under sail.

The next day we were back to motoring down another long channel and the wilderness continued to cast its lonesome spell over us. I discovered a steering innovation to break the monotony. Propping the deck chair on the cockpit seat with the fourth leg of chair supported by the fish box and two cushions, I was able to sit up like a shogun carried on a litter through his domain. My domain was unveiling itself one valley at a time around each new bend of Petrel Channel. Totally alone for ten straight days, the world could have gone to war or the stock market crashed and we would have been as insensible to it as the wood ducks or seals that swam around us. Like them, also, we were dependent on the sea for our sustenance. I remembered with relish the preceding evening at Captain Cove where Bo and I again penetrated a river's inner sanctum of grass and submerged mudflat to find our supper. The trout there proved so plentiful that we had to throw some back. I shook my head in amazement at such bounty and wondered at the sudden turquoise color of the water that tumbled alive and invigorating through rocky passes and around ragged promontories of this river kingdom.

I found the variety of colours in the water of this country intriguing. It changed from molasses brown where cedars discolored the rivers pouring into bays to a glacial milky green and even occasionally a pellucid blue. After many bends and turns, the channel poured us out near Anger Island and Principe Channel. Anger Island was a treasure island of small mountains and valleys intersected with mazes of saltwater channels. Picking our way around tiny islets and hidden reefs, we anchored in a small cove completely protected by rocks and trees, a land-locked harbour.

The pristine landscape just begged to be explored. Behind our little bay we found a maze of hidden channels, penetrating like blood vessels into the heart of the island. Usually the water was brackish in little estuaries such as these, but here a vigorous tidal flow kept the water sparkling clear, streaming with kelp and abundant fish. Racing through these channels at top speed like an airboat in the everglades, Bo and I skipped from one hidden world to another, a snorkeler's paradise, waiting to be discovered.

Ginette, Boaz and I decided to go fishing. Outside the safety of our sanctuary, the north wind blew strongly, discouraging us from venturing too far, but we could at least fish around the little islands close at hand. Soon we were bumping along in the chop and spray, anxious to find some good fishing. Suddenly, after half a mile, we spotted kelp right under us, and I cut the motor, quickly looking about sheepishly for the reef that kelp always signals. Twenty feet away I could see the pale outline of a rock only a foot under water. My initial scare gave way to the realization that this place had all the makings of a great fishing spot. Sure enough, Ginette got a fish on her pole immediately and I caught bottom. I left my stuck line and turned to pull her cod into the boat while thrusting the overly enthusiastic dog aside.

Boaz thought it his duty to greet every incoming fish by hanging over the gunwales on his elbows with his jowls a few inches from the water and his rump riding high, tail working vigorously. When the fish reached the surface, he would try to mouth it in the water and escort it through the air into the bottom of the boat where he would proceed to lick it unmercifully, all of which were good reasons to leave him behind on fishing trips. But if I did, I just couldn't bear his reproachful look on our return, so he usually got to come along, nuisance that he was.

While trying to restrain the dog and attend to Ginette's fish, my line suddenly gave two authoritative yanks and began moving off in a northerly direction. Bottom was alive! "I've got a fish. I've got a fish!" My two companions looked up from the rock cod flapping in the bilge. "It's really big!" I managed to splutter as fisherman's fever began to possess me. I knew whatever was on the end of my line had to be the largest fish I had ever encountered. It acted different—not the frantic flight for bottom of a rock cod, nor the stubborn yank of a ling cod that ran for bottom when it neared the surface, nor the dongy dong circling drag of a dogfish. It was a powerful gliding weight that peeled off my line like a running salmon, but it was deep, determined, and steady. At that moment I doubted if my curiosity about what it was would be satisfied because the tackle and rod were light, but nevertheless, I kept hanging on and fought it for twenty minutes. Finally a shape began to emerge.

Now, if one has never brought in a big fish in cold clear green water, it's hard to convey the awesome spooky feeling of catching the first glimpse of it coming up from the mysterious netherworld below. First there is only a dark shadow of movement, and then a dim outline begins to materialize with some distinctive marking that spurs a sudden shout of recognition. The fish always comes up headfirst, to meet you face to face with its googly eyes. As this one slowly levitated toward the surface, he wore a brownish leather-like jacket, and rippling along the edges of his kite shape was a luminous white underbelly. When it rose to meet me, the characteristic white bulbous lips and the broad flounder-like back elicited a shock of recognition.

"It's a halibut!" I shouted. "My first halibut!"

Ginette came bouncing to the back of the boat to see.

"Daddy, you caught a halibut! Yay, I'm so excited."

Halibut and chips was the foremost thing on her mind and, in fact, we had even asked God to help us catch a halibut for dinner. Then she saw the look of astonishment on my face and hesitated while I manifested my demented, crazy-man laugh and fumbled for a gaff. "It's huge! Look at it!"

In the frenzy of fisherman's lust and without thinking it through, I bent down and slipped the lightweight gaff under the monster's belly while greeting him nose to nose at the water's surface. I yanked upward with a mighty heave, and slid him heavily over the ten-foot boat's pontoon. He left only about three feet for the rest of us. I looked up with triumph to see Ginette and the dog crammed together in the bow with their butts hanging in mid-air, ready to back into the bay if necessary. Ginette's eyes were big as saucers and Bo, wanting nothing to do with landing this fish, contributed only a nervous little, "Wuff," to the effort. The fish sat stunned for a moment with its nose on the gas tank and its tail curled up over the motor while it worked its cavernous gills open and shut, spooking the forward mates even more. I sat panting for a moment as the realization dawned on me that what I had just done was not smart. I had just hauled a sixty-pound mass of pure muscle into a bathtub-size boat with three people already in it. The fish arched in a momentary curl and then erupted into a series of great ka-thumps, thrashing wildly as though he would shake the boat apart. I began flailing away at his head with a very inadequate wooden fish bonker while Bo snorted and backed up some more until his tail was in the water. Ginette shrieked, "I'm scared, Daddy. I want to go back to Mommy! Let's go home!"

I broke the stick whaling on him, and then broke the aluminum gaff, but he finally settled down to quivering shivers. I must have gaffed him in some vitals or the battle would have lasted longer. Now I understand why some fishermen shoot halibut in the head before bringing them aboard. We slowly motored the distance back to "Mommy" with our new passenger periodically throwing our boatload into bedlam with renewed thrashings. The next morning the deflated *Crayon* revealed he had punctured a hole in our boat with his sharp teeth.

Well, now Ginette had her own fish story and could hold her own around any campfire with her other siblings. The halibut's last fit occurred as we pulled alongside *Fred*, sending Mom to the other side of the deck with her mouth agape, thankful she hadn't gone with us. One time on our honeymoon I had traumatized her by throwing a speared, but still alive large ling cod in the dinghy with her when I was scuba diving. I then promptly descended back into the deep without a lot of consultation about the matter, and I had never heard the end of my need for sensitivity training because of such brutish behavior.

We dragged this brute ashore, dispatched it, cleaned it, and took lots of video footage. We could have eaten halibut for a year if we'd had a freezer handy, but we were eight hundred miles from home and as abundant as the provision around us was, we could only eat our little share and leave the rest for the multitude of scavengers above and below the water. I felt guilty about the waste, but I guess it wasn't wasted from the other creatures' point of view. We certainly were not in a land of people-centeredness.

Over the next few days we sailed down unfrequented Principe, then Squally Channel past the barren rocky peaks of Ayer Island, even skirting a few open spots of the broad Pacific. We would haul up the sails, then bring them down again as the wind alternately blew and quit. Huge swells, big as buses, rolled out of Hecate Strait, rocking us thirty degrees from side to side until we could finally turn to ride with them into Chappel Inlet as they crashed upon sharp rocks on either side of the entrance. The only boats we saw during that entire running period were a couple fishing boats off in the distance. We felt like vagabonds looking for a resting place. Civilization began to look good to us since our water tank was near empty, the propane tank was losing pressure, we hadn't had ice or showers for many days, and most importantly, we were running out of butter.

Hygiene is an interesting challenge on the boat where the only plumbing is a four-foot copper water line from the water tank to an old brass pump that serviced a foot square sink. We did dishes by heating kettles of water over the two-burner propane stove and pouring it into a Rubbermaid dishpan that could be emptied overboard. The toilet was a porta-potty mainly for the ladies' use, men having more direct options. Years ago *Fred* boasted a bona-fide marine toilet in the little rain closet, but one day my brother Tom and his wife, Ann, came back after a day's outing to find water a foot above the cabin floorboards. The toilet's open seacock had let water overflow in the toilet bowl, so it was summarily removed, saving us the embarrassment of one day having to explain that the boat sank on a calm sunny day because of an overzealous toilet. Nobody used it anyway, as it required a Herculean effort to squeeze into the closet, shut the door, squat and get out again. Space being at a premium, we much preferred a storage closet.

Bathing was another challenge that my fastidious spouse was especially ingenious in accomplishing, come hell or no water. Being made of coarser stuff, I generally dove in the salt chuck and considered the job done, but Lyza could sniff out a shower facility in almost any port. Even in Echo Bay, a tiny community made up of floating houses clinging to the edge of cliffs, she found a shower of particular charm. In a cedar board lean-to behind a small store, an old-fashioned claw foot tub was positioned under a metal showerhead suspended from the ceiling overhead. A person simply stood naked in the tub as the luscious hot water rained down. No shower curtains here. The sensation was delicious and spillage was not a problem as the water splashed down through inch-wide spaces in the wooden floor planks directly into the sea underneath. The lean to was tastefully decorated with quaint country touches and even a guest book containing names of former grateful 'showerees'.

Interesting people live in such places, like the father of a little girl Ginny had made friends with. (She did this in every port.) He found out, after pulling a warm beer out of his coat pocket and offering it to me, a total stranger, that I was a pastor. He then changed friendship tactics and asked me if I could tell him from Genesis 6:2 who the sons of God were who slept with the daughters of men and produced the giants of old, a fairly obscure and eccentric text to come up with from such an unchurchy looking man. I suspected some brief Pentecostal history followed by a little backsliding.

Between ports, Lyza was adept at contriving baths of various sorts—from the sun shower we hung from the mast to sponge baths in the cockpit while the rest of us were off exploring. She considered it a treat when we left her in the cockpit with a small tub of hot water, splashing and singing like a magpie in a birdbath. Other times we would all huff and puff in an icy glacial stream, then leap out on granite rocks, hopping and hooting in the sun. Definitely an elemental existence, but I did everything in my power to facilitate Lyza's priority of maintaining cleanliness because I knew, as my secretary, Patsi, would say, 'If Mama ain't happy, ain't nobody happy.'

Early the next morning we poked our heads nervously out of Chappel Inlet, hoping the massive rollers had subsided. We crept out from behind the protective islets into the open ocean again and gratefully greeted a relatively calm sea. As we proceeded, the shore to our southeast was rugged coastline penetrated here and there with a beckoning channel or inlet. Two months up here and we only had time enough to scratch the surface of exploration.

Passing into Laredo Channel, we came upon a pod of killer whales, which was the last item on Ginette's wish list. We played tag with them for an hour, exclaiming and snapping pictures. We passed the night in a small balloon-shaped inlet entered by a shallow thirty-foot wide channel. Nosing our way into the current that flowed out like a lovely quiet river, Lyza and Ginette were stationed on the bow looking for rocks when we were suddenly startled by loud splashing to the right and left. We had again stumbled upon a salmon run on their way back to their native stream. We became used to the constant leaping and tumbling which continued the entire time we stayed in Kent Inlet. Ginette actually hooked one all by herself, landed it, and later cooked it up for us, a gourmet's delight with her creative concoction of sauce, spices and garnish.

Finally, nearly a month later, we completed the circle and neared the vicinity of Bella Bella again. We had been incommunicado for two weeks, ever since leaving Prince Rupert.

One sacrifice Lyza had made in making this voyage was the possibility of being away when her second grandchild was due to be born. We had agreed beforehand that Lyza could fly home if we were anywhere near an airport when the baby came. But when we checked in at Prince Rupert (the last chance for such a flight) the baby's birth was not imminent, so Lyza had to let go of her grandmotherly yearnings as we headed out into the most remote places of our trip. She found it difficult that the baby might be born, or there could be problems, and we just wouldn't know anything for weeks. Besides, she had been in the delivery room when Irelynn was born and she just didn't want to miss out. After a good cry, she gave the matter to God's care and chose not to fret during the rest of our trip. However, she became antsy as we traveled down Meyers Channel and around Finlayson Channel to a tiny Indian village called Klemtu where we knew there was a small store, some fuel, and best of all, a telephone.

The boat's lines were hardly secured to the dock before Lyza charged up the float ramp to call home. Dave and Lori weren't home, but our good friend and neighbor, Christine, told her they had headed to the hospital just a few hours before. (Lyza also received the special added bonus of hearing the details of the birth of Christine's baby, Josiah, just the week before.) She gave Christine the Klemtu tollbooth phone number and we decided to wait until we heard something. A mere twenty minutes later, a local teenage girl walked up to Lyza in the store. "Are you Lyza Clarke? There's a phone call for you outside."

Lyza raced down the boardwalk, and grabbed the phone—"Hello?"

"Mom?" It was David. "It's a boy!" He shouted. "Born just twenty minutes ago. You should see him. He looks just like Dad!"

"Is he okay?"

"Perfect!"

"How's Lori?"

"Mom, you would have been so proud of her. She was a real trooper. She sailed through it."

"Thank God. What are you gonna call the little fella?"

"Get this—Finn David Vinal Clarke. Have to keep the Vinal name going, after all."

Though hundreds of miles away in the north, Lyza was able to share the fresh excitement of the moment and feel a part of it. What incredible timing, considering the variables of an unpredictable pregnancy and the uncertainties of our sailboat trip. Lyza believed it was the Lord's exquisite orchestration of the details of life and nobody would ever convince her the timing was a coincidence. Like our journey through the wilderness with its compensating treasures for all the troubles, we knew our lives were designed to reveal those little glimpses of God's care and His assurances of an inheritance prepared for us. What greater inheritance than to see the establishment of future generations. This grandpa was grateful that the Clarke name and his own mother's maiden name, Vinal, would be carried by the first son of the next generation.

Anchors Aweigh!

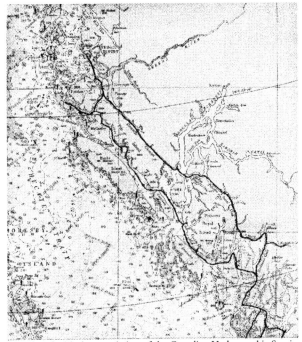

Reproduced with the permission of the Canadian Hydrographic Service

Greedy Desires at Kadesh Barnea, Numbers 11
The Eighth Temptation – Greedy Desires

The Ten Temptations: **8. Counterfeit Comfort (Greedy Desires at Kadesh)**

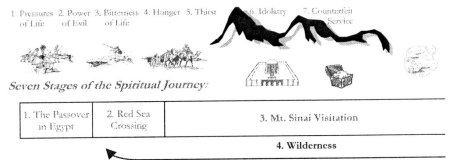

1. Pressures 2. Power 3. Bitterness 4. Hunger 5. Thirst 6. Idolatry 7. Counterfeit
   of Life   of Evil   of Life   Service

Seven Stages of the Spiritual Journey:

1. The Passover in Egypt	2. Red Sea Crossing	3. Mt. Sinai Visitation
		4. Wilderness

Chapter Twelve

Lyza and Ginette hugged me and then waved goodbye as they stepped aboard the little Cessna parked at the Bella Bella airport. Dick, my newfound friend from the spring trip to Malibu, had flown up with his son, Bryce, bringing with them my son Matthew. We were all a little emotional at the breakup of our little community of three, but the grandchildren exerted a special pull on Grammy's heart and I looked forward to spending some time with Matt bringing the boat down from Bella Bella. I was touched by Matt's choice to give up a planned Volkswagen van trip with his buddies to the Grand Canyon to spend two weeks with the old man.

We had once again restocked our supplies from the Bella Bella band store and were on the way out of town when Bo had an unfortunate run in with a local street gang of dogs. He tried to join the gang with his usual affable approach but the leader, more of a wolf than a dog, took issue and jumped him. He tore a small, deep hole in Bo's chest shattering what was left of his secure view of the world. Now on land and on sea he was never quite safe. No vet clinic existed in Bella Bella, but a kind doctor from the small local hospital stitched him up on the sidewalk at no charge. It was a good thing, too, because Bo didn't have his medical number on him. Licking his five stitches and his wounded psyche, Bo was glad to move on and leave that town behind. We were glad to be moving on as well.

Father and son headed off into the wild blue yonder. Matthew sat on the bowsprit, riding it like a cowboy over the rolling waves just as the kids had done together in the early years, lined up one behind the other like birds on a branch. We worked our way down through overcast days until we anchored one afternoon in a half circle bite off Fitzhugh Sound called the Koeye River. Koeye was a river whose deep channel penetrated into an isolated valley teeming with wildlife. We took *Crayon* almost two miles in, seeking trout, only to find a salmon run choking the channel. Under tall shadows of evergreens the dark gray backs of a thousand spawning salmon schooled, blotting out the river bottom, revolving slowly in a great ball of silent purpose. The insistent inner urging called them from the ocean depths to keep moving until they reached the gravelly shallows, fertilized their seed, and died, rotting in the streambed to provide nourishment for the next generation.

Our motor finally bumping on the river rocks, we let the current carry us back down toward the sea, drifting and casting for trout all the way. Splashing through the tumult where the river and the salty waves clashed, we went to our traps and hauled in a pile of Dungeness crabs. Matthew hooked a small salmon casting off the sandy beach while I cleaned the cod caught earlier in the mouth of the small bay. A humpback whale surfaced and spouted his way northward in the sound. Matthew thought he'd landed in heaven, but we couldn't stay—the anchorage was threatened by wind blowing swells into the shallow harbour. Koeye remained with us, an awesome memory as our course led us on to safer anchorage in Pruth Bay. There our voyage came to a halt as we got bogged down under a dismal low that settled over the area bringing blustering wind and rain. We waited it out playing Rummi-kub and listening to weather reports. A short hike through the woods took us to a sandy beach open to the Pacific while *Fred* stayed safely anchored in the lee of the forested strip of land. The visits to the ocean were invigorating, but our restlessness increased and our attitudes deteriorated as two days stretched to three.

Two things are especially important to remember on a sailboat voyage. One is you need a destination to head for and the second is you have to keep moving. If you stay in one place too long, its charm diminishes and restlessness sets in. A destination gives you a direction, a distance to cover, and a sense of accomplishment. When our children were young, we headed for Desolation Sound and back to Seattle on our summer vacations. They anticipated the special places along the way, like good old Sydney Spit, Hawkins Island, Bucaneer Bay, or Harmony Island, but we always hauled anchor and moved on to the next spot before they grew tired of each place's uniqueness. By the end of the trip we looked forward to the routines of home and were ready to get off the boat. But then we repeated the same cycle the next year and the kids never tired of it as long as we kept moving.

Life, too, needs a purpose or destination to keep progressing toward. We are meant to keep moving toward the inheritance through the lessons God has prepared, to a place where the intimate knowledge of God and a mature character are the goals. Without maturity as the goal, sometimes it's difficult to interpret the ports of call or the storms along the way. If the goal is personal happiness or freedom from trouble, the lessons of life can seem counter-productive or even destructive, but if the goal is maturity, every event along the way is constructive and purposeful. Likewise even a very pleasant place in life loses its charm if we are not growing. We have to move on and grow in character.

When Matt and I were stuck in Pruth Bay, we hiked to the ocean every day to keep up our spirits by exploring the beaches and talking about life. Matt, now twenty-three years old, was one of those people who came into life with his knapsack full. With an easy-going, likeable personality and a wise demeanor, he made friends easily and found favor with most people. He got good grades, was good looking and an excellent athlete, yet it didn't seem to go to his head. He wondered why his life should be so good when he looked at the rest of the world. He had a stable family, was part of a vital church, and opportunities abounded. He often felt bad that he couldn't truly identify with the suffering around him. At one point a few years earlier, being a fairly serious and spiritually-minded young man, he asked God for a deeper compassion to identify more with the pain of people. Although he didn't know it at the time, this was not a safe prayer.

In his late teens, Matt developed a serious back problem. For three years he sought relief, exhausting chiropractic help and many alternative therapies, but he remained in chronic pain, which altered his life and limited his opportunities. In the middle of a yearlong university exchange program in Denmark, he was forced to come home—he couldn't even sit through classes anymore. Our good-natured son struggled with irritability and depression, and coinciding with this physically and emotionally draining condition, Matt experienced an internal crisis of faith. How could he know for sure that the Christian way he grew up with was the only 'way' for him and others? Was there really a plan behind all this suffering or was it just life? As we walked on the beaches, we talked over his dilemmas. Whether his personal experience of suffering was God's way of answering his prayer to be able to empathize we couldn't say for certain, but he was definitely getting a firsthand dose of pain. He felt stuck in all dimensions, unable to rise above or move beyond his present state. He was suffering from spiritual and physical inertia. He was stuck in a harbour and wasn't sure what his destination was.

Kwakshua Channel was not an inspiring sight in the dull morning light but at least we were moving past it, a good sign after days of going nowhere. Once we were in the open waters, a hint of blue and a dash of sunlight broke through on distant hillsides lightening our way. Passing Aldenbrook Lighthouse, we finally came to rest at Fury Island in Rivers Inlet where I had felt such exhilaration on the way up. There we walked on the white-shelled beaches and fished for salmon in the rollers that came out of Queen Charlotte Sound. On our way out we finally caught one and then pointed our bowsprit toward Egg Island and the long exposed run around Cape Caution into Queen Charlotte Strait. Hoping to beat the next low predicted to hit that night, we motored ten hours straight, feeling our way in the darkness into a little cove in Wells Passage. We collapsed into bunks with the thought of home and missing my wife beginning to register. Both were still a long ways off, but we had crossed the divide and were back under the protection of Vancouver Island on the last leg of the journey.

Israel kept moving as well toward their destination and was learning in the process. Along the way were many camping places where the pillar of fire and cloud had stopped and so the people had stopped. These places were often times of testing or lessons to be learned and then they moved on, better equipped through their experiences to achieve their purpose and sustain themselves in the land once they arrived. They often got stuck in their campsites too. Some of them never moved beyond these places and died there because they would not learn the necessary lessons. In fact, most of them died before the forty-year journey was over. Some people stayed in campsites because they were satisfied and had enough of traveling. They liked places like Elim and said, "The rest of you go on. We've had enough and we like it right here."

You can find people like that in churches today, camped at some spot, unwilling to go any further in the spiritual journey. Some say, "I've experienced the cross, God's Passover, and that's all I need.

God's grace will get me to heaven and that's all I care about." Others are camped at the Red Sea, having experienced water baptism and say, "We're baptized, and we don't need anything more." Some, after experiencing a few tests in the desert, say, "We've had enough trouble in life and it is too hard. We're stopping here." Then there are the ones camped at Mt. Sinai. "We've seen God," they say. "We've experienced a baptism of the Spirit with power and that's what we're going to preach and that's where we'll camp," yet they are still far from the promised land with a Jordan River to cross and a land to occupy. They are fearful or unwilling to embrace some new challenge in their faith and they can't see the purpose of their suffering. Some get stuck in bitterness against God, complaining against His unfairness and feeling hard done by.

The purpose is made clear in the book of Hebrews—the purpose is maturity.

"Therefore leaving the elementary teaching about the Christ, let us press on to maturity, not laying again a foundation of repentance from dead works and of faith toward God, of instruction about washings and laying on of hands, and the resurrection of the dead and eternal judgment." (Hebrews 6:1,2)

We are supposed to keep moving, to press on to maturity, growing up into Christ. Things like salvation, baptisms in water or Spirit and doctrines of eternity or end times are just the foundations for gaining our inheritance. Yet, whole denominations have been built around one or another of these truths. The end of our faith is the nature of Christ formed in us for now and eternity. We're to let His nature be forged within us through life's experiences until our souls are at rest in a land flowing with milk and honey. Israel was not allowed to stay at Sinai, the scene of their great encounter with God. The experience at Sinai was designed to equip them to go forward under the guidance and command of God. This way of following God was in itself a new step of maturity.

Now in the second year, in the second month, on the twentieth of the month, that the cloud was lifted from over the tabernacle of the testimony; and the sons of Israel set out on their journeys from the wilderness of Sinai. Then the cloud settled down in the wilderness of Paran. So they moved out for the first time according to the commandment of the Lord through Moses. (Numbers 10:11-13)

It took the experience of Sinai, where they encountered God's manifest presence, to really get them moving under God's command. Sinai and its corresponding experience of Pentecost in the New Testament is when the Holy Spirit comes to write God's word on the tablets of our hearts. We then begin to move under the guidance of God's Spirit and actually want to live by the words that come from His mouth. The Israelites were moving under a new direct relationship with God, but their resolve didn't take long to break down as they faced another test. The problems began when the people started complaining about their lot in life.

Now the people became like those who complain of adversity in the hearing of the Lord; and when the Lord heard it, His anger was kindled, and the fire of the Lord burned among them and consumed some of the outskirts of the camp. (Numbers 11:1)

Evidently, complaining about our lot in life is big on God's hit list. Many people get lost in the desert because they see no purpose in pain (they feel God gave them a bum deal), and take to grumbling about it. One of the surest ways to halt our spiritual progress is to complain in adversity and become ungrateful. This crucial mistake is reiterated in the New Testament account of these events. *"Now these things happened as examples for us, so that... [we should not] grumble, as some of them did, and were destroyed by the destroyer"* (I Corinthians 10:6,10).

Once our forward progress stops because of grumbling, we become vulnerable to other kinds of temptation. When we are not going anywhere, we decide we might as well comfort ourselves with self-indulgence. We become susceptible to what the scripture defines as 'greedy desires'.

The rabble who were among them had greedy desires; and also the sons of Israel wept again and said, "Who will give us meat to eat? We remember the fish which we used to eat free in Egypt, the cucumbers and the melons and the leeks and the onions and the garlic, but now our appetite is gone. There is nothing at all to look at except this manna." (Numbers 11:4-6)

Although the issue presented in the story was about food (wanting meat instead of manna), it also encompassed the inordinate desire for other sensual gratification. When the Israelites became disaffected with God they turned to their senses. Sensual lust, the eighth temptation, is one of the more elemental temptations we might think was dealt with back at the beginning of the journey. Repentance and baptism may have dealt with sexual sins, but the ongoing tension between spirituality and sensuality is a lifetime challenge. We're not talking here about healthy desire, but that which goes beyond lawful boundaries—greedy desires. Craving evil things goes hand in hand with dissatisfaction with God. The temptation to trade eternal values for fleshly indulgence can be particularly potent when we camp too long in one place. A poignant Biblical example is King David at the height of his career. He made the mistake of hanging around home too long when he should have been out with his troops.

Then it happened in the spring, at the time when kings go out to battle, that David sent Joab and his servants with him and all Israel, and they destroyed the sons of Ammon and besieged Rabbah. But David stayed at Jerusalem. (2 Samuel 11:1)

We know that sap begins to rise in spring as do romantic desires, but we probably weren't aware that in old times kings went out to battle in spring to maintain their kingdoms. This time David felt he had enough of war, so he sent out his generals and decided to stay home and take it easy. Away from the action on the front lines, he became idle and bored. *"Now when evening came David arose from his bed and walked around on the roof of the king's house, and from the roof he saw a woman bathing; and the woman was very beautiful in appearance"* (2 Samuel 11:2).

One might wonder what David is doing getting out of bed in the evening instead of morning. That was his first mistake, sleeping on the job; the second was sleeping with Bathsheba. The ground had been prepared through an idle mind and a lazy day in bed to sow the seed of greedy desire. When he saw Bathsheba, he was tempted beyond the legitimate sexual needs of a married man into the arena of greedy desires. *"So David sent and inquired about the woman. And one said, 'Is this not Bathsheba, the daughter of Eliam, the wife of Uriah the Hittite?'"* (2 Samuel 11:3).

First, David was where he shouldn't have been, and second, he was looking where he shouldn't have looked, and now he was thinking about what he shouldn't have been thinking about. David stayed in the harbour too long. He didn't keep moving. He stopped fighting the necessary battles and so began losing the battle against sensual desires, first in his mind and then in his actions. Maybe he did a little murmuring like the Israelites, maybe he just got tired of going to war. Whatever it was, the stop in forward momentum set the scene for dissatisfaction, which opened the door for temptation, self-deception and eventually self-gratification. *"David sent messengers and took her, and when she came to him, he lay with her; and when she had purified herself from her uncleanness, she returned to her house. The woman conceived; and she sent and told David, and said, 'I am pregnant'"* (2 Samuel 11:4-5).

The rest of the story is a sad commentary on the tangled web of sin that springs from unchecked lust. David got Bathsheba pregnant and had her husband killed to cover it up. Even so, David was a man after God's heart. He represents the best of us and yet he fell. None of us are above this temptation nor are we exempt from the consequences if we fail. David was forgiven immediately, but he reaped consequences in his family for the rest of his life. All in all, this was not David's finest hour.

It was not the Israelites' finest hour either, as they lusted for meat and complained. Moses despaired at this latest blatant lack of spirituality among the Israelites—so much so that he became suicidal and asked God to kill him. However, God had his own way to deal with their lust problem.

> *"Say to the people, 'Consecrate yourselves for tomorrow, and you shall eat meat; for you have wept in the ears of the Lord, saying, 'Oh, that someone would give us meat to eat! For we were well-off in Egypt.' Therefore the Lord will give you meat and you shall eat."* (Numbers 11:18)

We should be careful what we whine about in God's ears, for He just might give us what we want. There is a big difference between what we want and what God knows we really need. It's better to leave our wants and needs in God's hands.

A greedy desire is not just pertaining to sex, but can be any desire that pushes us beyond God's boundaries. I have seen people lament over their single status while pining for marriage, until they finally engineer a relationship for themselves, which often turns disastrous. Then they whine in God's ear as though their choice was His fault. People plunge themselves headlong into the self-gratification of gluttony, drugs or alcohol until that passion becomes their odious slave master. Often people's lives become completely unmanageable before they are ready to be set free. Becoming completely overwhelmed with an overdose of our own greedy desire is actually one of the means God uses to show us the folly of our ways. He gave the Israelites what they were asked for, big time!

"You shall eat, not one day, nor two days, nor five days, nor ten days, nor twenty days, but a whole month, until it comes out of your nostrils and becomes loathsome to you; because you have rejected the Lord who is among you and have wept before Him, saying, 'Why did we ever leave Egypt?'" (Numbers 11:19,20)

It's like the father with the son who wanted to smoke so he gave him a pack of cigarettes and insisted he smoke every one. By the end, the boy was so sick he couldn't stand the sight or smell of another cigarette. This is really last resort parenting, but as we've already seen, God's discipline can be extreme when He's making a point.

Now there went forth a wind from the Lord and it brought quail from the sea, and let them fall beside the camp, about a day's journey on this side and day's journey on the other side, all around the camp and about two cubits deep on the surface of the ground. (Numbers 11:31)

You want meat? You got it! A pile of birds fell three feet deep all around their camp. *Go ahead, gorge yourselves until it comes out of your*

181

noses! They got what they wanted and a lot more. Then a lot of them died, struck with a plague. Maybe God was punishing them or maybe they experienced the natural consequence of so much meat sitting around in the desert sun. Are STDs the judgment of God or just the natural consequence of crossing the boundaries? Whichever way we want to interpret it, acting on our greedy desires ends in death, if not physically, then certainly spiritually. Many of these Israelites did not receive their inheritance because they died before they could get to the Promised Land, but a more subtle loss occurs from yielding to the temptation of greedy desires. An inner dying inhibits the growth of God's life in our souls.

That loss is best illustrated by Abraham's heir and grandson Esau.

"See to it that no one comes short of the grace of God; that no root of bitterness springing up causes trouble, and by it many be defiled; that there be no immoral or godless person like Esau, who sold his own birthright [inheritance] *for a single meal."* (Hebrews 12:15,16)

The King James Version says, *"He sold his inheritance for a bowl of soup."* The bowl of soup story illustrates how we can trade a valuable, enduring inheritance for passing, immediate gratification. Esau came in from a hunting trip, totally famished, to find his brother Jacob making a savory soup. Overcome with hunger, he traded his right of firstborn inheritance to Jacob for a bowl of it. The vernacular of his statement is revealing. "Gimme some of that red stuff, for I am famished and what good is my inheritance to me if I should starve to death?" His immediate desire for physical gratification overshadowed his better judgment and the more enduring values. Who in their right mind would trade a rich future heritage for one lunch? And yet this is essentially what is at stake in the battle we all have to fight to keep sensuality at bay.

Fidelity is obviously crucial in the domain of family life. There is no greater destroyer of the orderly and peaceful transfer of a natural inheritance than the tearing apart of marriage and families. A family's estate can be dissipated in a generation through divorce and its related complications. In terms of the spiritual inheritance, the effect of giving in to greedy desires can be subtler, yet involves the same disenfranchisement. Esau lived in the present without thought of the future and without a clear purpose in his life. In the same way, if we lack a clear purpose and have no worthwhile destination, the slide into moral oblivion is much easier. The philosophy becomes, "Let's eat, drink and be merry for tomorrow we die."

Lust is a particularly subtle thief because it is a counterfeit for spiritual passion and can bring our forward progress to a standstill without us hardly knowing it. John tells us, *"Do not love the world nor the things in the world* [the lusts of the flesh, etc.]. *If anyone loves the world, the love of the Father is not in him"* (1 John 2:15). These two loves are mutually exclusive. A Christian continually neutralized by sensual lusts may ultimately make it to heaven but be robbed of his inheritance along the way. This temptation is one of the greatest 'disinheritors' of them all because sensitivity to God's guidance becomes buried under an addictive physical appetite.

The remainder of Matt's and my voyage passed by quickly as we retraced Lyza's and my route through the cluster of islets at the end of Queen Charlotte Strait and back down to Johnstone Strait. One morning, while trying to tighten the bolts on our stern bearing stuffing box, I accidentally twisted the bolt right off, creating a major disaster. The constant anxiety on *Fred* was that some engine failure or malfunction would render us helpless somewhere in the wilderness or in the midst of a treacherous sea. I always wondered what would happen if the two leaking bolts around the propeller shaft came off or broke. My dad always warned me to keep those bolts tightened, but hadn't told me what ominous consequences might result if I didn't. I was about to find out. My first inclination was to stay put. Fear of the unknown on Johnstone Strait and visions of water pouring into the boat through the propeller shaft immobilized me. We were a good sixty miles from Lund, where I knew of a mechanic. There was nowhere to turn in the wilderness so we had no choice but to keep moving and hope for the best.

At least we were now within cell phone range, so I called Clyde, the boat's mechanic, in Seattle. Through the static-filled connection he increased my fears by telling me I'd better get to a mechanic quick and sail rather than motor as much as possible to put less stress on the remaining bolt, which held the stern bearing in place. So we unfurled the sails before a thirty-five-knot northwesterly and sailed through the mountainous wind tunnel amid foaming whitecaps for forty miles. The morning consternation melted away into the most glorious day of sailing I can remember, sometimes reaching twelve knots in the wind and current. The mechanical crisis forced us to enjoy a day of sailing. Two days and fifteen sailing hours later, we made it to Lund and discovered the problem was not as dire as I had imagined. The mechanic assured us that if the stuffing box had fallen apart completely, the bilge pump could have handled the incoming water. It wouldn't have been fun, but we wouldn't have sunk.

Over the years my brother and I had endured numerous mechanical breakdowns and crises but every one of them resulted in some blessing. I developed a greater knowledge about boats and engines and how they work, and therefore a much greater confidence as a captain. One time the engine just quit in a storm in the middle of the Strait of Georgia. I had to take the fuel lines apart to clear the sediment that clogged the lines. Another time we ran out of fuel in Bellingham Bay and had to figure out how to bleed the injectors to get started again. Then there was time my brother put the boat in reverse off Sucia Island and backed the propeller and shaft right out of the boat until it caught on the rudder. He had no choice but to tow the boat up on the beach and wait for the tide to go out so he could pound the shaft back in and reattach it. He didn't know whether the boat, over on its side like a beached whale, would right itself when the tide came back in or just fill up with water and sink. Happily it floated at the last minute just before the water reached the cabin portholes.

'Trial by error' was our usual learning method through the years and there certainly were numerous incidents to complete our education. I'm sure there are safer and more expeditious ways to learn, but most of us approach the basic challenges of life in just this way. Whether the trials come from our own stupidities or whether they just happen to us, God turns them into training for life. If we keep moving forward through the perplexities we eventually become equipped.

In our years of ministry we have encountered perplexities, despair, setbacks, heartaches, deaths and disappointments and yet insights, helps, blessings and revelations all came along through the same processes. It may be frightening, we may experience failure, but we take the adventure that befalls us, pull up anchor for the next port, and believe that eternal hands are steady on the most important tiller. Fear immobilizes us but faith leads us forward. The testings of life are tools in God's hand to channel our life force in the right directions. This might seem to be an unending challenge but it is designed to bring us home to heaven with a richness of experience and character that nothing else can instill. My hope and prayer for my son, Matt, was that through all the trials he was presently experiencing, he would persevere and move on to a deeper experience of God's reality.

We made the last six-hour run down the coast to the cabin site where Lyza and Ginette switched with Matt as my crewmates for the last leg back to Seattle. The summer days were waning, leaving a burnt hue upon the Gulf Islands where red arbutus and yellow maples littered their leaves over rocky crags and golden grasses. As we drifted down with the ebb tides, we remembered the flood tide of our emotions in the spring when we had followed this route northward. I was happy we had done it; I was glad we had pressed beyond our comfort zone. I remembered the wavering point in 'Bludgeon' Harbour and the trip beyond Cape Caution into the rich experience of the north. Looking over the chart of the north coast, I knew it personally now. I had navigated its waterways, viewed its mountainous beauties, penetrated its coves and rivers, braved its weather, and tasted of its seafood bounties. It was not the awesome unknown anymore, but rather, it was an awesome experience. We had become acquainted; I had become equipped.

Another piece of the picture puzzle slipped into place as we finally tied up the boat with the heavy bowlines against the winter storms on Lake Washington and I gave my dear mother an embrace. This voyage was part of God's design for me, part of the picture He was painting through my life, part of His workmanship created in Christ from the foundation of the world. Some may not think a sailboat trip to the Alaskan border is very spiritual, but I think, in God's economy, it fit together in the overall picture. It was something He had placed in my heart to do as much as serving Christ in pastoral ministry.

So we put *Fred* to bed and headed back to White Rock to visit a very dear friend, Marge, completing the final leg of her journey in a bout with cancer. She was our former pastor's wife. While checking in with her on the phone from Prince Rupert, I had promised her I would conduct her funeral service. At that time I had hoped she would still be with us when we got home, for we knew she might not have more than a few weeks to live. Now it looked as though I would be there to celebrate both her sixty-sixth birthday and my fiftieth, which were only a couple of days apart. Life was shuttling by so fast. Old friends were dying and I was already half a century old. Yet we all were really only moving on to the next milestone, the next port. Marge was about to pull up anchor for the last time to head for the most beautiful coast of all and I needed to bid her bon voyage.

Safe at Home Base

Miriam and Aaron's Rebellion, Numbers 12
The Ninth Temptation – Usurping Authority

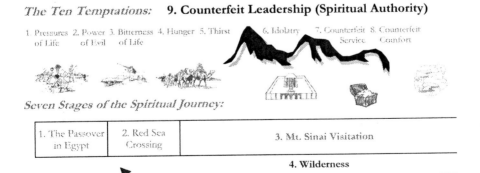

The Ten Temptations: **9. Counterfeit Leadership (Spiritual Authority)**

1. Pressures of Life 2. Power of Evil 3. Bitterness of Life 4. Hunger 5. Thirst 6. Idolatry 7. Counterfeit Service 8. Counterfeit Comfort

Seven Stages of the Spiritual Journey:

1. The Passover in Egypt	2. Red Sea Crossing	3. Mt. Sinai Visitation
		4. Wilderness

The heavy oak and beveled glass door swung noiselessly open into a solemn ornate room. A pink casket lay open on the dais. Sitting in velvet covered pews and standing about on the richly carpeted floor was an almost merry group of people hugging, talking, laughing and crying with one another. This was Marge's close circle of family and friends coming to bid her farewell and comfort one another. Their presence lightened the somber atmosphere of the high-ceilinged funeral chapel.

There, lying primly with her hair done exactly how she would have liked it, was Marge, who wore death as victoriously as she had managed life. She lay waxenly peaceful, a single rose laid in a velvet box for her Master. I had not gotten home in time to converse with her, but she was still alive when I got to the hospital. Even then her indomitable spirit prevailed in the hospital room. As Lyza and I sat in her room with two of her children, Rick and Karen, she let us know she was listening in little ways, especially when Rick was telling stories on her. Marge determined to be as fully engaged as possible right up to her last breath, and we figured that she had probably picked her birthday as an appropriate day to go home to heaven. We delayed our flight to the east coast, the next leg of our sabbatical, for her funeral.

I couldn't help but reminisce, being back home for this brief time at the halfway point of our year away. It didn't seem very long ago that Verne and Marge were pastoring the church and we came in as young adults learning the ways of Christian community. It was all so new and different for us in the beginning, the Sunday morning and evening services and the Sunday afternoon dinners. I could still remember those dinners after church—a full meal at midday, roast beef with gravy and all the farm vegetables, dessert and coffee—in neat Canadian homes where you always took your shoes off at the door. Whether it was Saskatchewan farm culture or church culture, or both, we quickly slid into the same habit. In many ways we learned the essence of building a sense of community in those early years. And in the middle of it all was Marge, always active, always cheerful and demonstrating the kind of hospitality we learned to emulate.

Verne was a stocky Irishman with a twinkle in his eye that always let you know that life was best taken with a sense of humor rather than taking yourself too seriously. Like many married couples, they seemed complete opposites and managed to balance their differences in a mutually beneficial tension. I remember one time, on Marge's 40th birthday, when the two of them stood, as always, at the door to greet people after the service. Someone wished Marge a happy birthday and Verne was ready with a comment.

"Yeah, I thought maybe it's time, now she's forty, to trade her in for two twenties." He was grinning and chuckling over his cleverness.

"Well, dear," she didn't miss a beat, "that's all very well, but I don't think you are wired for '220'."

For eighteen years, Lyza and I served under Verne and Marge's leadership. Although I sometimes strained at the bit, God had prepared a place for us to learn and grow without the extra pressure of being in charge of the church. The Lord brought us to a place where we could learn the important lessons of responding to someone else's authority.

Paying my last respects to the slight form in the funeral chapel, I felt a special kinship with and affection for this spunky lady. Only the two of us really knew the ways God had tested us. Only the two of us knew the pain we had caused each other and the difficult twists of fate that had helped refine our characters. Marge and I, at different stages of our lives and from completely separate vantage points, had needed to learn the lessons of the ninth temptation. We had to learn how to trust God to work for our good through very fallible people.

It was as the Israelites neared the Promised Land that two of Moses' relatives demonstrated this test of responding correctly to the human authority God puts in our lives. Miriam was a prophetess in Israel and a close relative of the 'big guy', Moses. She was Aaron's and Moses' sister and the one who picked up the tambourine to lead the whole nation in triumphal worship after crossing the Red Sea. She had a powerful spiritual leadership capability in her own right with deep insights into the purposes of God. A person with such abilities is always a prime candidate for the sifting of God's ninth test.

Then Miriam and Aaron spoke against Moses because of the Cushite woman who he had married (for he had married a Cushite woman); and they said, "Has the Lord indeed spoken only through Moses? Has He not spoken through us as well?" And the Lord heard it. (Numbers 12:1,2)

The grammatical particulars here indicate that it was Miriam who led the criticism of Moses. This may account for the events later when she receives the brunt of the consequences. Miriam's criticisms had a legitimate base. Moses had married a Cushite (Ethiopian) woman, which was against the rules God laid down for them. Israelites were not to intermarry with other peoples because these nations served other gods and would corrupt the message God was forging in the Israelites.

Usually deeper issues are at work beneath the surface when a person criticizes a leader. Miriam's issues had to do with jealousy and pride. *"Has the Lord indeed spoken only through Moses? Has He not spoken through us as well?"* (Numbers 12:2). In other words, "Don't you people remember how I prophesied over Israel and led the nation in worship? Don't you think I can hear from God too?"

Moses was not much of a public speaker. Whatever oratorical skills he had as a prince in Egypt were completely dissipated after forty years in Midian. Moses had been out keeping sheep in the backwoods of Midian for too long and was very reticent to put himself forward. As Canadians would say, Moses was 'bushed'. That means he had spent so much time in the bush (wilderness) that he could no longer socially relate. Whatever illusions of grandeur he might have had were long abandoned after his bungled attempts at leadership in Egypt. It is interesting that what Moses interprets as a shame and a failure the scripture records as an entirely different quality. *"Now the man Moses was very humble, more than any man who was on the face of the earth"* (Numbers 12:3). (It might undermine the point, however, if we point out that most scholars agree Moses was the author of this passage!)

Regardless, Miriam had not spent forty years looking after sheep in the desert like Moses had, and was unaware of the unexposed motivations propelling her into this conflict. She only saw the clay feet of her brother and felt the flush of exhilaration when God's Spirit moved upon her. Miriam made the mistake of believing that because God had used her, she was now ready to assume the leadership. God's blessing upon us and the power released through us is not necessarily in direct correlation to the maturity of our character. In fact, failure and frustration often do more to build our character than success and recognition.

Leaders always have clay feet. They have unrefined character issues, weaknesses in their leadership styles, personality quirks and sometimes even grave spiritual liabilities or besetting sins. That is what makes the ninth test a test. If God only used people without any unregenerate dispositions, He would have nobody to use. Through His amazing grace, He chooses to use us in spite of ourselves. Understanding this should deter one faulty human being from discrediting and undermining another faulty human being that God has seen fit to put in spiritual authority. Authority comes from God and is bestowed by grace.

When Miriam spoke against Moses, the scripture says, *"… the Lord heard it."* What followed for Miriam was a head-to-head with God who didn't even deal with her complaint about the Cushite woman, but talked about His own relationship with Moses.

> *"Hear now my words; if there is a prophet among you, I, the Lord, shall make Myself known to him in a vision. I shall speak with him in a dream. Not so, with My servant Moses, he is faithful in all My household; With him I speak mouth to mouth, even openly, and not in dark sayings, and he beholds the form of the Lord. Why then were you not afraid to speak against My servant, against Moses?"* (Numbers 12:6-8)

This was not just a vindication of Moses; it was a vindication of God's order and initiative. God started this thing with Moses. It was God's work, not man's, and Miriam was thinking comparatively, in human terms. Even Jesus, while excoriating the scribes and

Pharisees, honored the authority of the religious system that had its roots in God's initiative.

> *"The scribes and the Pharisees have seated themselves in the chair of Moses; therefore all that they tell you, do and observe, but do not do according to their deeds; for they say things, and do not do them."*
> (Matthew 23:2,3)

In other words, excel them in character but don't contend with their authority. We will always have to work out our spirituality in the context of people and in relation to some spiritual authority. Many a spiritual journey comes to a halt around this issue. People can't see God at work in their context so they lead a group of other disgruntled people off to form their own group. If they leave in a wrong spirit, they soon are committing the same errors. We're all made of the same clay. We can't build a positive future on a negative foundation. Miriam's punishment is a warning to those who commit her error.

> *So the anger of the Lord burned against them and He departed. But when the cloud had withdrawn from over the tent, behold, Miriam was leprous, as white as snow. As Aaron turned toward Miriam, behold, she was leprous.* (Numbers 12:9-10)

Leprosy is a very visual disease where the flesh rots off of the body. Usurping authority is a work of the flesh in a spiritual sense. It is man projecting himself through his pride into the spiritual domain. The result of this is usually a kind of spiritual leprosy where that person, instead of becoming more spiritual, becomes more fleshly in a way that is obvious to all, and they often become guilty of the very weakness they criticize. Miriam's consequence for exalting herself was leprosy, and she was isolated from the people. Only through the intercessions of Aaron and Moses was she spared a life of leprosy. They prayed and she was healed. God's mercy can override our mistakes.

This ninth temptation was well placed because the people were nearing the Promised Land and a switch of leadership from Moses to Joshua was about to take place. They needed to have their eyes of faith upon the Lord Jehovah and not upon their longstanding human leader. It is necessary to look past human personalities and weaknesses to discern the leadership God has established in our lives. Only as we learn to respond to spiritual authority do we develop the foundation of character, which is needed to steward whatever gifts God has given us.

Many people become frustrated because they don't know how to use their talents in the context of spiritual authority. They want position or recognition without securing the trustworthiness and maturity that grows while working under authority. In a world that glorifies outward success, many Christian leaders think they have some great ministry to fulfill, which others are hindering. However, it is not external recognition, but the reflection of Christ's nature in our character that is the measure of success and the procuring of our true inheritance. Perhaps there is no escaping the pain that accompanies this process.

After we became part of a church, I realized more and more that pastoring was a natural fit for me. Not having any pastor types in my family lineage that I knew of, it had never really entered my mind before to consider the vocation of a pastor. Even when we made the radical move toward the coffeehouse ministry, it never registered that I was heading toward becoming a minister. Finally, when they started paying me to be a youth pastor, it began to sink in and I thought that maybe I should get some training. Lyza and I settled into an apprentice position, comfortably working under the direction of Pastor Verne and Marge as well as receiving training from other pastors in the area, especially Les Pritchard. Verne let me start preaching and taught me the practical pastoral skills of conducting weddings, visitations, and funerals. Mostly I imbibed his heart toward people and his attitude about service in God's house. We learned that church was really an intergenerational family and we came to appreciate the broad diversity of age and background in our church community.

As time went on and more leaders and ministries were raised up in the church, the differences of gifting between Verne and me became more apparent. Verne was a wonderful pastor of people who liked nothing better than to visit everyone, help them with needs and give practical advice. I was more of a visionary type, with my head in the clouds, wanting to get revelations from God and work with leaders towards various goals and purposes. Some tension arose over our differences of focus, but mostly Verne and I respected each other's differences and appreciated the balance we had together. We became fast friends, enjoying each other's company and playing golf. I had learned principles of spiritual authority early on and tried to put them into practice, entrusting myself to God's leadership and to the pastor I served. Verne gave me a lot of rope, enough to hang myself at times, and he even put me in charge of areas that normally only a senior pastor would do. He trusted me and I didn't want to break that trust.

Sometimes I was frustrated at being given certain levels of responsibility that were difficult to fulfill without having the authority to make final decisions. As we worked diligently to improve ways in which our giftings could complement each other, we became a model of compatibility. Many people commented over the years on how well we worked together. So many stories of conflict and church splits arise from power struggles in church leadership; it can be a major cause of disillusionment for people in a church.

Sometimes, however, you can try to do everything right and still get in trouble. King David was one who tried to do everything right and still got in trouble. After David gained great notoriety by defeating Goliath, Saul, the king, took him into his house as his primary lieutenant. The king eventually became jealous, persecuted David, attempted to kill him, and chased him around the countryside for years. If anyone ever had just cause to resent and usurp the authority over him, it was David; instead he became the greatest example of a man who entrusted himself to God in the test. His most famous responses to Saul while being chased in the wilderness are instructive to us all. After refraining from killing Saul when he could easily have done so he said, *"Far be it from me because of the Lord that I should do this thing to my lord, the Lords' anointed, to stretch out my hand against him, since he is the Lord's anointed"* (I Samuel 24:6).

He persuaded his men not to rise up against Saul, but to simply cut a piece off of Saul's garment to prove he could have slain him if he wanted to. Later, as he spoke to Saul from the cave mouth he said,

"Now, my father, see! Indeed, see the edge of your robe in my hand! For in that I cut off the edge of your robe and did not kill you, know and perceive that there is no evil or rebellion in my hands, and I have not sinned against you, though you are lying in wait for my life to take it. May the Lord judge between you and me, and may the Lord avenge me on you; but my hand shall not be against you. As the proverb of the ancients says, 'Out of the wicked comes forth wickedness'; but my hand shall not be against you." (I Samuel 24:11-13)

David understood that God rules over the kingdoms of men and gives authority to whomever He will (Daniel 4:32). Every one of us will undergo this test of honoring people in authority, the ninth test in the wilderness. Is God big enough to work through faulty institutions and fallible people? God was preparing David to be the king. We also are being prepared for our inheritance, to rule and reign with Christ. Many people go round and round this issue, fighting against the authorities God has placed in their lives and frustrating their own futures because they don't comprehend God's sifting of their hearts through this process. It is most important to remember the lessons when we are in the crisis points.

One Sunday afternoon, in 1990, we got a phone call. Lyza was talking on the phone to a friend when the operator cut in on her call with an emergency message from Bob, Verne's brother-in-law.

"I just got a call from Marge. Verne has had a serious heart attack at their cabin and was taken to the hospital. It doesn't look good."

Later that evening we were all in the church service, praying for a miracle, when we got the news. He was dead. Verne, as far as we knew, was in great health. A little overweight perhaps, but not much. He was conscientious about health issues because early deaths from heart disease were in his family genetics, so we fully expected another twenty years of his fatherly presence. We were shocked and his family was devastated. What followed was a very difficult time for all of us with a great deal of confusion and pain.

The primary shock was grief and bewilderment, for we were losing someone we all deeply loved and depended on for guidance. Marge was suddenly a widow, the children, though grown, had lost their father, and the congregation its pastor. A secondary issue underneath those was that we were in a sensitive and vulnerable place in our leadership development and Verne's death left us all in limbo.

A couple of years earlier Verne made a decision that he was going to be the head pastor for three more years and then he would turn over the church leadership to me and a new group of elders. When he died, we were in the middle of a training process to put this new leadership team in place, which in some ways was very providential, but in other ways left us vulnerable because we were in transition without all the details worked out. Communication was incomplete with many of the people involved, including Verne's family. In the midst of bringing forth a new structure, the chief architect was suddenly out of the picture, leaving many unanswered questions and opportunities for misunderstanding.

Verne felt he had a clear direction from God, and although he had some personal struggles over his plan for transition, he was sure it was right. I was to find out that husband and wife were not quite on the same page about this. There was a lack of communication and perhaps even lack of agreement about just how this plan should work and tensions began to rise between us as we tried to hammer out the specifics. On the last day before Verne and Marge went on vacation to their cabin, we had a disturbing talk, which revealed that the terms of this leadership transition were not clearly understood. Verne was going to continue as a father in the church, but exactly what this meant and what it meant for me to become the new head pastor was not clearly negotiated or accepted. We agreed to keep working it out when they returned from holidays, but Verne died while they were away. I don't know if I'll ever understand God and the ways life plays itself out, but I am convinced He knows what He is doing.

Needless to say, this put Marge and me in an excruciatingly difficult position. It was pretty clear in everybody's mind—the elders, and Marge, too, for that matter—that Verne had appointed me to succeed him. Verne had perhaps exercised more wisdom and foresight than any of us knew to have already initiated such a plan, and we all discovered later that he knew more about his heart condition than the rest of us.

Marge was suddenly put in a terrible position and in a very great test of her own. In one stroke she suddenly lost her husband and her identity in the church. She was very much part of the pastoral ministry with Verne, and part of her struggle with Verne's changing role was that, in the transition plan, she wasn't sure what her place and role was going to be. Grief and shock put Marge into an emotional crisis. On top of that, Verne had shared some of his emotional struggles about the transition with his full-grown children and there were a lot of misconceptions and confusion about what Verne's plan intended. Most of my communication had been between Verne and me, and I thought we had a pretty clear understanding. Being close friends, we were open about our lives and even able to talk about our conflicting emotions surrounding our shifting roles. Now I was left with a grieving widow, four children and a lot of misconceptions. What could I say that wouldn't sound self-serving or contrary to some of the impressions they had?

The days following Verne's funeral brought a sorting out of issues on the surface, but underneath, grief and hurt continued simmering, especially for Verne's family and Marge. My time of entrusting myself to the leadership I was under was over. I was now the senior pastor overnight. Somehow all it felt like was a weighty burden—one that was fraught with uncomfortable feelings and perceptions, yet it was really the same test as when I was under authority. Either God is in charge, orchestrating events, or man is just muddling through alone. I chose to trust that God somehow allowed all this discomfort and was orchestrating the details of all our lives for good.

Marge, particularly, had to wrestle with trusting God's sovereignty in all of this. Her whole life was turned upside down. Marge and I had always loved and respected each other deeply, but during this time she felt that I was somehow partly responsible for what had happened. There were murmurings that perhaps Verne's heart attack was partly precipitated by pressure I had put on him over this transition. There were intimations that I had usurped his position. These feelings were verbalized in a couple of painful encounters with Marge where she expressed she felt I had been like Absalom to Verne.

To be considered like Absalom precipitated a deep personal crisis for me. Absalom was King David's oldest son who became disaffected with his father, turned the affections of the people from his father to himself, and eventually ran David out of town, even seeking to kill him. I told myself that Marge was distraught and so she could not be fully responsible for making such awful accusations, but it appeared at the time that all my good intentions and decisions to support this couple were for naught. I had fancied that I had acted quite David-like through the years, standing behind Verne's decisions, fending off criticisms, and even deferring an opportunity to be the head pastor in another large church. Now, whether accurate or not, the widow of the man I had served for eighteen years deemed me an Absalom, and as far as I knew, his children felt the same.

The irony of it left me on the floor one night, prostrate before God, feeling utterly broken. I experienced three days of sickness where my head throbbed with a splitting, flu-like headache that kept me in bed. Something about being sick and in extreme pain reduces you to your elemental motivations. During this time I managed (when the shooting pains in my head subsided periodically) to read a book by C.S Lewis called *Till We Have Faces*. In the book, the main protagonist had a pronounced misperception of herself known to the reader, but not to her. At the end of the story, she finds herself in a courtroom pleading her case to God. As she hotly and bitterly defends her case to God, it's obvious that she is guilty and totally blind to her own motivations. And here I was, possibly an Absalom, thinking all this time I was more like a loyal David. I lay with my head on the floor, a Bible open before me, and said, "God, am I really an Absalom?"

To my surprise, the response came, *"Yes, son, there is Absalom in your heart.... But there is David there as well...Don't worry, I am pleased with you."* It was like, well, what's there to defend? The heart is deceitful and desperately wicked, who can know it? I may have thought I behaved myself honorably, and yet God knew some of my motives and actions were not pure. That is why God does put us to the test with authority in our lives. It is a purifier to bring our motivations to the surface. This turn of providence put Marge into a position where she had to sort out her motivations as well. That was her battle. None of us are innocent. Later, I was greatly helped by Gene Edward's book, *A Tale of Three Kings*. In it, he powerfully makes the case that Saul, David, and Absalom are in all of us. There are no pure Davids and no pure Sauls. They are characters who help us sort out the mysteries of our own hearts. We all have choices to make which reinforce our motives, whether for good or ill.

Marge and most of her children left our church during the next few months, and saddened, we all went on as best we could, allowing time and the Lord to heal our wounds. Relationship healing cannot be forced. A few years after Verne's death, Marge, Lyza and I sat in our family room and talked. It was at Marge's initiative and we were struck by her humility as she shared with us some of her journey out of that grief-stricken experience. We talked honestly about the struggles we had all gone through, expressing feelings that were a great relief to be able to share at last. Marge came back to the church after that, which was a tremendous witness to God's grace. We renewed a trust and love that was deeper than before.

For the next eight years she continued to pour herself out, doing missionary work in Russia and Haiti, serving in a prison ministry, and giving away most of her substance to those in need. Many, under the circumstances she went through, might have retreated into bitterness or focused on self-preservation, but she was an inspiration of cheerful, joyful, optimistic service to God. None of us know what conditions will bring out the ministry of God within us. Paul said he learned to be content in whatever state he was in; whether abased or exalted, he would serve Christ. Whether in authority or under authority, we are taught to serve and leave our works with God. Nothing can ultimately subdue a victorious spirit. Lyza and I count it a great joy and privilege to have served together with Verne and Marge and their family for over thirty years in the same church.

Now Marge's casket was laid to rest next to Verne's. A multitude of family and friends filled up our sanctuary for her memorial service. Looking down from the podium, I saw that the first four rows, more than 120 seats, were filled by relatives—brothers, sisters, aunts, nephews, nieces—and in the front row sat the immediate family— Rick, Gail, Karen, Tracy, their spouses and children, with thirteen grandchildren and even one great grandchild. It had been ten years since all the turmoil after Verne's death and a profound peace was in the air.

Looking over at the children, I couldn't help but marvel at God's reconciling power. Most of her children were back in the church after some stints in other churches. Marc and Karen, who had stayed through the whole time, were beloved elders in the White Rock church, and of great personal support to Lyza and me. Tracy, the youngest, had moved back to B.C. from Alberta with her husband, James, and baby, Blake, and we felt her love and support. Rick and Carol were instrumental in our church's school ministry and fully committed to God. Gail and her husband Joe had raised four boys who had all attended the church's school founded by their grandparents. All had gone through their own siftings and had made their peace with God and with us. Now, at their mother's memorial they spoke eloquently of her impact on their lives. I felt an overflowing gratitude for everything the Lord had put us all through.

When we get to the other side of the tests, we realize why they were necessary and that they were worth it, preparing us for the true inheritance. The church organization was not Verne's nor was it mine to bequeath or control. The church is the possession of Christ and He allows it to be stewarded as He chooses. We all need to have the eyes of our hearts opened to see beyond the particular church we belong to and who is currently in charge of it to see the sovereign God at work to shape our lives. People who jump from church to church because of conflict with leaders or other people risk forfeiting a part of the inheritance because they never stay in one place long enough to personally change and grow. They may seek for the perfect church, but when they finally find it, that church is no longer perfect because they just joined it.

Lyza and I, however, would be hopping from church to church for the next six months as we traveled on the east coast. It would be a strange experience going to a different kind of church every Sunday, but I wanted to get a feel for other church traditions and appreciate the preaching of other pastors. As we caught our plane the day after the funeral, I looked forward with anticipation to this new stage in our itinerant life.

Newfoundland

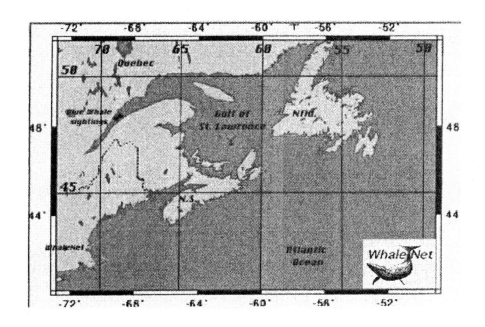

Unbelief at Jordan—Numbers 14
The Tenth Temptation—Doubt and Fear

The Ten Temptations: **10. Doubt and Fear (Unbelief at Jordan)**

1. Pressures 2. Power 3. Bitterness 4. Hunger 5. Thirst   6. Idolatry 7. Counterfeit 8. Counterfeit 9. Counterfeit
of Life   of Evil   of Life   Service   Comfort   Leadership

Seven Stages of the Spiritual Journey:

1. The Passover in Egypt	2. Red Sea Crossing	3. Mt. Sinai Visitation
		4. Wilderness

Chapter Fourteen

A hand shook me awake in the dimly lit dormitory. The whole room swayed from side to side, disorienting me, and then I saw the rows of two-tiered bunks and remembered we were in the North Atlantic. "C'mon. You've got to see this!" Lyza said, patting my brow.

My splitting head had sent me to the bunk several hours ago with two Tylenol. As I stumbled after her down the passageway, I was surprised how much this sturdy ferry rocked and heaved. The seas weren't even that rough as I stepped into brilliant sunlight sparkling on a windblown sea, but the ocean swells rolled us anyway. We had been in gray open ocean when I went to bed. Now the scene before me snapped like a photograph upon my retina, exactly matching pictures I had seen of east coast fishing villages, but this was living color complete with salt spray and wind on my face.

The bright sun, breaking for this moment through the overcast, made the black reefs glisten like the backs of whales frozen in time. Wild white caps crashed over them casting the spray high. Barren headlands barely sheltered battered square buildings squatting among granite humps and hollows. My first reaction was alarm at the nearness of the land as the ferry slid at a good clip through a narrow channel into a small rock-hewn harbour. Gray stone, a backdrop for the buildings of Port au Basques, stretched off in the distance as far as I could see, where exposed stony plains, hills and mountains were carpeted with scrubby shrubs and grasses. It was a land unashamed to reveal its secrets and I scanned its naked contours.

Hardly stopping in the little port, we soon sped between conical peaks, circled broad bays of steely blue sea, and coasted over miles and miles of terrain. Low-lying spruce trees interspersed with yellow swampy meadows and blue ponds mirrored a sky of unsullied blue. We glided so effortlessly along the well-maintained highway we felt almost airborne. It was supposed to take four hours to cover the 409 kilometers to Springdale, but we did it in three. I could not keep my foot off the pedal as the empty road often revealed fifteen-mile straight stretches with few vehicles. I rocketed through this vast land as Lyza fell asleep.

I glanced fondly at my mate as she dozed in the seat next to me. The waning yellow sunlight cast a glow over the Newfoundland landscape and rested on her face. The warm glow also emanated from within as I basked in the unbroken intimacy and companionship we were experiencing in the last week and a half. It was great to be so comfortable, so completely yourself with another person. The last six months had mended some of the frayed edges of our emotions. This extended time without the constant intrusion of outside pressures was restoring our deep bond of affection.

Exploring the Maritimes alone together sealed this work of restoration God was doing. Lyza and I were on our anniversary leg of the sabbatical, discovering the Canadian east coast together. After Marge's funeral, we settled Ginny for a month with her adopted 'Auntie Linda' and flew to Prince Edward Island for a delightful stay at the Inn at Bay Fortune on our thirtieth anniversary. We toured PEI for a week and then headed up the coast of Nova Scotia in our rental car to the North Sidney ferry for the crossing to Newfoundland. Staying in bed-and-breakfasts, eating out, walking on the beach—it was a romantic and fun time, and we were reminded that we really enjoyed one another's company more than anyone else's in the world. The truth of the matter, however, was that we also had been harder on each other and had caused more pain to each other than anyone else in the world. The greater the intimacy, the greater the potential for hurt. Now the silent, surreal journey across the breadth of Newfoundland was taking us to Springdale and then to a tiny fishing village clinging to the rocky north coast. We were headed just about as far away as we could drive from everything we knew.

Our hosts in Springdale (whose house we rolled into late that night) were Ray and Juanita Whalen. They were real Newfoundlanders whose forefathers sailed schooners to the coast of Labrador to load up with cod, salt it in barrels and sell it to the European market. Ray's father had been a Pentecostal pastor converted in the revival at the turn of the century. He helped bring the gospel and 'Holy Ghost fire' to the coasts of this province, braving poverty, persecution, and hard-hearted communities. On the way north to their fisherman's shanty the next day, Ray took a side trip down gravel roads into La Scie, another tiny fishing village. He pointed across the slate sea to large islands in the distance.

"Those are the Horse Islands. I lived on the one on the right for five years." I looked at him incredulously. I thought we were already just about at the ends of the earth and these islands looked like they were off the edge. "I was nine years old and lived there till I was fourteen. My father brought revival to those islands. A wicked bunch of people lived there but my dad baptized most of them. He was a man of prayer. I remember waking up some nights in the cold seeing my father on his knees under four or five blankets."

Ray had moved away from home when he was fifteen, living hard and rebellious until he came back to his spiritual roots in his twenties. Some people thought he wouldn't amount to much, but he became a successful businessman and a strong support to his church. He and his wife were now spending summer vacations helping an Inuit community in Labrador. They were into it heart and soul.

When I heard the story and testimony of how they got involved there, I just marveled. Ray had led a convict to the altar, a person who turned out to be the most despised man in the Inuit community of Nain. Like good Samaritans, Ray and Juanita helped him get back on his feet, filling his house with furniture, and helping him get re-established in his community when he got released from prison. Their persistent love for this man and his family affected the whole Nain community, and people eventually accepted that the changes in the man's life were genuine. The government and sometimes the organized church throws money and personnel at such situations to try to help, but only God penetrates hearts so thoroughly and He delights in unorthodox methods. I was reminded again of strange fire and God's fire, and of making a difference one life at a time. I thought, "Ray, you may not have been a fisherman like your grandfather or a pastor like your father, but you have been effective just being yourself. There is surely a heritage of spiritual passion in you, which has prepared you for this unique calling."

Ray and Juanita had picked up a couple of old fishing houses hanging on the cliffs of Round Harbour when the price had been right and made it their business to periodically ensconce wondering friends and acquaintances in their favorite one. They led us down back roads for almost two hours and finally drove us down into a lost world—a tiny community built entirely around a small circular harbour, raw-boned and wild, carved out of solid rock. To get to the house we were to stay in, we had to hike two hundred yards along the base of a cliff by way of a path that wound among boulders, over tilted boardwalks and behind disheveled houses. The winds blew one way and then another over the spiny mountains and cliffs, through the cracks in the boards of the houses and underneath the door stops. Twenty feet off the front porch of their cabin they said I could catch a lobster.

Behind the house were jumbles of huge boulders interspersed with coastal heather and scrub spruces that climbed the high ridges of jagged rock towering behind us. The Whalens loaded us down with halibut, cod steaks, frozen rabbit and seal meat, and left us to fend for ourselves and keep the home fires burning. We settled down the first night feeling totally cut off from all that was familiar, hanging over the eastern edge of the continent, as far from White Rock on the Pacific side as we had ever been.

Waking up in a different place every day was having the effect of making dream life and waking life more difficult to distinguish. Squinting early the next morning at the bright sun pouring through the white crosses in the ancient window panes, I attempted to roll off my aching back to shift my weight and became stuck, encased in a cocoon of tangled quilt, warm Lyza and a sponge cake mattress. The night before we laughed out loud as we attempted to balance our two bodies and five blankets on top of that mattress. The blankets slid left and right as we both rolled inexorably together into the generous crevasse in the middle. Changing positions in the night was accomplished on signal. One of us would groan and say, "Roll", and we would shift in unison into a new position, sinking back into its spongy embrace.

I stared up at the ancient white-washed planks of the ceiling a mere foot and a half from my face and then around the tiny bedroom to the small square window panes through which I could see the fantastic angular landscape surrounding us. The desire to light a crackling fire in the friendly kitchen stove and the desire to linger in the warm bed briefly sparred with each other until, jerking awake from another strange dream, I realized the bed had won.

With a supreme effort I planted my feet on the cold planks and stiffly maneuvered my way down the precipitous, creaking stairs to ground level. Ground level was a platform of planks nailed to ancient grayed timbers, which were balanced on log rounds wedged and braced on the boulders below. A rickety deck surrounded the entire structure. Outside, the cold wind rattled among the old timbers and combed through the sea village wreckage. The thought of retreating back to the upstairs cocoon was quickly forgotten as the crackling fires in the old woodstoves confronted the cold with smoky penetrating warmth.

The central wood-burning heater, fueled largely by the remains of surrounding tumbledown cabins, had a finicky personality of its own. Rudimentary instructions were given, but between opening the bottom vents, adjusting the baffle and keeping the piece of tin properly placed over the broken glass front, I lost my way somewhere. After filling the place with smoke, I had to pry open the wood-latticed windows and let the cold wind blow through to clear it out. This happened several times before the perverse heater settled into a grudging flow of air through its mysterious innards that produced a steady warmth once it got in the groove. Then it was good for the day, except when we threw in new wood or the wind blew a little too hard and created a downdraft. Then a puff and a billow of smoke would roil out of every seam of the stove like a teapot losing its temper and we would have to open all the windows and doors again to clear it out. By the time we left the little house we smelled like smoked codfish.

Leaning back against a worn sofa and propping my feet on an old stool, I peeked incredulously out upon this newfound land from the corner of the room. From my vantage point, rock and water and a brilliant blue sky filled the old warped windowpanes, which produced a romantic scene akin to looking through a Japanese glass float. I kept saying to myself, "This is the real thing." People actually live their whole lives in this remote world, catching codfish, drying them on rocks and pointing the exaggerated prows of their fishing boats out through the narrow opening of the cove into that cold north Atlantic I could see surging endlessly at the mouth of the cove. The sun shone brilliantly while a brisk westerly swept the wave crests past an open boat stoically pursuing the ever-diminishing codfish on the wide-open sea.

We were in awe of this place, a vestige of the past where Irish, Welsh and English ancestors lived in this very house 165 years ago making their living from the sea. It was only a few years ago that the rock at the head of the bay had been blasted away to bring a road to the village. Before that, they came by boat or hiked in, enforcing isolation for the twenty or so wooden houses balanced on the rocks around the little cove. As I later walked the stony paths and picked my way through boulders to the lookout points, I felt the independent, self-reliant spirits of the fathers and grandfathers. I heard their voices among the craggy ridges whispering, *"We get our living from the sea, we take our meat from the forest. We live off the land as our fathers and their fathers have always done."*

We walked up above the houses, feeling like intruders from another planet. Lyza and I gingerly stepped among the gravestones of a tiny cemetery, reading names on the tombstones—Snow, Fudge and Collins—when a man came up the hill on his four-wheeler and caught us in the act. All smiles and good humor, Bryce Fudge charmed us with an almost childlike manner and a narration of his fishing affairs and of politics. His wife had been taken out to Saint John's because of severe arthritis and other physical ailments. She wasn't coming back. We felt sad for him as we realized life as he had always known it was about to change for good. "Sometimes I feel lonely in the house," he volunteered, "Not when I'm in my boat. I can just about fall asleep in my boat. It's when I come back to the house..."

I contemplated the kindly face and imagined him hauling out codfish and crab all day then chugging cold and stiff back into his harbour home at day's end. The house windows on the cliff face would be lit, the warmth and smells of the kitchen would be beckoning and the warm embrace of his wife would crown the day. It was a rough-hewn life, but it was all that he had known, and now it was slipping away. The inexorable forces of time and age were beginning to call an end to this life and Bryce was one of the last to cling to it.

Most of the houses in Round Harbour were empty now and only two or three families remained—mostly the parents of children who were scattered across the country, university-educated and forging strong paths of their own, drawing upon iron roots. Down around the bay, here and there an old house lay between the others, a pile of collapsed timbers and poles reminding us of the families that had lived in them and were now gone. Bryce was planning to follow his wife to St. John's.

"But I don't want to live in the city. I'll have to come back here sometimes." Perplexity was written on his face, but I knew he would manage his latest adversities with courage and resignation, from the same core of resolution he had carried in this rough, beloved place.

Even here, I thought, the inheritance of generations, of a way of life, was never finally secure. Nothing seems to be sacred on this earth. Old men want to preserve a way of life, a heritage of homes, lands, or business, but it slips beyond their control. Children move off and are forced to break new ground, finding new answers to old questions: Where shall we live? How shall we live? What shall we live for? I was glad that at least we had the privilege to glimpse the tail end of a lifestyle that was passing away.

I could only imagine how those first people must have felt when they came to this brand new northerly land with its appalling abundance. The waters were teeming with codfish and lobster and the mountains and valleys were filled with game. We had read on a restaurant wall in Prince Edward Island that lobsters had been so plentiful on the east coast that they fed them to convicts and spread them for fertilizer on the fields. Some lobsters found back then were five feet long. The first people built their homes close to the sea and reaped its bounty year after year, decade after decade, until the resources were finally depleted and the New World's charm was blunted and worn.

It must have been similar for the Israelites as they finally stood on the Jordan River and gazed across at the Promised Land. Imagine the excitement and anticipation after four hundred years of Egyptian slavery to contemplate a new land of abundance, flowing with milk and honey. It was described to them as a land whose rains came in their season, a land that the Lord watched over and in which He brought forth abundance. At that time it was not the denuded land of modern Israel, but a land of forests, streams, and fertile valleys. After the sweatshop of Egypt and the trials of the Sinai Desert, it would have appeared a veritable paradise. Moses sent twelve spies to check it out and they brought back reports of a glorious land, with bunches of grapes so heavy it took two men to carry them. There was only one problem. The inhabitants of the land were giants.

> *Thus they* [the spies] *told him, and said, "We went in to the land where you sent us; and it certainly does flow with milk and honey, and this is its fruit. Nevertheless, the people who live in the land are strong, and the cities are fortified and very large; and moreover, we saw the descendants of Anak there. Amalek is living in the land of the Negev..."* (Numbers 13:27-29)

The people were about to face the last and most pivotal test in the wilderness. In the latter half of their journey in the desert of Paran, God's people had passed through four temptations since Sinai—the test of idolatry, the test of strange fire, the test of greedy desires at Taberah, and the test of Miriam and Aaron's rebellion. Now they were on the verge of entering into their inheritance, the Promised Land. God had trained them and was ready to fulfill the promise He made to Abraham some five hundred years before to give them a land flowing with milk and honey and to multiply their descendants in it. All they had to do was go into it and trust God to give them victory over its inhabitants. They were facing the most important test of all, the test of faith and the temptation of unbelief. Could the God who miraculously brought them out of Egypt and through the desert actually bring them into the fulfillment of the promise? Was God able to finish what He started? They had to consider side by side the great richness and exceeding abundance of God's inheritance, and the seeming impossibility of its attainment.

This has very incisive bearing on the essential struggle of the Christian life. Many people have experienced God's power to bring them out of a sinful life of bondage, but fail to believe the same God can bring them into a life of righteousness, peace and joy. Instead, they are held captive in unbelief by some terror of the inner man or some unconquered stronghold of self. The critical importance of this test is underscored in Hebrews 3 where the Holy Spirit summarizes the main reason the people failed to enter their inheritance of rest:

*"And to whom did He swear that they would not enter His rest, but to those who were disobedient? So we see that they were not able to enter because of **unbelief**."* (Hebrews 3:18,19; emphasis added)

The main reason they failed was not because of their many sins and rebellions along the way, but because, in the final testing, they would not believe God. We begin the Christian life in faith but we also conclude it in faith, and many fall in-between the beginning and the end by losing the heart to believe, usually because of disappointments and hardness of heart. Faith is the foundational issue through all of the ten temptations, since the right response in any test is to entrust ourselves to God, but a particular insight relative to this tenth temptation reveals why faith is so sorely tested at this juncture.

That understanding has to do with the symbolism of the giants in the Promised Land. Anak, the father of the Anakim, was a giant and the father of a race of giants. Anak literally translated means 'the long-necked one'. Being long-necked or stiff-necked is an image of the stubborn self-nature of man. Anak and his sons represent the independent, unfettered characteristics of man asserting self-will and self-exaltation. Now, these giants all lived on a hill or mountain called Kiriath Arba. 'Kiriath' means stronghold and 'Arba', in its root meanings, can be interpreted as the strength of Baal, the strength of natural forces or of the natural man. So here we have giants of self-will living in a stronghold of the natural man.

A person is victimized by the vicissitudes of life, evil social structures and poverty. He is also influenced and victimized by demonic temptation, but after all is said and done, a person is his or her own greatest enemy. The greatest obstacles to a man or woman obtaining his or her inheritance are the strongholds of self-will within. The giant kings who held the Promised Land captive against the Israelites were the internal strongholds of self, with names that can be translated 'self-righteousness', 'self-pity', 'self-consciousness', 'self-effort', 'self-justification', etcetera. Some have interpreted the Promised Land to symbolically represent heaven, but if that is accurate, what are enemy giants doing in heaven? Although the final inheritance is certainly heaven, the symbolism of the Promised Land has more to do with an inheritance and a place of rest found within ourselves while we still are living on this earth.

When we are up against the unregenerate dispositions of self, we are most likely to become hopeless, disillusioned, and lose our faith. This discouragement is felt most keenly in the intimate relationships of life in marriages, in families, or even in the close bonds of Christian relationships. These strongholds thwart intimacy with others as we withdraw, building walls and getting hard, to protect ourselves from the pain of relationships. We often settle for uneasy truces and live with the sorrow of unfulfilled longings in our most important relationships. At worst, we break away from the committed relationships of marriage, family or church community or try again in another relationship to find what eluded us the first time. The destructiveness of this pattern is all around us in fractured families and divided church communities. The more brokenness we experience, the harder it is to approach intimacy again. Some people simply give up on relationships altogether.

So when we see how the children of Israel lost their faith considering those giants, we can understand their fear and unbelief. They were despairing over the strongholds of human nature that create unassailable walls of alienation between family members. They were staring at your mother's unreasonable anxieties, or your father's uncontrollable anger, or your brother's stubborn pride, your husband's inordinate jealousy, or your own controlling moodiness. These seemingly inexorable forces tear apart marriages and produce the children of divorce who themselves feel handicapped and untrusting in relationships. Ten out of the twelve men who viewed the Canaan possibility concluded: *"We are not able to go up against the people, for they are too strong for us"* (Numbers 13:31). In God's sight, this evaluation of the situation is called unbelief. When we give way to fear and helplessness in the face of these strongholds, it is also unbelief.

However, two of the twelve, Joshua and Caleb, saw the same giants and the same fortifications but came to a different conclusion. *"We should by all means go up and take possession of it, for we will surely overcome it"* (Numbers 13:30). This assessment of the situation is called faith—not basic faith in God or even faith for our daily bread, or for healing, or for our future (the challenges of faith that have accompanied every temptation along the way)—but faith that believes God will bring under His dominion the strongholds at the core of our human nature. Just as we were incapable of conquering overt sins in our lives and needed the grace of faith, we are totally incapable of conquering the self-nature within without that same grace and faith. The ten spies weakened the faith of the whole nation of Israel so that they gave in to unbelief. The spies said,

> *"The land through which we have gone, in spying it out, is a land that devours its inhabitants; and all the people whom we saw in it are men of great size. There also we saw the Nephilim (the sons of Anak are part of the Nephilim); and we became like grasshoppers in our own sight, and so we were in their sight."* (Numbers 13:32-33)

If we are grasshoppers in our own eyes, we easily become grasshoppers in relation to our fears and problems. Soon our fears become an overwhelming reality and unconquerable emotions run rampant. Our own statement defeats us: "We are grasshoppers."

> *Then all the congregation lifted up their voices and cried, and the people wept that night. All the sons of Israel grumbled against Moses and Aaron; and the whole congregation said to them, "Would that we had died in the land of Egypt! Or would that we had died in this wilderness! Why is the Lord bringing us into this land, to fall by the sword? Our wives and our little ones will become plunder; would it not be better for us to return to Egypt?"* (Numbers 14:1-3)

Some would call this emotional flooding. We get to a point where all reason (and all affirmation of faith) is swept away by negative emotions of frustration, fear and anger. Spouses often give way to this overwhelming flood during arguments and say and do things they wish they hadn't afterward. In this state they try to storm each other's strongholds, but only succeed in entrenching themselves in their own strongholds and aggravating their partner. Afterward hopeless despair, disillusionment and self-pity descends, making it feel like things will never change and the relationship is irrevocably damaged. Demonic spirits then prey upon these strongholds to amplify and further entrench them. It is a conspiracy of the flesh and the devil to keep mankind in its chains even though the Son of God has set us free.

The generation of Israel who failed to press into faith was consigned to wander in the wilderness for forty more years. God forgave them, but they forfeited their inheritance. God said to Moses,

> *"I have pardoned them according to your word; but indeed, as I live, all the earth will be filled with the glory of the Lord. Surely all the men who have seen My glory and My signs which I performed in Egypt and in the wilderness, yet have put Me to the test these ten times and have not listened to my voice, shall by no means see the land which I swore to their fathers, nor shall any of those who spurned Me see it."* (Numbers 14:20-23)

Here the scripture confirms the ten temptations and culminates them all with this crucial issue of faith. At this final test an irrevocable note of consequence sounded. The books of Numbers and Deuteronomy record that from then on they went through more testings, but they were the same tests as before. They went around the same issues again and again until they died. Any one of the ten temptations can become the place where we lose faith and go around in circles, sometimes until we die. At a certain point we lose the ability to respond anymore and the area becomes lost to us. All of us lose something along the way, but it is tragic to lose marriages, relationships with sons and daughters or good friends. Most importantly we lose a level of intimacy with God that the test would have taught us if we had responded rightly.

Caleb, one of the two spies with the positive report, is the embodiment of the attitude necessary to press into our full inheritance. His name means 'bold'. It's a bold faith that stands up to the most difficult challenges of life. God said of Caleb,

> *"But my servant Caleb, because he has had a different spirit and has followed Me fully, I will bring into the land which he entered, and his descendants shall take possession of it."* (Numbers 14:24)

Caleb lived out those forty years in the desert with those who were dying because of their unbelief. The inheritance only grew more glorious in his mind and heart until forty years later his passion was still unabated. He said to Joshua,

"I am still as strong today as I was in the day Moses sent me; as my strength was then, so my strength is now, for war and for going out and coming in. Now then, give me this hill country about which the Lord spoke on that day..." So Joshua blessed him and gave Hebron to Caleb...for an inheritance. (Joshua 14:11-13)

He persevered and asked Joshua for his piece of the Promised Land. And the plot of ground he claimed? Kiriath Arba, the hangout of Anak and his sons. It was renamed Hebron which means 'union with God'. He set his sights on the most resistant stronghold of self and unflinchingly believed God could deliver it. Caleb's attitude should inspire us to press on, in our few short years, to go for the gold. We admire the Olympic athletes who go for the gold, but may have no conception of the spiritual challenge in front of us to believe for eternal gold. Paul warned us to be careful that no one takes our crown. It's our choice to be a Caleb or to die in the wilderness.

Strangely enough, Olympic gold was part of our experience in the old fishing shack in Round Harbour. Perched on a corner table in the front room was a small television. It only could pick up one channel, but it was a Canadian station, which carried coverage of the Sidney Olympics. Several evenings we watched in awe the discipline and sacrifice athletes give to their passion.

The splendor of the Olympic facilities was a stark contrast to our Spartan surroundings, but we were observing our own kind of Olympic gold by celebrating thirty years of marriage. Just the week before, on our anniversary, we dined on carpaccio at one of the top ten rated restaurants in Canada. This week it was wild rabbit and codfish in a rickety cabin, east of nowhere. Not exactly a honeymoon suite, but it put me in mind of a few of the other places Lyza had consented to live with me over the past thirty years. There was the three-room counselor's quarters we started out in, the tent, the beach house without any furnace, the church farm with no privacy, a six-week stint in the dead of winter in a Bella Coola cabin, the many *Fred Free* trips with three children and a dog, and the privations of Nelson Island cabin building. She's a good woman. That's Olympic living!

The Olympic gold medal of marriage is unity. The discipline and sacrifice needed to attain a successful marriage relationship can be as great as that of an Olympian. Probably the greatest challenge in all relationships—with God, our spouse, our family, friends, our community—is to forge a union that allows for diversity and yet stays in harmony. The strongholds of Anak prevent it. If we persevere to conquer these strongholds, they become renamed Hebron, or 'Union with God'.

One of the best places to illustrate the battle over Anak's strongholds is where it affects us most personally, so Lyza and I have agreed to share our own challenge of faith. After thirty years we still knew what it meant to struggle through painful marriage conflicts and some of those led right up to our year off. This year was also a sabbatical from the marriage tension that the pastor's life aggravated for us. For us these particular strongholds of Anak had roots that went way back.

We were married September 18, 1970 at 8:00 PM in a church overlooking a high school football field. As Lyza walked down the aisle to me, the sound of fans cheering the kick-off was her accompaniment. The guests at the wedding included about forty young people from our work in White Rock along with many relatives and my dad wearing a resigned look on his face. It really was the kick-off for a whole new life.

Lyza and I had not found it hard to be romantic. Our love for each other started on the right foot of building a friendship and centering our relationship on spiritual values, but we had passionate icing on the cake. Our cake was made from a diverse set of ingredients. Our backgrounds were very different. Mine was stable and supportive, though somewhat emotionally stilted. Lyza's was unstable. Her parents split up when she was five years old and in subsequent years she moved from place to place. I had undergone hardly any disruption in my life while she had experienced the tragedy of losing her closest brother to suicide when they were in their teens. Our temperaments were very different. I was a phlegmatic, laid-back, unemotional sort of person, although intense about the deeper issues of life and faith. Lyza was talkative and outgoing, quick to respond and react in situations, engaging and people-oriented. These differences played into the dynamic of our relationship through the years and created certain vulnerabilities in our interactions.

My greatest liability was not being very emotionally in touch with others and myself and consequently not very nurturing. Coupled with this was a kind of self-righteous pride, of being above it all, with a certain disdain for what I perceived as emotional weakness. We carried a sort of British stiff upper lip attitude in our family, and we held to high ideals such as integrity and loyalty. Although love and respect was a given in our family, not much expression of feelings was encouraged, so a large gap existed between the ideals of integrity espoused by my father and my behavior as a partying high school student. (I would rather have been turned into the police than face my father's disappointment if caught in some wild escapade in those days.) This lack of emotional connection with others and myself was liability number one, and to complicate matters, I viewed this liability as a strength. Anak was encamped with his sons around a self-sufficient and self-justifying 'Nothing's wrong with me' attitude. Later on a real subtle operator called self-pity would join these characters.

Built into the other side of the equation were Lyza's vulnerabilities. The mechanisms she developed to cope with her difficulties were forged in the fires of broken relationships. Lyza learned early on that men in general could not be trusted in a crunch. They came into her life periodically, but never stayed around too long. She formed an incredibly strong bond with her brother, John, but he deserted her too, in her sixteenth year, in a devastating disappearance and death. This tragedy helped propel her towards seeking the purpose of life and shortly after, a whole new world of hope and comfort opened up to her through a relationship with God. A year after that, she met me and our romance caught fire as a new John entered her life. We bonded to each other with a fervor born of sorrow, emotional need and a whole new realm of intimacy with God and each other.

The seeds of mistrust and anger in Lyza's life didn't really come to bear upon my weakness until a number of years into our marriage.

She obviously trusted me greatly to have followed me to Canada and to have lived through our many adventures and unorthodox living situations, but emotional difficulties arose between us over time when she felt unprotected under the inevitable onslaught of people's opinions, judgments, and personal problems that arrived with regularity on the doorstep of a pastor's house. I was ill-prepared to provide assurance at these times and she would feel abandoned by me, with the thought running through her head, "There is nobody there for me".

One time early in our life in the church, Pastor Verne had a vivid mental picture as he was praying for Lyza. He saw her standing alone in a forest of small trees, not knowing which way to go and waiting for someone to come and show her a way through, but nobody came. After a while she simply forged a path off in a direction of her own. Translation: "If no one is going to take care of me I'll just have to take care of myself." This is where the anger surfaced. Anak's stronghold in her life was built around self-protection and subsequent self-reliance and self-sufficiency. The emotional arsenal guarding this stronghold was anger, withdrawal and control.

Now add to these mechanisms another liability of mine, a great aversion to anger, especially capricious anger, which was rooted in a fear of my father's infrequent angry outbursts. When Lyza would get hit with some broadside, her longing was that I would protect her from these situations or at least provide comfort, which I invariably failed to do. Failing to foresee, prevent, or avert the given emotional trauma, I was also very inept at providing the validation that could have made it more bearable.

In my mind the beginning of breakdown in our communion was Lyza's anger; in her mind it was my lack of response. A chasm would open up underneath us at this point and we would get mired in frustration, blame, defensiveness and lonely withdrawal. This miserable state would last an hour or a day or two until we somehow found grace from God to climb out of the pit and reconcile. In between these infrequent conflicts were great periods of sweetness and light, sometimes even intensified closeness. We fiercely clung to each other, but at the same time could not seem to avoid being hurled periodically into this horrible pit of anger and coldness on her part and self-pity and resentment on my part. I felt victimized by her anger and blamed her as the primary catalyst of our conflicts, my self-pity blinding me to the emotional nurture I was failing to give. It would not do any good to try to talk our way out of it, for we both would keep beating the same old drums.

This syndrome grew in intensity over the years, fueled by a ministry life that deeply engaged us with people and their struggles. Other people's problems became our problem because they exacerbated Lyza's need for protection and my need for peace. We could not keep out of the soup and were increasingly worn down by both the tension of pastoring together and the pressure of our respective relational tendencies, especially in the last couple of years before the sabbatical as Lyza's church responsibilities grew.

Lyza and I would fall in this pit time and again and just when it felt like we were getting beyond it, the dumbest little issues would send us tumbling back down. It wasn't like we were fighting every day. We could go for weeks experiencing connubial bliss and then, like an alcoholic, we would slip off the wagon. Sometimes after we had put it behind us, we tried to remember what on earth the big deal was, and we couldn't even remember the issue. But the emotions and the fear of falling into them again could become all too present at a moment's notice.

Many people in such relationships, after repeated painful experiences, put up walls of defense and retreat into silent isolation. One day Lyza and I watched an older couple in a Maritime restaurant endure an entire lunch without saying a single word to each other. They munched their lunch mutely, staring at the ceiling, the floor, out the window. They were past anger and reactions, living in a silent truce or temporary cease-fire. Unable to realize unity, they settled for an unsatisfying stalemate.

The unity of two people is nowhere more tested and refined than in a marriage. Marriage is God's boot camp for learning the meaning of unity. Unity between people is probably the most tangible evidence of the grace of God at work and one of the final goals of the inheritance journey. Jesus best expressed the heart of this unity in His prayer for His disciples and the world, just before His crucifixion:

*"I pray Father …that they may all be one; even as You, Father, are
in Me, and I in You, that they also may be in Us, so that the world
may believe that You sent Me…"* (John 17:21)

Jesus prayed that we, His people, would be one with each other,
learning oneness by his example and the power of His reconciling life
and death. This unity characterized His relationship with his Father
and is the primary evidence to the world around us that Christ is who
He said He was. The true mark of a Christian is his ability to remain
reconciled to God, his wife and family, and other believers. Therein
lies one the greatest tests of life. Lyza and I knew this testing not
only in our own marriage, but also in the marriages of some of our
best friends. Three of our closest friends had become separated in
the last few years, and one of them was divorced and remarried. Part
of our enduring sorrow was that the hallmark of our faith was
supposed to be reconciliation and yet, as Christians, we so often
failed to attain it. At the crux of Jesus' work of reconciliation was a
cross, but we just couldn't quite bear that cross.

Genuine unity among Christians often seems as difficult to
attain. *"One faith, one Lord, one baptism, one God and Father over all,"* the
scripture says. Yet so many denominations separate Christians.
Even in the early church, the saints were admonished about divisions,
and church splits were commonplace. What a mess believers have
made all through church history. It's no wonder the world at large is
skeptical of the church. We have demonstrated our immaturity and
lack of true spiritual power by our failure to walk together.

One morning, while climbing the hill above our Newfoundland
retreat, a building across the harbour caught my eye. Later that
afternoon I made a closer inspection. The simple building had a
green roof and looked like many other houses in the village, except
for its arched windows, the little white cross atop it, and an old bell
near the peak of the roof. The whole building, not more than a
thousand square feet, was nestled into the surrounding rock in a way
that made it look as if it had grown on the ledge of grass dotted with
yellow daisies.

Pushing the old door inward, I was immediately drawn into the
cool serenity of a tiny Anglican chapel. A sense of reverence and
peace transported me back to little Gulf Island chapels I visited as a

child during our summer vacations. Tight wood pews were ornately carved and an arched beam held up a vaulted ceiling. Sitting quietly in one of the pews, I could see past the colorful trappings of Anglican liturgy through diamond-latticed windows to a monolithic cliff face. To my left, a foot or two outside the windows, was a rock face covered with heather, grasses, and berries as red as drops of blood. To my right the northward view revealed the houses of the parish around the harbour and the Atlantic Ocean beyond.

A palpable sense of sanctuary pervaded the little outpost where a handful of human beings had been born, lived, and died, and I worshiped the Lord of all such churches. On the front wall, beside the trinity of latticed windows, hung a plaque. It read:

Erected by Saint Andrews
Sunday school. In memory of
Fred Arthur Fudge
Born September 27, 1902 and was drowned
December 15, 1930 when the schooner
Warren W. Culp was wrecked on
Burnt Point, Cape Breton.
"Save, Lord, we perish", was their cry,
"O save us in our agony"
The word above the storm rose high,
"Peace, be still"

That is what we need in the midst of our storms—a word to bring peace, a word of faith to answer the test of unbelief. Only through Him can we realize that unity typified by Hebron, and attain our inheritance of righteousness, peace, and joy.

I thought of the graveyard further up the hill and Bryce Fudge who we'd met. Later Bryce informed me Fred Arthur was his father's cousin. The church had been built a hundred and twenty years ago. He and a handful of others still attended this church once a month when the itinerant vicar came around to do a service. As they lived and fished, families in this cove had a place of worship where they were christened, married and buried.

Gazing around me at the evidence of faith I thought, "Why do we judge one another so often as believers? Who are we to judge another man's servant? To his own master he stands or falls." So many arrogant words ascend to the ears of the One who prayed that we all would be one.

"Those Anglicans aren't truly born again, stuck as they are in their liturgy…Those Pentecostals are just caught up in emotionalism, not substance." Would that we honored one another, respected the differences, learned from each other and were served by each other's strengths. As for me, I was glad for my Anglican brother, whoever he was, who served these people and tended their griefs and joys through the years in a far-flung corner of Newfoundland. The next morning, as I climbed the cliff at Round Harbour under a gray sky, a sudden shaft of sunlight pierced the canopy from somewhere out in the Atlantic and illumined just the little church on the hillside as if to say, *"My special light and care is over all My churches."*

Lyza and I knew His love and care was over our marriage as well. He patiently taught us unity and strengthened our fainting hearts in the face of Anak and his tribe. Sometimes we just hung on to the faith to not quit. We stayed committed because God stays in committed covenant with us. This staying power is rooted in a will that is surrendered to faith, to the humility of entrusting our very self to God. If Christ's death on the cross conquered the power of sin, it can also conquer the power of self holding us in bondage. As we wait, God reveals a way for victory and transformation. Our weakness and failure actually become stepping-stones of grace to overcome the self-giants in the land. As we learn to depend on a power greater than our own, we gain more and more of the Promised Land.

Hitting the Wall

Crossing the Jordan, Joshua 4
The Death of Self-Reliance

The Ten Temptations: **Crossing the Jordan**

1. Pressures 2. Power 3. Bitterness 4. Hunger   6. Idolatry 7. Counterfeit 8. Counterfeit 9. Counterfeit 10. Doubt
of Life   of Evil   of Life   5. Thirst   Service   Comfort   Leadership   & Fear

Seven Stages of the Spiritual Journey:

1. Passover in Egypt	2. Red Sea Crossing	3. Mt. Sinai Visitation	5. Crossing Jordan River
		4. Wilderness	

Chapter Fifteen

The rocky coastline, bays and estuaries of Yarmouth, Nova Scotia, were bathed in the waning yellow light of the afternoon sun and soon vanished out of sight in a swirling mist of white. I stood at the back railing, transfixed by the operation of the Fastcat Ferry transporting us from Canada to Bar Harbor, Maine. Blustering along at fifty miles per hour, the huge sea locomotive spewed out a great steamy rooster tail of broiling seawater. I could not imagine what it would be like in a rough sea. Apparently they kept a water hose handy to spray off the back deck after seasick passengers lost their lunches in rough crossings. Prince Edward Island, Nova Scotia, Cape Breton, and Newfoundland receded into a satisfying memory as we crossed the Bay of Fundy to the next camping place of our sabbatical wanderings. After Newfoundland we had driven the Cabot Trail around Cape Breton, enjoyed a Gaelic music festival in North Sydney, and given ourselves a week to drive down the winding roads of Nova Scotia's east coast.

Autumn color peaked during this stage of our trip and we drove the rural routes surrounded by brilliant reds, yellows, and oranges. We contemplated the history of this land and the people who had lived in these places. We stopped in the town of Guysborough to investigate some family roots for one of our close friends, Linda Jenkins. Crossing a picturesque bridge four miles out of town, we came to Jenkins Road, a narrow gravel track that ran along a stream bank to a small farm. The austere looking house and barn stood in a meager clearing surrounded by colorfully painted low hills. We tried to imagine Linda's father growing up there and how this little homestead in Nova Scotia was connected to us through Linda.

Linda was the adopted auntie in Ginette's life. She still cried when telling anyone the story of Ginny's life and actually had a special bedroom outfitted for her in her condo. As a single person she had never had children and Ginny filled a special place in her heart. Linda was also a godsend to us, someone we felt comfortable leaving Ginette with. We liked to call ours a 'symbiotic' relationship.

Many others in our congregation on the west coast had farmer or fishermen forbears from Nova Scotia and other Maritime provinces. That hardy stock had carried forward some spiritual genes to their descendants judging by the many white steepled churches standing sentinel over every village.

The ferry slowed in the gathering twilight as it passed outlying islands in Bar Harbor, bringing into view the lights and clean lines of summer homes in America's vacation land. An hour's drive south from there, we had arranged to rent a summer house on Penobscot Bay for two months. I began to fall in love with Maine that first evening as we drove down the winding rural routes underneath the thick arms of oaks and maples resplendent with fall foliage. Passing in the dark through Blue Hill, East Brooksville, South Brooksville and North Brooksville, we ended up driving around Cape Rosier twice before our destination, 'The Pipers' Nest', materialized, a light in the woods at the end of a long lonely gravel drive. It was a summer home on a hundred acres of forest owned by relatives of my parents' next-door neighbors on Mercer Island. Peter, our host, met us at the door ready to show us the ropes of Cape Rosier living, which included chopping wood, running the wood stoves, picking mussels, and manning the boats.

I was ready to unpack our bags and live like New Englanders for a while. In Maine, I would continue to write and we would investigate some of my family roots on a nearby island called Vinalhaven. We picked up Ginny from the Boston airport after a month's separation and the next day we settled into the fall season in front of the Rumford fireplace.

After forty long years of wandering in the desert, Israel was also ready to settle into the land, build houses, and enjoy the resting place God had provided. The children of an unbelieving generation had wandered with their parents all those years and finally stood again at the edge of the Jordan River, ready to enter their inheritance under Joshua's leadership. Moses himself had disobeyed God, and as a consequence, was not allowed to go in, having died in the wilderness along with everyone in the previous generation except Caleb and Joshua. However, their children had learned from their mistakes.

"Your children, however, whom you said would become a prey – I will bring them in, and they shall know the land which you have rejected. But as for you, your corpses shall fall in this wilderness. Your sons

shall be shepherds for forty years in the wilderness, and they shall suffer for your unfaithfulness, until your corpses lie in the wilderness. According to the number of days which you spied out the land, forty days, for every day you shall bear your guilt a year, even forty years, and you shall know My opposition. " (Numbers 14:31-34)

Lasting damage to the lives of the older generation was the result of the sin of unbelief. God forgives us for our failures, but He doesn't always remove the consequences. Some windows of opportunity never open again and the benefit we would have gained by trusting is forever lost. New opportunities come and God is always willing to bless us, but it's important to pay attention and not jeopardize our possibilities. Many times we are brought around in a circle to face the same test again and again until we learn the lesson. If we don't learn it, we repeat the cycle and can eventually die in unbelief as Israel did. Any one of the ten temptations—such as dealing with bitterness, or trusting God for provision, or dealing with the issue of authority—can become one of these repeating cycles of unbelief.

Multitudes die in the wilderness in every generation. Only a few follow the Lord fully as Caleb did, conquering the strongholds of Anak and possessing a full inheritance. Perhaps all of us have some areas in our lives that we win and some places that we lose out. God is very patient and does not quickly resign us to our folly. He even allows life to play itself out in such a way that we are forced to face our core issues. Sometimes when we totally exhaust our efforts to make something work and end up in failure, we hit the wall and cannot go any further. Our defenses are stripped and we stand face to face with our Creator. At these times God wants to do a work of freeing us from ourselves. This is the special lesson of the Jordan River.

To equip us to confront the strongholds of Anak in the promised land, God prepares the 'death to self' lesson of the Jordan River, reminiscent of the death experience to sin in the baptismal waters of the Red Sea, but with a deeper level of application. Israel failed to enter their inheritance by their own wisdom and their own strength, but now the children would overcome their parents' failure by learning to completely rely on faith.

Up until then they only knew the desert life. They probably grew up hearing old Caleb's stories about Canaan around the campfire. Not jaded, not disillusioned, they were idealistic young people who had caught his passion and heard his vision. They were ready to believe God to go all the way and win their inheritance. So it is that God often preserves a remnant of a former generation to inspire a coming generation to new heights. Their parents may have become cynical and disillusioned. They may have failed in their marriages or left the church. They may have been bound in some habit or settled for religious mediocrity, but the children want more. They say as much to Joshua on the threshold of Canaan.

> *"All that you have commanded us we will do, and wherever you send us we will go. Just as we obeyed Moses in all things, so we will obey you; only may the Lord your God be with you, as He was with Moses. Anyone who rebels against your command and does not obey your words in all that you command him, shall be put to death; only be strong and courageous."* (Joshua 1:16-18)

These people were serious as they faced the death experience of the Jordan River. Joshua instructed them to go forward into the midst of a flooding river, just as their parents walked down into the midst of the Red Sea and trusted God would bring them out the other side. This time the water represented not a death to sin but a death to self and self-reliance.

> *"Moses My servant is dead; now therefore arise, cross this Jordan you and all this people, to the land which I am giving to them, to the sons of Israel. Every place on which the sole of your foot treads, I have given it to you, just as I spoke to Moses."* (Joshua 1:2,3)

The initial step into the Jordan River was the first of many steps into the strongholds of Canaan. The river was in flood stage and without God's help such a step meant certain death. In the same way, every battle they would fight for every city in Canaan would require plunging in under strict obedience to God's direct instructions. Before they stepped into the Jordan they were to wait for the Levitical priests to carry the ark of the covenant (God's presence) down into the midst of the river.

> *Joshua said, "By this you shall know that the living God is among you, and that He will assuredly dispossess from before you the Canaanite...Behold, the ark of the covenant of the Lord of all the earth is crossing over ahead of you into the Jordan... It shall come about when the soles of the feet of the priests who carry the ark of the Lord, the Lord of all the earth, rest in the waters of the Jordan, the waters of the Jordan shall be cut off, and the waters which are flowing down from above shall stand in one heap."* (Joshua 3:10,11,13)

When they waited for God's presence to go first, a miracle happened similar to the one that happened in the Red Sea. The power of God to deliver them from the land of bondage was still available to bring them into God's promises of provision. *"...Do not come near it, that you may know the way by which you shall go, for you have not passed this way before"* (Joshua 3:4). Truly the Israelites had not gone this way before—the way of depending completely on God. This was very different from the impulsive and presumptuous ways their parents first attempted to enter the Promised Land. After refusing to go in when God told them to, they decided later they would go in on their own time even though Moses warned them not to do it, for God was not with them. They wouldn't go when God told them to, but they would go when He told them not to. This was Anak self-will in action.

Many of our troubles in life are not the result of evil actions but of presumptuous ones. We just do what we want to do when we want to do it without acknowledging that God has a say in it. We may bewail our failures and even blame God for them, but God is not responsible for choices made independent of Him.

Now the Levitical priests proceeded to carry the ark of God down into the river bottom and stood there while all the people passed through this barrier to their inheritance. Their action is a metaphor of intercessory prayer.

> *And the priests who carried the ark of the covenant of the Lord stood firm on dry ground in the middle of the Jordan while all Israel crossed*

on dry ground, until all the nation had finished crossing the Jordan. (Joshua 3:17)

Jesus went down into the valley of the shadow of death in order to usher all of us into the promise of eternal life. Intercession means that someone stands between two parties to mediate. As we needed Christ's mediation to get us out of our 'Egypt', so we need His mediation to go through the process of dying to ourselves so we can enter our full inheritance. To truly come to the end of ourselves is a very painful process and there are no shortcuts to get us there. It is essential for others to pray for us and to recognize that Jesus prays for us as we go through the process. Whenever we pray we are admitting that our needs are beyond our power to fulfill. Otherwise we would not pray; we would simply attend to it ourselves. It is God's supernatural ability to bring us through these 'coming-to-the-end-of-ourselves' experiences that demonstrates to the world who God is. What God starts He is able to finish.

"For the Lord your God dried up the waters of the Jordan before you until you had crossed, just as the Lord your God had done to the Red Sea, which He dried up before us until we had crossed; that all the peoples of the earth may know that the hand of the Lord is mighty, so that you may fear the Lord your God forever." (Joshua 4:23-24)

Some history from the book of Genesis helps explain the Biblical significance of the Jordan. It is the story of Jacob, the son of Isaac, the son of Abraham, direct heir of the promises of inheritance. Even before Jacob was born, he was in conflict with his twin brother Esau. God explained to his mother Rebekkah what the conflict was about as the two children struggled in her womb.

"Two nations are in your womb; and two peoples will be separated from your body; and one people shall be stronger than the other; and the older shall serve the younger." (Genesis 25:23)

Esau, symbolic of the fleshly nature, was the one who sold his inheritance for a bowl of soup. Jacob and Esau also symbolize the struggle existing between the flesh and spirit inside each one of us.

As Jacob and Esau fought with each other in Rebekkah's womb, so the spirit and the flesh fight with each other in the heart of every person.

This struggle between the good and evil impulses of human nature is demonstrated graphically through Jacob's personal struggles. Even the meaning of his name was 'heel catcher', 'trickster', or as some translate it, 'deceiver'. Although in the end he overcame and became a spiritual man, his life story was full of scheming, deceit, and manipulation to get his own way. He conspired with his mother to steal the inherited blessing from the firstborn brother by deceiving his blind father into believing he was Esau.

Later, fleeing from his brother's wrath, he came into a working relationship with his uncle, Laban, and was on the receiving end of deception when Laban tricked him into bedding the wrong bride on his wedding night. However, he managed to turn the tables and steal away most of his uncle's wealth from under his nose through some clever manipulation of his own.

His life became more complicated when he met up years later with his still unpacified brother Esau. Through God's blessing and the strength of his scheming efforts he had gained much wealth, but he also reaped a lot of conflict and trouble. Like all of us, he was a mixture of both spiritual motivations and fleshly ambitions, and in the end only God could sort out the two natures within him. His meeting with his brother on the outskirts of the Promised Land was a very significant encounter, illuminating the essential truth we all need to confront at the River Jordan.

Esau heard of Jacob's impending arrival and rode out to meet him with four hundred men. Jacob, aware that it did not require four hundred men for a welcome home party, was greatly afraid for his life and devised a plan of appeasement. While Esau was still a ways off he divided up all his flocks as gifts and sent them in successive droves to meet Esau as he approached. Then he crossed a tributary of the Jordan to put some space between him and his brother.

So the presents passed on before him, while he himself spent that night in the camp. Now he arose that same night and took his two wives and his two maids and his eleven children, and crossed the ford of the Jabbok. He took them and sent them across the stream. And he sent across whatever he had. Then Jacob was left alone, and a man wrestled with him until daybreak. (Genesis 32:21-24)

These circumstances were all very strange, and yet they perfectly reflected the work that would be accomplished with Jacob's descendants at the Jordan River five hundred years later. It was no accident that Jacob was alone on one side of a piece of the Jordan and all his worldly possessions were on the other. The Jordan River experience is what separates us from all that we cling to in this world and casts us utterly upon God, reducing us to a face-to-face encounter between Him and ourselves.

Then Jacob was left alone, and a man wrestled with him until daybreak. When he saw that he had not prevailed against him, he touched the socket of his thigh; so the socket of Jacob's thigh was dislocated while he wrestled with him." (Genesis 32:24,25)

At first the reader is not aware of who wrestled with Jacob. The scripture just says "a man" wrestled with Jacob. We realize later that it was God. It is also left unclear who was wrestling with whom. Was Jacob wrestling with God to get something out of Him or was God wrestling with Jacob to get something out of him?

Then he [the man] *said, "Let me go, for the dawn is breaking." But he* [Jacob] *said, "I will not let you go unless you bless me."* (Genesis 32:26)

The man (God) who wrestled with Jacob won the wrestling match by dislocating the socket of Jacob's thigh, but Jacob still held on until he got what he wanted. This has got to be one of the most extraordinary narratives in the entire Bible. It is a picture of God and man engaged in a grim struggle, each intent on getting satisfaction out of the other. Never has the conflict between the human and the divine been so poignantly illustrated.

Man, from his entry into the crucible of life, wrestles with God, asking himself, "Why must I struggle and suffer in pain while I endure the setbacks and inconsistencies of life? Why do I often feel shut outside the door as an alien when I clamor to be let inside as a son?" God, who created man in His image, wrestles with man and strives to build within him the image of His character. He wrestles with man to render him submissive and surrendered to a plan lovingly laid down for his good.

In this wrestling match between Jacob and God we see man, not vanquished immediately under omnipotent power, but elevated to a face-to-face athletic contest. God obviously could have squashed his opponent like a bug, but He consented to go at it all night. He waited for Jacob to recognize that it was not a man, but God Himself he was wrestling.

Sometimes it takes us a lifetime to recognize that behind all our struggles with our fellow man there is a God with whom we are dealing. He allowed Jacob to wrestle Him to a standstill before shrinking the flesh of his thigh, effectively disabling him. He lets us give it our best shot in our own strength before He reveals the futility of our human efforts. The thigh is the center of physical strength for a man. God shrank Jacob's flesh at that crucial spot just as He touches the core of our self-will, revealing our inner motivations in order to free us from ourselves. However, Jacob was tenacious as well, and would not give up without getting satisfaction.

> *"...I will not let you go unless you bless me". So he said to him, "What is your name?" and he said, "Jacob." And he said, "Your name shall no longer be Jacob, but Israel; for you have striven with God and with men and have prevailed."* (Genesis 32:26-28)

The man who will not let go of God even after being disabled is the man who will discover the secret of blessing, of obtaining the inheritance. But God will not let go either until He gets the admission he wants from man. *What is your name?* As if God didn't know! Jacob had to confess it. "My name is Jacob (supplanter, trickster, deceiver)."

Only after we admit that the core of our nature is contrary to God can we receive the new name God gives us—'Israel', meaning 'prince with God, prevailing with God'. The very name of God, 'El', is contained in the name 'Isra-el' and gives evidence to whose power transformed the deceiver into a prince. Jacob became Israel, which became the name of God's people. The people of Israel have prevailed through persecutions, pogroms and dispersions, and are a nation today, albeit one torn by strife. The evening news is still dominated by Palestinian uprising and Jewish reprisal, threatening to bring the whole world into conflict. And yet God's work transcends any particular nation. It is always about His kingdom prevailing in the heart of every person in every nation. The drama of history and of life is designed to bring into focus the true battle between the flesh and spirit.

> *Then Jacob asked him and said, "Please tell me your name." But he said, "Why is it that you ask my name?" And he blessed him there. So Jacob named the place Peniel, for he said, "I have seen God face to face, yet my life has been preserved."* (Genesis 32:29-30)

"My God," says Jacob, "I've seen God's face and I'm not dead." It has always been God's intention to deal with us face to face. He walked and talked with Adam in the garden. He still walks with man, His face veiled for our sakes. He is near to us, wrestling with us. Perhaps if we will just admit our 'Jacob' state, we will also discern the hand of blessing, see the face of God and hear the fatherly benediction on our life, 'Israel—prince with God'.

> *Now the sun rose upon him just as he crossed Penuel, and he was limping on his thigh.* (Genesis 32:31)

Life and death struggles with God leave their mark. The places where we have seen our greatest weaknesses can become our places of greatest strength. The places where we may think we have done permanent and irretrievable damage are often the sources of purest grace. The places where we have come to our wit's end and the utter exhaustion of our strength are where we see the face of God.

So it is understandable that Jacob's descendants, five hundred years later, standing on one side of the Jordan with their inheritance on the other side, were at a significant juncture. They were standing on the site of their greatest failure, the place where they had flunked the test of faith. They spent forty years of frustration and struggle in the desert where unbelief and self-reliance were being purged out of them. The analogy of their story helps us understand the same workings of God in our lives to bring us into our inheritance.

It is important to grasp the heart of God in this work. We tend to see ourselves as either good or bad, and God as either for us or against us. The reality is that God is neither impressed with our goodness nor put off by our badness. He is a father—weighing, measuring, and monitoring our progress in His grace. His favour toward us was determined long ago by the righteous act of His Son through which He redeemed our souls and adopted us as sons and daughters. Now that we are His children we are heirs and subject to the discipline of training. Like Jacob, all of our scheming and convoluted ways come inexorably under the microscope of God's scrutiny. The excellent surgeon of heaven has scheduled us to come under His knife to excise the Esau nature out of us.

It is perhaps difficult to recognize when this death of self is happening in our own lives. It happens slowly along the way, but specific 'Jordan crossroads' in our lives cause us to meet God face to face and get a glimpse of ourselves as we really are. It is usually at the point where we've finally run out of gas and there is nothing more we can do. Long distance runners know this state. It is the point in a race where they realize they have hit a wall and there is no physical resource left—nothing left to boost their performance. Ironically the same runners testify that if they just persevere at this point, some sort of supernatural reservoir kicks in to take them beyond where they could go. God allows similar 'hit the wall' experiences in our spirit and in our souls so that He can supernaturally lift us to a higher plane.

The Israelites had reason for their unbelief. On a human level, they could have never overcome the giants. But God never expected them to conquer them in their own strength; He expected them to put their trust in Him. So, in our affairs God knows our limitations. He gets us to the place where we recognize them, too, and acknowledge we can do no more. This is right where He wants us— at the end of ourselves and our strength—for this is the beginning of His power unleashed in our lives.

As I began my sabbatical year, I was probably at the culmination of a few Jordan experiences in my own life, which helped me realize it was time to step back from ministry for a time. In some ways we could have just kept chugging along, but in other ways I was hitting a wall emotionally and spiritually. For thirty years we had just kept going, but the time was ripe for a strategic change. Then, just as we began our break at Nelson Island at the beginning of our time away, a disturbing experience happened to me on a physical plane to remind us of our human limitations. How suddenly and unexpectedly our vulnerabilities can be revealed to us.

A kaleidoscope of blue, gray, tan, and white circled around me and rocks with barnacles, sea, sky and trees flashed like strobes in the periphery of my field of vision. I felt far away, drifting, and then, sky and tree branches focused above as I realized my head was cradled on a rock. Why was my forehead pulsing? But incongruously I felt peaceful. Vulnerable. I almost felt the urge to laugh at my ridiculous position. This was really strange.

I began to recall my walk to the rocky point at the entry to our cove. *"My God, I guess I've got a real problem."* I lifted my head to assess my predicament. Half-dressed, blood all over. I felt a tinge of fear. Then a sense of being totally undone. I laid my head back on the rock and rested, waiting to feel better, afraid to get up in case I might pass out again. *"Well, God, look at me now. Here I am in all my glory. What are You going to do with me now?"* I just lay there for a while, feeling safe, almost amused, cradled in the arms of nature even though the craggy rocks were not exactly a soft pillow.

The inclination to chuckle had a history. Feeling helpless and not in control of certain areas of my life and emotions resonated with this physical state I now found myself in. Embarrassing as it is to have a major uncontrollable intestinal bleed, it was kind of the icing on the cake. I had always been a very robust individual as far as health was concerned. I had never had any major ailments. The only time I had ever been a hospital patient was when I donated a kidney to my brother and that was because I was so healthy. Now, for the first time in my life, I was feeling the emotions, consternation, and helplessness relative to a weakness in my physical body. I slowly gathered myself together and dizzily stumbled the couple of hundred yards back to the cabin where my condition shocked Lyza and sent her into panic mode. It was an unnerving experience for her to be in charge of running the boat eight miles back to civilization and driving another hour on curving roads at breakneck speed to the nearest hospital.

If nothing else, I had always counted on my body, my physical health. Our cabin retreat world was built by and dependent on my two hands to keep it operating. I chopped the wood to keep the cabin warm, serviced all the boats, kept the water system running, and even brought in the seafood for dinner. The goal of taking *Fred* to Alaska was totally dependent on the strength of my body. Now my physical state was in question. At first, I was kind of in denial about it, ready to just shrug it off, my usual way of handling ailments and minor injuries. Then I began to think about the possibilities, especially after seeing how seriously the doctors took my condition, submitting me to various medical indignities. Some close friends had died of colon cancer so the worst case scenarios began to play with my mind.

I wasn't overly fearful, but it did seem ironic to be faced with such fears at this particular juncture. I wondered, *"Okay, God, is this it? Is it all over?"* I thought to myself, "Well, what if it is? Would I feel incomplete as a person or as a pastor? Would I feel my life work and purpose was unfinished?" As a matter of fact, yes, I would. If nothing else, I wanted to get this book written before God called my number. I also wouldn't have minded a little more success in a few areas, like seeing thousands come into the kingdom of God. For sure I wanted to be a grandfather for a while. Then again—what if my time was up? What if God in His estimation determined that His purposes for my life were finished?

Sometimes we overestimate our significance. I was learning that I was expendable as a pastor. Maybe I was expendable period! Some might feel this was a somewhat negative consideration, but actually, to me, it was quite liberating. What if this was a permanent sabbatical? I remembered those near-death experiences I'd read about where people afterwards approached life on a completely different basis. Sometimes it takes looking death in the face to see life as it should be seen.

As it turned out, there was no such dire prognosis. Every test for every possible disease proved negative and the doctors were left scratching their heads about what it was and I was given a clean bill of health. I think it was an extreme case of God testing my resolve to trust Him. The timing was unique, happening at the beginning of our time of extended reflection. I think He just wanted to remind me to lay it *all* down—to remind me that my life and ministry were totally in His hands. Physical strength was one of my last bastions of self-reliance. He might as well have it, too, just another area of self-life to be brought down to the Jordan River for last rites.

Hitting the wall can happen in many different areas of our lives. For Lyza and me, our marriage was one of the most intense and most personal areas of this test. There were times when the strongholds described in the previous chapter would bring our emotions to a complete immobilization. Nothing more could be done that we hadn't already tried and we were undone. We could only cling to God's covenant and cling desperately to each other and say, like Jacob, "We won't let go until you bless us."

Slowly the stubborn strength of self ebbs away and the hardness softens. As love and acceptance seep in, we become transformed into new people with new names. Some people feel they've already gone way past such a point, but it is usually way past the place where we think it should end that God brings us to change us. Sadly, in marriage many come short of their inheritance by not holding on beyond the 'hitting-the-wall' experiences.

Women are generally better than men at marriage. I think they work harder at it. They seem to have an internalized marriage manual and they know where marriage is supposed to go. Men sometimes seem oblivious to it, outwardly focused, goal-oriented, not intimacy-oriented, and often too proud to submit to the program, not able to acknowledge their need until it all starts to unravel. I'd seen the scenario too many times. A wife working very hard at making her marriage work, holding it all together, putting up with abusive patterns, ready to go for counseling and help while the husband just motors on. Then one day something snaps inside and it feels like it cannot be mended. She gives up. Once this happens it seems very difficult to turn around. It takes a long time to get to that point, but once she's finished, she's finished, and the husband wakes up one day to find out it's over. She hit the Jordan wall and later he hits the Jordan wall after losing her. What God wanted to use to bring death of self and real change becomes the death of the marriage through unbelief. The result—Jordan is never crossed in that area of life.

In those painful days following Verne's death, I felt a similar 'hit-the-wall' feeling. I thought I'd given it my best shot to serve those over me in the Lord, and had been perceived negatively despite my good intentions. Some could have said at this juncture, "Come on, pull yourself together. Life is full of setbacks. Get up and go at it again." But there is a certain point, after we've gotten up and tried again enough times, that something new, something different must happen. Getting up and giving it another go would only be another effort in the strength of Jacob. Our number is up and we know it; we have to stop wrestling against God and start clinging to God. Our tenaciousness becomes an intercessory prayer and God begins to move us into the Promised Land.

Lyza, Ginette, and I were now ensconced in a pine-paneled house in Maine surrounded by a hundred acres of New England forest. We were living a pleasant life with a simple rhythm. Up in the morning to light the wood-burning drums in the basement and back to bed until the house heated up. Then coffee and breakfast around the Rumford fireplace in the living room. The Rumford had a shallow firebox, so the fire seemed right in the room with us while the flames played up the angled bricks to deflect heat into the room. It became the centerpiece of our New England existence. We spent the mornings home-schooling Ginette and working on the manuscript. By afternoon we were outside in the crisp October air under brilliant blue skies. Wild blueberry bushes splashed crimson brush strokes on the surrounding multi-colored hillsides where we hiked and explored. In the evenings, after dinner, we read around the fire, watched the news and played Rummi-Kub.

For thirty years such a basic life had been foreign to us. Meetings three or four nights a week were commonplace. I didn't resent it, for it came with the territory, but sometimes I longed for a slower-paced uncomplicated lifestyle like this. I reveled in not being responsible, not having to be somewhere at night, not having to live up to anyone's expectations. Some people actually lived this way all of the time.

I had recognized a few months previous the inner mechanisms of guilt that kicked in if I stayed still too long. Soon I would be thinking, *Shouldn't I be doing something constructive?* Going somewhere? Helping somebody? Yet I had to ask myself when I thought this way, was I driven by duty or was I motivated by genuine love? I wondered how many of the people I was trying to serve back in the pastor life could tell the difference between the duty call and the genuine heartfelt visit from me. The sabbatical was deepening its effect on me. I was beginning to discern how stupid that whole way of thinking was. I began to just exist and love God for His own sake and the love for my fellow man became renewed as a natural result. How simple the call of God really is. It all really boils down to *"Love God with all of your heart, all of your strength, all of your mind…"*

Maine was certainly not the Promised Land, but for me it was close enough for that time. It was the land of my forbears and it elicited a deep response of peace and contentment within as though ancient friendly hands reached up to me out of the ground to welcome me home and voices called to me from the sea. Although it should have felt like a foreign land, it was familiar to me. I felt rooted and grounded again in native soil—the soil of God's love for my spirit and the soil of Maine for my soul. I was transitioning into a new season of rest.

Rosier Roots

Grandpa Clarke
Governor of Iowa
(Paternal Great-Grandfather)

Grandpa Vinal
(Maternal Great-Grandfather)

Fred & Mabel Clarke
(Paternal Grandparents)

Elwyn & Grace Vinal
(Maternal Grandparents)

Ted & Lee Clarke
(John's Parents)

Possessing the Land, The Book of Joshua

The Ten Temptations: **Possessing Canaan**

| 1. Pressures of Life | 2. Power of Evil | 3. Bitterness of Life | 4. Hunger 5. Thirst | 6. Idolatry | 7. Counterfeit Service | 8. Counterfeit Comfort | 9. Counterfeit Leadership | 10. Doubt & Fear |

Seven Stages of the Spiritual Journey:

1. Passover in Egypt	2. Red Sea Crossing	3. Mt. Sinai Visitation	5. Crossing Jordan River	6. Conquest of Canaan
		4. Wilderness		

All three grandchildren:
Tate, Finn & Irelynn

Son Dave with new son,
Tate, born January '03

Julie & Lyza in Maui

Ginette in Maui

Matt at the cabin

Daughter-in-law Lori, Daughter Julie, Lyza's mom, Julia

John, Bo & Ginette on boat
trip up the coast

Dave & Lori

Julie & her fiancé, Chris

Chapter Sixteen

Two things began to have new meaning for me during our time on the coast. The first was cemeteries and the other was my middle name. While driving up Rural Route 15, Lyza suddenly cried out for me to stop, just as I was swinging right onto Route 175, which led to Cape Rosier where we were living. (She had a nasty habit of telling me to stop or turn while we were going 50mph and parallel with some sight she wanted me to see). This time as I backed up a hundred feet toward some greenhouses, I realized it was a tiny cemetery that had caught her eye. Although it sounds a bit strange, cemeteries had become a real point of interest to us ever since we hit the Maritimes.

On the west coast, cemeteries are usually great municipal acreages where all the graves are consolidated into one big amorphous spot. I'm sure this practice prevents the problem of buying a piece of property with someone else's family members buried on it, but it lacks the charm and character of these eastern cemeteries. We found family plots in the fields, next to road allowances, and even in the middle of woods overgrown with trees. These plots were still preserved and respected in spite of the progress of civilization taking detours around them.

On one hike through deep woods, we came across a tiny square, fenced with granite posts, where a few headstones lay, one of which was adorned with a small American flag. It recorded the death of a fifteen-year-old at Gettysburg. The tombstones in such quiet spots were tipsy with time, leaning over little hillocks and stumbling across gnarled old roots swelled with age. Often these places were on prime real estate, overlooking a bay, shaded by great maples, oaks, or elms, silently bearing witness to the lives, history and mortality of people who were once full of hopes and dreams. We read on stones of drownings at sea, of young men sent home from war in a casket and of family tragedies and sorrows.

On this cold day Lyza climbed up on the grassy mound off highway 15 to view a handful of headstones a few feet off the gravel shoulder. Just a block up the road was a gas station and some tumbledown greenhouses. Two small headstones side by side recorded the names of one- and two-year-old siblings who had died on the same date, February 17, 1823. Their mother lay beside them, dead only seven years later in 1830 at thirty years old. Most likely no one now could tell us the story behind the stones and so we were left to ponder them 160 years later.

Others had stood on this ground before us and left a mark for us to consider. It made me think twice about our habit of scattering ashes to the winds as so often happens now. It's good to have ways to connect with the past for it helps us define who we are in the present. An inheritance comes out of a past and leads us into a future. We do not just appear and disappear like a flower. We have roots that connect us to a larger family and a greater history. That is one reason why we have last names and middle names because they connect a person to their past heritage.

This was the other thing I gained a deeper appreciation for when I was back east—my middle name. Middle names are a sensitive issue with a lot of folks. At least I know it was with me. It seems that every odd moniker hanging on the family tree gets inserted into that unused spot to satisfy some aunt or great uncle who wants their name preserved in the family progeny. Some really embarrassing names are bestowed this way, lurking to expose their namesakes to childhood ridicule.

Vinal was my middle name. It was my mother's maiden name and I always thought it was a little strange, but it became worse when my friends got hold of it. I started hearing things like, "Hey, Linoleum, you wanna go play football?" The situation deteriorated further when a well-meaning vice-principal mispronounced my name in the high school graduation ceremonies. Confused by the fancy writing on the diploma, he thought the 'V' was a 'U' and said 'John Uinal Clarke' when calling me forward to receive my certificate. From then on it was, "Hey, Urinal, you wanna go play football?" When we moved to Canada I escaped the abuse, and looking for a fresh start, I didn't tell anyone my middle name. Later on I learned of its noble origins and then began to throw it around with pride, being especially gratified that my first grandson's name was Finn David *Vinal* Clarke.

In the last days of November, seeking to learn about my mother's side of my family history, we found ourselves poking around in the cemetery on a rather large island in the middle of Penobscot Bay called, of all things, Vinalhaven. There, in the middle of a hundred or more grave markers, was a six-foot high stone with that middle name of mine inscribed in bold dark letters, proud and confident, laying claim to a respected heritage on this granite island. Scattered around were many other Vinals hailing back to the 1700's and two miles out of town by the old family homestead was another plot dedicated to Vinals. The cause of embarrassment in my youth was actually the token of a rich family legacy.

Searching among gravestones in the cemetery and reading in the files of the adjacent historical society, we confirmed that the Vinals had a long and thorough investment in the history of America. Anna Vinal came to Massachusetts in 1636 with her husband, Stephen, and was widowed shortly thereafter, leaving her to raise three children: Stephen, John, and Martha. She settled, built a house and from her three children, a family of descendants grew in the new world. Her husband was descended from William of Vine Hall who bought the Vine Hall Estate in England in 1450, taking the name of Vinal. His descendants were granted a coat of arms in the 1660's. This was a definite promotion for me—elevated from being a floor covering to a descendant of English nobility. The records included a line of soldiers, sea captains, and legislators down through the Civil War. In fact, it was a point of interest to me that the last living survivor of the Civil War had been my ancestor, Wooster Vinal. The island of Vinalhaven was named in honor of John Vinal who expedited the incorporation of the islands in 1789. His son, William, pioneered and helped populate the island with his descendants.

There was something bracing about getting an overview of my ancestors' lives. As we walked around the little graveyard and surveyed the saltwater bay, the lobster boats, and the old granite quarries, I imagined the hardy lives of William, his sons, and the generations whose existence I knew nothing about before now. My mother had told me as a child about my great-great-great grandfather, William Vinal, (descended from Anna's other son, Stephen), who sailed as a whaling captain out of New Bedford, Massachusetts, in the 1830's. Another of his descendants, John Vinal, was a colonel in the Civil War whose six-foot saber my grandfather had inherited and kept in his home, an item I found fascinating as a boy.

249

What talents and interests had filtered down through the generations? Perhaps my love of sailing had its east coast roots. Of even keener interest to me was that Anna Vinal was a Puritan who must have sown the truths of the eternal inheritance of Christ in the hearts of her children. I didn't learn of any preachers in the family line, but their names were definitely found on the church rolls, giving testimony to their faith. Maybe those spiritual genetics passed down through the decades and came to expression in my brother Charlie's and my call to the ministry. Perhaps Anna had prayed over her descendants in the new world and the robustness of her line was the fruit of her faith. Now here I was, 364 years later, paying tribute to her faith, sniffing around the relics of her 'Canaan land of promise' and writing a book about the value of a spiritual inheritance.

We hiked back to the ferry dock past old buildings lining the main street of the town of Vinalhaven where a Vinal had been postmaster for over fifty years in the 1800's and another one had been the longtime proprietor of the Paper Store. Later, as the ferry threaded a channel among the many outlying islands, we got a broader view of Penobscot Bay where we had been living for almost two months. We drove the rolling rural roads and frequented the ancient fishing villages—Castine and Stonington—wandering their narrow streets, learning their histories, and buying fresh lobster off the docks.

On Cape Rosier the little country store, garage, and post office of Brooksville in Buck's Harbor became 'our town'. We hung out on the front porch of the store, savoring sticky buns and mugs of hazelnut coffee while the fiery colors of autumn leaves drifted around white-sided houses and cluttered fields and lanes. We marked time firsthand by the subtle changes of the season upon the trees, the scents in the air, and the changes in the sky instead of the turning of daytimer pages. We watched the holiday decorations change on the porches and in the yards from Halloween to Thanksgiving to Christmas and I was reminded that New England with its pilgrims, turkeys, and white-steepled villages draped in snow was the fount of America's most deeply engrained holiday images.

As the seasonal events came and went I realized many of the special holiday touches my mother created in our home growing up came from New England and were passed down from her mother who was born and raised in New Bedford, Massachusetts. This area was a place I could have loved and called my own with its farms and forests, its coastline and its old wood boats. I was tempted to imagine another life there on Cape Rosier tending to quiet rural pursuits, but it was not to be so. My ancestors moved west. My maternal grandfather, Elwin Vinal and his bride from Massachusetts, Grace Tripp, met up with my paternal grandfather, Fred G. Clarke, who had moved west from Iowa to Mercer Island, where their sons and daughters grew up and were married.

So I grew up loving the west coast instead, although living on the east coast enriched that love as the joining of my ancestors enriched the heritage of their children. In the same way God used the natural genealogy of Abraham and the land of Canaan to teach the world of the richness of the eternal inheritance of Christ, He uses our natural histories and experiences to teach and enrich us.

Even though Lyza and I were transplanted from our natural roots when we moved to Canada, God built for us a new richness of heritage in Canada. He taught us about our 'roots' in the heritage of Christ and the deep bonds between His people. Our church family roots became identified with the brothers, sisters, fathers and mothers of the faith and our inheritance began to be identified with the promises of God. In those days our understanding grew of the inheritance wrought for us by Christ in the spiritual realm, the Lord began to use miraculous provisions in the natural realm by demonstrating His love and generous heart toward us in the area of our housing needs...

A line of dump trucks rolled down the half-mile gravel road toward our place, churning up dust behind them. My friend, Erich, was in high spirits, enthusiastically waving trucks on to the hog fill track, which covered the frozen mud, and directing them behind the house foundation. Simultaneously he gave orders to the bulldozer driver and called to the driver of the other big grade-all machine to dump some of the sandy gravel inside the foundation. This was all in a day's work for my Mennonite general contractor, a veteran of many subdivisions, who had been raised on hard work from his childhood as a refugee in Paraguay. He immigrated to Canada at the age of eighteen and had made good through his industriousness, which he still demonstrated now, thirty years later. He and his wife, Elsie, and their three sons had become close friends and had been of inestimable value to our church community as it grew through the years. At this moment he was particularly exuberant because his construction problems relative to our little dream house had been miraculously solved in a matter of a couple of days.

The biggest problem was mud and the next biggest problem was the lack of available sandy, gravelly material to build a septic field. It had become apparent towards the end of October that the health inspector would not give us septic approval without raising the ground's level two feet. The septic field had to be built behind the house, not in front, which put it about two hundred feet from the road on this five acre farm plot. Not only did we have a real problem getting trucks back there through the mud, but we had a problem stretching the budget to cover one hundred truckloads of suitable fill at ninety dollars a load.

Just before this dilemma occurred we had a little test of faith over the price we had paid to the neighbor for the piece of land. He had incurred a much greater expense than he expected in digging us a well for the property and I felt God prompting me to pay an unsolicited two thousand dollars more for the land as an act of good will. This was in the early 1980's and it was a lot of money to me. Shortly after this act of obedience, I was hit with this extra expense of my own and I almost considered going over and asking for the money back. Instead I entrusted our affairs to God and looked for some divine intervention.

The solution to our problem began with a storm in the Caribbean. Mel, another friend, was chased home to Surrey early from a Caribbean cruise when a volcano and a hurricane struck. At the same time an anomaly in the weather pattern of British Columbia produced a cold snap that persisted for a number of days, freezing the ground solid. Even the slug population was caught off guard and was decimated the following year. As the ground hardened, Mel came home and went back to work where he was clearing two lots in White Rock only minutes away from our building site. The lots needed to have a great amount of dirt hauled out of them and when he talked with Art Mckay, the excavator, he offered it to us for free if we paid for the trucking, reducing our previous trucking estimates from ninety dollars from Aldergrove to ten dollars a load from White Rock. Twenty trucks moved it all in one day and the material was so good we used it in the foundation as well, saving expenditure on sand.

The final bill? Two thousand dollars, the exact amount we had given away. Of course there are skeptics and those who would think it egocentric to believe God arranged hurricanes and cold snaps to provide me a septic field... but what can I say? It happened. This was not the first time we experienced unusual circumstances that helped us get established in our natural inheritance.

The beginnings were back in the early seventies when we first moved out of the church farm we were living on. At that time Lyza and I didn't have many expectations of buying our own home because we assumed we had left material advantages behind. We had moved from the tent into the beach house gratefully and then after two years were offered a small house to rent. It actually had delightful luxuries, a real furnace and wall–to–wall carpeting (even if it was gaudy red). Less than a year later we left our cozy rental house for the church farm. We were finally earning a small wage from construction and then from the church after our immigration papers had come through, but we just assumed we would probably 'rent till the rapture'.

One day, while living at the church farm, Lyza and I were driving around and just started talking about what kind of place we would like to live in if we ever could afford to buy one. We agreed we would both love a little house on acreage.

A few weeks later, Erich, the same friend who later built our house, came to talk to us about our future. He said God had put it on his heart to help us get started in a house. We were blown away to think that anybody cared that much. We became the beneficiaries of a rich community heritage of shared material things that sprung from the Penners' Mennonite roots. They had done well financially, but felt it their responsibility to wisely help others along the way. Months later we moved into a small farmhouse on nine acres that Erich had traded for something else in a business deal. If we took over the mortgage and paid the taxes (a fairly big stretch for us in those days), he would give us a share in the property's value when it was later sold—an amazingly generous offer. We lived there for the next few years, extremely satisfied, raising a few chickens and steers, and adding three children to our family. Then the property sold and we moved on to the 'Christian Corner' subdivision carrying a reasonable mortgage. Who would have believed we would be living in our own house ten years after starting out in a tent?!

But it didn't stop there.

After living in the subdivision for five years with four other families from the church, including Erich's family and Pastor Verne and Marge, another opportunity came out of the blue. This time part of the plan included blending back together our spiritual inheritance with our natural one. An economic downturn in the early eighties created an opportunity for us to purchase a five-acre parcel of land for a rock bottom price just off the agricultural land reserve in South Surrey and across the road from where Erich and Elsie had moved a year before. Simultaneously my parents had to sell two lots they owned on Mercer Island because of some family pressures, and one of those lots would have been my inheritance.

At this stage my parents gladly agreed to make available some of the money from the Mercer Island lot to secure the five acres. My father and mother were just amazed and grateful that our life had turned out so well after initially fearing we would end up in disaster when we had married so young and penniless. Within only a couple of weeks we sold our house and contracted with Erich to build a house on the five acres, the place of our septic field 'miracle'. We stood amazed at God's blessing and provision for us. Jesus' words to Peter's blunt question rang true in our own experience —

> *Peter said, "Behold we have left our own homes and followed you."*
> *And He said to them, "Truly I say to you, there is no one who has left*
> *house or wife or brothers or parents or children, for the sake of the*
> *kingdom of God, who will not receive many times as much at this time*
> *and in the age to come, eternal life."* (Luke 18:28-30)

Before we bought the acreage, I remember walking through the picturesque stretch of woods on that property feeling like it was my promised land, but it just seemed too good to be true. I almost felt guilty. Why should I get this? What about other people and their financial struggles? I was afraid it could become a distraction from my real calling.

My son, Dave, then about thirteen, was praying about it in church one day. When he told me he had prayed about it, I was touched. But when he told me what he thought God said to him, I felt humbled. "Dad, I think God said, 'I'm giving it to you and you can have it for keeps'." I took Dave's word for it and also the growing assurance I felt from my Father, and in childlike delight we went for it. When our cute country house was built, with a vegetable garden and four acres out back fenced for sheep to run in, I would wander in the woods and pour out my heart to God. I felt like David did when God had established him in his kingdom.

Now it came about when the king lived in his house, and the Lord had given him rest on every side from all his enemies, that the king said to Nathan, the prophet, "See now I dwell in a house of cedar but the ark of God dwells within tent curtains." (2 Samuel.7: 1,2)

In other words David felt his house was doing a lot better than God's house. David went on to tell Nathan he wanted to build a house for God to live in. I had left our street ministry to join the church with a single-minded desire to build a house for God. I had to admit that most of the time I felt I hadn't done a very good job. Building up God's house was a constant struggle full of setbacks and difficulty, yet in the matter of our own housing we just walked into blessing and supernatural help. God appeared to be building up my house behind my back while I was busy trying to build His house. We were now living on the five acres in a cozy new farmhouse with a low mortgage.

But it didn't stop there, either.

Our five acres was located in the midst of an undeveloped area where no other houses were even visible except for the Penners' who had the five acres facing us on the other side of the road. After three of four years, one other family bought a five–acre piece adjacent to ours and built a beautiful house overlooking a large pond they dug out behind his house. A successful developer, he took a year off to build the house exactly as he wanted it, with many special features. When it was finished and landscaped, we would admire their view of the pond with a little island in the middle. Like a private park, Canada geese visited it as did mallard ducks. One day, five years after he moved in, I was out raking branches around our sheep barn when Wayne, our neighbor, leaned over the fence from his driveway to ask me a question.

"John, are you at all interested in selling your place?" I blinked at him in surprise.

"I don't think so. We love our place. But why are you asking?"

He then explained to me, with a kind of suppressed twinkle in his eye, that the consortium that had been buying up properties across the street from us was now expressing interest in our two parcels. None of us had thought that these parcels would have any investment potential when we first came out there because we were too close to the Agricultural Land Reserve. Times had changed, however, and a company was assembling hundreds of acres to build a top-level golf course with executive home subdivisions between the fairways. Wayne said that if I were willing, he wanted to discuss a proposal with the prospective buyers. I told him to check it out.

Two weeks later, he showed me the offer they were prepared to make for my hobby farm. After picking me up off the floor, I told him maybe I was willing to sell after all. They were offering us five times what we had paid for the place ten years before! Suddenly, after years of financial discipline and raising a family within a moderate pastor's salary, we were facing the prospect of an altogether new kind of financial freedom. It was ironic that only three months earlier we had paid off our mortgage by doubling up payments over the years. Again, I was amazed at God's administration of our lives. It was as though He kept us under the discipline of the desert until He deemed we were ready to handle greater liberty and responsibility.

I went down to Mercer Island soon after and told my dad what had happened. He just shook his head slowly, stared at me, and then burst out with his great bellow of a laugh. I think he was really tickled by it all. Being financially well established was a language he could understand. It was kind of a reverse prodigal son story. The son who had left home for a far country to preach the gospel and serve God had come home, not empty, but full.

"Then it shall come about when the Lord your God brings you into the land which he swore to your fathers, Abraham, Isaac and Jacob, to give you, great and splendid cities which you did not build, and houses full of all good things which you did not fill, and hewn cisterns which you did not dig, vineyards and olive trees which you did not plant, and you eat and are satisfied, then watch yourself, that you do not forget the Lord who brought you from the land of Egypt, out of the house of slavery." (Deuteronomy 6: 10-12)

"Cities you did not build and houses you did not fill." The blessings they did not earn they were given as gifts of grace to confirm his covenant. When we watched Wayne build his house years before with its nine-foot ceilings, five thousand square feet of finished living space, and the quality touches of a builder building his own home, we never dreamed he was building it for us. In the midst of the conclusion of our deals to sell our properties, Wayne again said to me over the fence, "You should buy my house because the buyers are willing to sell us both back our houses in order to save themselves some capital investment after subdividing off the acreage part. It would not be to either of our advantage to buy our own houses because we would be liable for capital gains tax, but there's nothing saying you can't make the deal with them over my house."

He then explained that the rough figure they determined his house was worth was assigned without looking at it and was below the actual value. "You have all those people coming over all the time for meetings and your kids are getting to be teenagers now. My house would be perfect for you and you wouldn't have to move out of this area that you like so much." Here he was, thrusting his house upon us in a good-natured way, and we really didn't know him and his wife that well. It was like, "Here! Have this house that you did not build." We ended up making the deal and have lived in that house for the last seven years. The house and its location have been a tremendous blessing to our family and others, and many financial details in the arrangement have worked to our advantage over the years.

We were left shaking our heads in wonder. The couple who came to this community with nothing but two thousand dollars, few enough possessions to fit easily into a van, no job and just some faith in a loving God, had come a long way from living in a tent like Abraham. We were now living in a spacious home on one of the largest lots in one of the most prestigious developments in the whole area. Again I felt humbled, like David must have felt when Nathan the prophet was instructed, *"Go and say to My servant David, 'Thus says the Lord, "Are you the one who should build Me a house to dwell in?"'"* (2 Samuel 7:5). In another place God says, *"Heaven is My throne and the earth is My footstool. Where then is a house you could build for Me?"* (Isaiah 66: 1).

I often thought, *Why are you doing this, God? Why are you blessing me this way?* I knew it wasn't because of any virtue on my part. It had to be simply an expression of God's goodness and an illustration in our lives of the inheritance that God wants to bring us into in the spiritual realm. God delights to bless his children. In a later place He said to David,

> *"I gave you your master's house and your master's wives into your care, and I gave you the house of Israel and Judah; and if that had been too little, I would have added to you many more things like these."* (2 Samuel 12:8)

Besides expressing His love, the purpose of God's blessing in natural ways in all of our lives is to confirm His covenant. I think our story of getting established in houses and land was to confirm our life message of the inheritance. God purposed to give us a land flowing with milk and honey that we did not deserve and could not attain by ourselves.

> *"But you shall remember the Lord your God, for it is He who is giving you power to make wealth, that He may confirm His covenant which He swore to your fathers as it is this day."* (Deuteronomy 8:18)

Financial blessings confirm His covenant, and His covenant is about the inheritance. Not only has Christ saved us but He has also opened the way for us to enter into all that His salvation has gained for us. As it was completely by grace that we entered into our birthright so it is grace that allows us ultimately to appropriate our inheritance. I don't believe financial miracles like we experienced will be the portion of every person who walks in the way of faith, but God is a creative God who chooses to reveal through these situations His intentions to bring His people into a land of blessings and into the riches of the glory of the inheritance.

Remember Caleb, the lone survivor besides Joshua from the generation who went through the wilderness? After waiting forty years he claimed the mountain called Kiriath Arba, the stronghold of the giant Anak, and his sons. The record reveals that he drove them out and conquered that mountain, settling there with his family and bequeathing it to the following generations. Caleb and the rest of the Israelites became established, putting down roots in the land that God had promised them. Their life as itinerants came to an end. The land had become their own as God had said it would to Abraham and his seed five hundred years earlier.

We had become attached to our cozy life at the Pipers' Nest, sitting around the fireplace, but we had already gone through most of the seasoned wood, leaving in its place the five cords of neatly stacked green firewood that I had bucked up in the basement. Christmas with our children and grandchildren on the west coast beckoned us. Even so, I found it hard to leave this particular chapter of our sabbatical journey because of the deep sense of roots I felt there. Our time in Cape Rosier was coming to a close and Marjorie Bancroft, the owner, and her stepson, Peter, came to close up the house against the Maine winter, which had already frozen the ground solid and dusted it with snow.

The Bancroft family had their own seafaring tradition steeped in wooden sailboats and coastal adventures. After their retirement Marjorie and her husband, Den, had spent three years sailing in a forty-two-foot ketch called the *Dovekie*. They crossed the Atlantic, made it to the British Isles, sailed around Europe into the Mediterranean, and then back to the Caribbean and up the Atlantic coast back to Maine (and I thought we had been adventurous on *Fred*!). Theirs was another life, another family, and another story, yet I knew all of our stories find their ultimate meaning in God's story of the human race. I remembered God's promise to Abraham, *"In your seed all the nations of the earth shall be blessed"* (Genesis 22:18). The legacy of all families only finds ultimate significance in relation to the eternal heritage.

As we prepared to leave, I reflected on our evenings in the cottage watching Alex Haley's video series "Roots". We were deeply touched by the true story of the generations of Kunta Kinte, the African captured and sold into American slavery. Alex Haley was able to trace his generations only by some miracles of circumstance and the strength of the oral traditions passed from generation to generation in Africa. Alex's roots went all the way back in Gambia, Africa, to the Kinte clan where the oral historian of the tribe could recite their family history back five hundred years. As he recited their history, he came to the actual account where Kunta Kinte went into the forest to cut a drum out of a hollow log and was captured by slavers and lost to the tribe. Haley was able to complete the circle of his generations and connect it back to his family roots in Africa.

As the full story of his forbears' sufferings under the injustice, cruelty, and inhumanity of slavery in America unfolded, I couldn't help but realize that it was the very antithesis of my own progenitors' history in America. Yet through courage, pride in their God-given origins and a Methodist faith that gave them a foothold in the eternal perspective, their family made it through the degradations of slavery and racial prejudice to carve out an inheritance in the New World and a heritage of character in their family.

The power of Haley's story lay in making connections through the family history and preserving a sense of identity through knowing where he had come from and what his name really was. Early slaves were not even allowed to have last names, which was part of their disenfranchisement. When you know who you are and where you come from, it also helps you know where you are going. Alex Haley also wrote the autobiography of Malcolm X, the highly controversial Black Muslim activist of the 60's, who for a time justified the use of violent means in the racial struggle. Malcolm took the last name X as a refusal to acknowledge the slave name the white man gave his ancestors. Part of Haley's motivation to verify his own name, Kinte, came from this sad void of having no real last name and no traceable roots. One's first name is often enough to identify us in everyday usage, but our last name identifies us in the larger context of history and time.

Slavery was definitely one of the darkest chapters of American history, yet there is even a more pernicious disenfranchisement that has been perpetrated in the spiritual realm for centuries. Man became a slave to sin and has been bound in the darkness of Satan since the beginning. Blinded by various ideologies, philosophies, traditions and the distortions of religious systems, man's true roots and his true identity have been lost to him. He has forgotten that he was originally made in the image of God and his destiny was to rule and reign in creation with his Maker, having dominion in the earth and filling it with his seed, his descendants. Separated from these roots, he has given himself to vain attempts to gain a security in this life through money, pleasures, and power that will all be stripped away from him upon his decease. The eternal riches of the inheritance are hidden from him, but Jesus Christ, the great liberator, broke the chains of his slavery to sin and made an emancipation proclamation of freedom, which is the gospel of the kingdom, the good news. All men can now have legal status as adopted sons of God and legal right to the inheritance God has promised.

It doesn't matter if we can trace our natural heritage or if we can lay claim to property or riches in this life. Even if we have been disenfranchised, stripped of possessions, of family relations, or even of personal dignity by the ravages of sin, we can now be inheritors of all that God has promised from the beginning of time. By being adopted into the family of faith, our lineage consists of all those great saints from the beginning of time until now who have walked in the way of the promises of God. Abraham, David, Isaiah, Peter, John, Augustine, Luther, Wesley are all relatives of mine to give me a sense of roots, destiny, and purpose. When Jesus was informed that his relatives were outside looking for him, Jesus answered, *"Who is my brother my sister, my mother? Whoever does the will of God is my brother, my sister, my mother."* As Alex Haley did with his African origins, we all need to take a penetrating look through the distortions of our past to connect with our true roots. Our real spiritual roots are found in the person of God Himself who created us originally and who reinstated us as true sons and heirs of all that He is and has through His son Jesus Christ.

Paradise Lost and Found

Rest in the Land
Hebrews 4, Joshua

The Land of Promise and Rest

6. Idolatry 7. Counterfeit 8. Counterfeit 9. Counterfeit 10. Doubt
            Service   Comfort   Leadership   & Fear

Seven Stages of the Spiritual Journey:

1. Passover in Egypt	2. Red Sea Crossing	3. Mt. Sinai Visitation	5. Crossing Jordan River	6. Conquest of Canaan	**7. Rest in the Promised Land**

4. Wilderness

Chapter Seventeen

What could be better than this? I was with my two sons overlooking our Maui paradise, seated in a padded lawn chair on the condo balcony and engaged in conversation about life and its meanings while sipping guava nectar, my feet propped on the table. My daughters were swimming in the ocean breakers two stories below. The water near shore was opal green, deepening to turquoise and then to royal blue out beyond the coral reefs. A subterranean painter's palette of white sand and brown coral mixed with the tricolor sea and the trade winds whipped up brush strokes of white over all.

Across the water a crown of clouds billowed above the peaks of Molokai, accentuating by their shadow the magenta valleys cloven in the hills of green, casting a Bali Hai mystique over the island. If ever there was a promised land on earth, it had to be the Hawaiian Islands. The palms swaying in the winds, the gorgeous array of tropical flowers forever in bloom, and the perpetual sunshine far exceeded anything I ever saw in modern Israel. As far as I was concerned the actual real estate of the Promised Land, after centuries of conquest, was hardly worth fighting for, a denuded land of desert, rock and barren hills. Maui, on the other hand, was 'the closest thing to heaven on earth', according to the tourism pamphlets in every store and this was where we landed for the last months of our sabbatical year.

Barely escaping the bite of Maine's winter, we flew to wet Vancouver for Christmas with the children and then boarded a jet shortly after the New Year, managing to skip winter altogether. We could not believe our good fortune, ensconced as we were in a condo overlooking the Pacific, living like retirees with nothing to do but write and explore the island.

'Benign' is a fitting word to describe Hawaii. The temperature is a near constant eighty degrees with the cooling trade winds blowing almost every day. The ambience of the place is soothing and gentle, inviting rest and relaxation—truly the place to have a holiday. This land harboured no poisonous snakes, few obnoxious insects or major weather disturbances, and very little crime, political turmoil or social

265

unrest took place here. It was a perfect place to consider the end of the inheritance journey where Israel finally experienced rest from war and peace in the Promised Land. A place like Dr. Seuss' 'Solla Sollew', where "...they never have troubles, at least very few."

Gazing placidly down from our lookout on the balcony, I wondered why Julie suddenly raced toward shore, swimming the crawl faster than I thought she knew how. Lori did her best to follow, shouting something unintelligible after her. I assumed a race was underway and turned back to the conversation with the boys. Five minutes later Lori burst breathlessly through the door.

"Dad, Dad, come quick! Julie is bleeding really badly. Something happened on the reef—I think something bit her." I stared at her as though she were some kind of actor in a play. She couldn't be serious.

"What do you mean, 'bit her'? There's nothing out there that would bite her. She must have scraped herself on some coral."

"No, it's not like that—you should see her leg. Just come; it's really bad!" Hustling next door to where we were staying, I found Lyza bent over Julie's ankle fumbling with a makeshift bandage as blood streamed to the ground. Julie, wide-eyed in shock, twisted around to get a good view of her wound, as Lyza dabbed carefully to clear away the blood from the three inch long rent in my daughter's flesh. There is something obscene about an open wound, especially on a loved one.

Julie was already thinking about what this was going to do to her vacation, fighting back tears. This wasn't what any of us had pictured at all. What malign creature had inflicted such an insult in the midst of those sparkling sunny seas? After we rushed her to the clinic, the doctor matter-of-factly pointed out the teeth marks and informed us that a large moray eel inflicted the wound. By her estimation, one at least three feet long. The doctor said it was quite rare to see such unprovoked attacks, but not unheard of. She thought perhaps the eel was disoriented in the pounding surf and Julie was just in the wrong place at the wrong time.

As Julie lay on her stomach, still in her wet swimming suit, the doctor closed the laceration with thirteen stitches. I was amazed at Julie's attitude; she was determined not to let it ruin her vacation. "Well Dad, at least it's going to make a good story—bit by a three-foot moray eel while swimming in Hawaii. What a killer scar I'm going to have, huh?" I had to admit that was a good one.

The significance was not lost on me. Here we were in the Promised Land ('heaven on earth'), getting bit by a sea serpent. Eve was warned about such things. Speaking of man's relationship to the snake that had deceived Eve in the Garden of Eden, God said,

> *"And I will put enmity between you and the woman, and between your seed and her seed; He shall bruise you on the head, and you shall bruise him on the heel."* (Genesis 3:15)

The timeless enmity between humankind and Satan, between man and his fallen nature and his fallen world, follows him everywhere. No place of safety on earth protects us from the sudden bite of the serpent. We are not exempt from pain or trouble no matter where we flee and no matter how we attempt to insulate ourselves. What we can take solace in is that the last half of that verse in Genesis promises ultimate victory. The serpent may wound us on our heel, but we will crush his head. Ours is a temporary infliction of pain while his is a permanent and utter defeat. Satan stole our inheritance from us, tempting us to take our future into our own hands. We lost everything, but God in His mercy through Christ has completely restored to us that inheritance. We progressively crush the serpent's head with each victory over temptation until we rest in a place of confidence that God has already made a way of victory in every battle we face. Rest in the Promised Land does not mean we will never get bit again—it means we wear hobnail boots and we know how to use them to abide in a place of security and confidence.

My Julie could have been robbed of the rest of her vacation in Hawaii by resenting what happened and complaining about not being able to swim, but she already had been learning in other areas of her life to keep her eyes on God and entrust her happiness to Him. She was grasping the inheritance truth that joy ultimately depends on internal attitudes not on the external circumstances.

Our external circumstances were sure nothing to complain about for the two and half months we lived in Honokawai on the western shore of Maui. We walked three or four miles every morning, swam afterwards in the ocean in front of the condo, and then worked together writing and editing. We spent our afternoons and weekends exploring, driving around different parts of the island, and exclaiming at the sights, the diverse climatic zones, and the lush vegetation.

What an interesting place with a fascinating history! The missionaries and the whalers had come in the early 1800's. The former came for souls and the latter for sensual solace. They both left their mark on the island's history and psyche. Although some mistakes were made, the missionaries, for the most part did much for the well-being of the island's people

The Hawaiians were ripe for Christianizing in the 1800's. The nobility themselves were looking for something better than the human sacrifice and Kapu system that had originally come with the first natives from Tahiti. The merciful God of the Bible appealed to the people, and the message of the gospel was initially warmly embraced. What did not go down well over the long term was the tendency of the missionaries' descendants to go into business, marry royal Hawaiian women and end up with all the land.

By the late 1800's a few powerful families, whose roots traced back directly to the missionaries, owned much of Hawaii. Through illegal circumstances, these families with powerful business interests eventually helped orchestrate the downfall of the Hawaiian monarchy and the annexation of the islands by the United States. And even today a simmering sentiment exists among some Hawaiian descendants because their land was stolen and given to the Americans. It is a sad reality that those who were sent originally to bring the native people into their spiritual inheritance ended up with the Hawaiians' natural one.

Many fail to obtain their spiritual inheritance by becoming enamored with the temporal inheritance of lands and riches. If God gives us wealth in this life, it is to teach us about the true values. Ironically, some scramble to obtain an earthly inheritance only to lose their eternal one. They have neither time nor inclination to cultivate an appetite for their real legacy because their hearts are consumed with a counterfeit. People wrongly assume wealth will bring peace and rest by keeping want outside the door. Yet, those who attain wealth often seem to experience the least amount of peace and rest in their lives. True rest is only found in the fellowship of Him who said,

> *"Come to Me, all who are weary and heavy-laden, and I will give you rest. Take My yoke upon you and learn from Me, for I am gentle and humble in heart; and you will find rest for your souls."* (Matthew 11:29-29)

The Israelites finally experienced this rest of soul in Canaan. They had traversed the desert, fought all the battles for Canaan, and now they rested in their Promised Land. They retired to their homes and farms and fulfilled their dreams of living in peace and plenty amid the beauty of the land. God came through just as He said He would. All His promises were fulfilled.

> *And the Lord gave them rest on every side, according to all that He had sworn to their fathers, and no one of all their enemies stood before them; the Lord gave all their enemies into their hand. Not one of the good promises which the Lord had made to the house of Israel failed; all came to pass.* (Joshua 21:44,45)

The promises had become a provision and the people experienced God's bounty firsthand. The land flowing with milk and honey was a land that took care of itself because God was watching over it, and man did not have to labour to experience its abundance.

> *"But the land into which you are about to cross to possess it, a land of hills and valleys, drinks water from the rain of heaven, a land for which the Lord your God cares; the eyes of the Lord your God are always on it, from the beginning even to the end of the year."* (Deuteronomy 11:11-12)

The inheritance of spiritual rest that God is bringing about within us is also a condition that God watches over and sustains. It is a place of fruitfulness where God brings forth the fruit of the Spirit in its season. The book of Hebrews describes this rest as a place where a man ceases from working out of his own strength.

"There remaineth therefore a rest to the people of God. For he that is entered into his rest, he also hath ceased from his own works, as God did from his. Let us labour therefore to enter into that rest, lest any man fall after the same example of unbelief." (Hebrews 4:9-11 KJV)

The land of rest is a place where we cease striving in our own efforts to accomplish the works of God. Man needs to come to the conclusion that not only is he bent on doing evil, but also he is incapable of doing good. We can labour for years, even when serving God, and find that so much of our effort is rooted in self, not in the rest of the Holy Spirit in righteousness, peace and joy. We are warned to be careful not to miss living in this rest.

"Therefore, let us fear if, while a promise remains of entering His rest, any one of you may seem to have come short of it." (Hebrews 4:10)

The analogy is clear. A whole generation came out of Egypt and was baptized in the Red Sea, but most of them died in the desert. They came short of living in their full inheritance. They never saw or lived in God's provision for them because they would not believe in God's ability to provide it. This rest (that we, too, can come short of) means to cease from striving out of our own resources and to rely fully on the strength that comes from God. In order to enter the kingdom of God in the first place, we have to recognize that there is absolutely nothing we can do to commend ourselves to God. All our works of righteousness cannot please God. It is only by receiving grace and faith and resting in the work that Christ did for us that we obtain a right standing with God—salvation. All through the journey we continue to rely on that same recognition. Our work and service for God has to be totally wrought by Him, by His grace working within us. Ephesians 2:10 says, *"For we are His workmanship, created in Christ Jesus for good works, which God prepared beforehand so that we would walk in them."* As we progressively embrace this revelation, we will act more and more from that purified motivation and we truly will fulfill the 'works' God has planned for us to do. This is an odd paradox of 'ceasing from our own labours' in order to truly work the works of

God. It often takes a lifetime to recognize that the grace that saved us is the grace that enables us to live for Him.

Our time in Hawaii was drawing to an end and our year off was almost over. Maui was proving to be the hardest place for Lyza to leave. She seemed to be floating along in a world of color and peace with a lightness of heart and spirit. I wanted somehow to bottle the essence of Maui and take it with us back to White Rock, so she would never lose it. Surely I was catching a glimpse of God's rest in my beloved and in the way my own spirit found such serenity over the past year. Could we still live in such a way when the pressures came back? Could we rest in the midst of our labours? Only re-entry and time would tell, but I hoped there was a residual power in what we were experiencing, not just because of the extended break, but because of the place God had brought us to in our journey.

We had come too far. We knew too much. The sabbatical had passed quickly and slowly at the same time, which is how I think eternity must be. Forever is caught in a moment and a moment can last forever. In God, a thousand years is as a day and a day is as a thousand years. As we boarded the plane and headed home for a last few days at the cabin before 're-entry', I hoped our peace could be sustained in the midst of fighting the good fight.

The rain spattered on the slippery planks of my brother's cabin deck and tapped a rhythmic staccato on his metal roof, as I stood, alone and pensive. The *Grady* was at its float, ready to take our stuff and us back to White Rock, to the life of a pastor, to our home again. My feelings were mixed—renewed and excited to get back to the people we loved and the challenges of our big church family, and apprehensive when I considered the stress and the expectations commensurate with such a life. Of course, I also felt sorrow at leaving behind this more free and contemplative lifestyle. I would miss the time with Lyza and the special times with Ginette—the walks and talks, the writing, the books, and the various people we had met along the way. It was Thursday, March 29, almost exactly a year since Dad's funeral in Seattle.

Something about the rain brought comfort to me. As a west coast person, I had webbed toes, moss in my armpits and gills behind my ears. I loved the solitude one feels in the rain, especially when lying under a noisy roof with the sight and smell of water dripping off the trees, running down the gutters, and soaking into the soil. Perhaps that comfort feeling went back to my childhood growing up in the soggy Pacific Northwest. When I was a boy, I used to climb up into the attic of my parents' home to sleep in the winter. I would pile up three or four old mattresses and cover them with heaps of blankets and sleeping bags, then crawl in under the whole pile like a squirrel in his nest of leaves. My mother thought I was a bit strange, but I loved sleeping in the dark under the uninsulated roof, my eyes peeping out in the cold, listening to the consoling sound of the rain. Now, as I stood getting ready to go back to the busy world, I felt a reluctance to crawl out from my cozy cabin hideaway and face it all. Childish, perhaps, but I somehow wanted to preserve within myself a secret place of rest even in my regular life. I wanted to live all the time out of the intimacy I had experienced with God and my spouse.

Three months 'back in the saddle' later, in July, I stood with my hands in my pockets, staring over the green pasture to the limitless flat horizon of Alberta farm country—not a mountain in sight. This land did not feel like home to me with the only sea nearby a green waving expanse of barley stretching for miles on one side of the gravel road and a sea of yellow canola rolling over the plain on the other. Huddled among the grove of aspens and cottonwoods to my right was a rough assortment of plywood and two-by-four bunkhouses, a white-washed cookhouse and a barn-shaped chapel that made up Pembina Bible Camp.

The camp was built alongside the Pembina River on a piece of the Seatter family farm, and for the last fifty years or so families from the surrounding areas like Dapp, Slave Lake, or Athabasca came for summer family camps and spiritual renewal. I was to speak in the evening meeting in about ten minutes and was trying to get handles on why I didn't feel quite right about my message direction for the second night in a row. There is nothing worse than being the main speaker in an unfamiliar situation and feeling like you're not quite hitting the ball. The night before I felt as though I was straining at it, working at it. It wasn't flowing like warm oil over the congregation and I knew I wasn't really getting to the sixty or seventy young people in the first six rows. (I could tell by the way the ten-year-old boys were jabbing each other in the ribs.)

It seemed odd to be here, once again far from home, just three months after returning to White Rock. But the irresistible tug of the Holy Spirit had been upon this invitation to be the speaker at a church Bible camp in Alberta, and although I didn't know why, I knew by now that to obey that urge was the wisest course. The morning adult studies were going great, but I was definitely off my game as the featured speaker in the evenings. Maybe my problem was partly due to the pressure I felt from Lyza and Ginette's pre-service counsel the night before. "Now, Dad, you're going to be funny, aren't you? Remember there is a whole bunch of young people there so you need to keep it exciting and interesting." That is all a fifty-year-old preacher needs to hear to make him feel self-conscious and irrelevant. So I struggled through the second night trying to get my bearings.

Afterwards as I walked dejectedly into our cabin, Lyza gave me that 'where is your anointing' look and muttered something about Bible camps not being her cup of tea as she reached for a book to bury herself in. As I prayed fervently early the next morning, I felt as if God said to me that I was too worried about focusing on the young people. I had moved off my inheritance foundation theme and was speaking topically in the evening meetings, thinking the inheritance perspective was too involved and broad a subject to relate to the youth. The Lord made it clear I was to trust Him and impart the truths of the inheritance to the whole congregation at the camp.

The young people came forward to the altar that night en masse and were spread about the floor, weeping and calling upon God, some lying prostrate on the floor under the power of the Spirit and some in huddled groups of intense prayer. The Dapp camp was my rare opportunity to preach the inheritance message within the context of twelve sessions through the week. As it turned out, the young people were the most hungry to hear that God had designed a purpose and destiny for them to be conformed into the image of His Son. The Old Testament stories painted a picture for them that they could understand, and as I waded in the third night to backtrack and explain to them the whole picture, the Holy Spirit riveted even the ten year olds to their seats with a desire to understand the eternal inheritance God had prepared for them. 'Light bulbs' were going on all over the chapel as people from eight to eighty began to see that all the events of their lives were orchestrated by the Lord's sovereign purpose.

Bill Seatter, the patriarch of the camp, epitomized this fresh response as he, after nearly eighty years of life and Bible camps every summer, expressed the refreshing he felt at the consideration of what God had planned in His wisdom. Bill had no trouble relating to the value of a rich heritage. His father had come to this country at the turn of the century from Scotland to stake a claim to northern Alberta farmland about the same time my grandfather went out to the west coast from Iowa. With a bag of oats on his back and a twenty-two in his hand to shoot rabbits for food, Bill's father crossed the Pembina River with a vision to turn the scruffy peat land into a farm. Nearly ninety years later, that piece of land was one of the best producers in the area.

Bill told the story of how a traveling evangelist held meetings one year, preaching a fiery 'conviction of sin' message. On the way home from one such meeting, his mother expressed to his father her dislike of 'those kinds of messages'. His dad responded by saying, "That was the only message that ever did me any good!" His children knew something had happened to him. From that time on the air no longer turned blue from the cussing that used to erupt when his ornery old machinery refused to cooperate. After that the Seatter family not only laid claim to the Pembina land, but they also laid claim to the spiritual territory, sponsoring revival meetings and eventually providing the farm for the Bible camp. Bill's brother, Les, and his family eventually moved to the coast to become a pillar in our White Rock fellowship, and have continued to nurture strong spiritual stock, both their own offspring and many others.

We left Alberta encouraged that the inheritance message was vital and on the plane home we began to formulate how to teach these insights in some kind of seminar format. The promises made to Abraham those millennia ago still reached down to find us in the twentieth century, confirming that the land and the seed were ours. When God first came to Abraham to make covenant with him, He told him to look upon the sand by the seashore to see if he could number the grains. And God declared that, *"So would his descendants be."* Later, after all the testings of his life, when Sarah and he were beyond child-bearing years and in their nineties with no children of their own, God came to meet with him again, this time telling him to look up at the number of stars in the heavens. Again the Lord declared, *"So would his descendants be."*

At that point, the impossibility of such a feat could not be lost on Abraham. It was something only God could perform. Abraham was still childless, living in his tent with no land to call his own, but the promise was as sure and solid as God Himself. The scripture says that Abraham believed God and it was counted to him as righteousness. Even God changing the metaphor from sand (something of the earth) to stars (a heavenly phenomenon) reflects this shift from earthly dependence to God's supernatural power for its ultimate fulfillment. Abraham's focus shifted from looking down to looking up.

About a week after returning from the Alberta camp in quite a buoyant frame of mind, our peaceful transition back into church life was abruptly jarred. We had been back to work for the previous three months and fully engaged with people, preaching and pastoring with a new sense of peace and purpose. I had presented some ten-year goals to the church's leadership in June, which included a renewed dedication to reach our city in cooperation with the other churches in the area and a plan to build a new church sanctuary and school facility on a property we had located. It all seemed to be received with a great sense of enthusiasm and unity and we headed into the summer looking for great prospects in the future, so suddenly experiencing some turmoil took me by unpleasant surprise.

We began hearing news of several families we had known for a long time leaving the church. There didn't seem to be any particular issues on the surface that I knew about, but after talking with some of them, it sounded to me like my leadership was under question and there was a crisis in confidence in some of the areas of church ministry. Perhaps it was due to some deficiencies in my leadership style, some insecurities produced by my protracted absence, or maybe it was just the season our church fellowship was in. Whatever it was, during the summer time, with vacation absences accentuating our weaknesses, a lot of pressure came on me from some key people to make things better. I found myself at a crossroads, torn between resting in God or falling back into my pre-sabbatical mentality that it all depended on me.

Here I was, completing a book on the rest of God and experiencing some upheaval, with the underlying pressure that I as a pastor had better do something quick to fix our problems. Suggestions were made that I should hire some people to fortify our areas of weakness and questions arose about our ability to move forward into a building program. A pervasive doom and gloom atmosphere began to descend almost inexplicably. It is amazing how quickly human nature can move to extremes of emotion. After thirty years of stability in our church, one would think we shouldn't have been able to feel so shaken. It was uncanny how it all happened so suddenly and we couldn't help but feel something was happening in the spiritual realm to test our resolve and our message. I was tempted to think that while I was contemplating the inner pilgrimage of the inheritance, the practical world of our church life was going to hell in a hand basket. While I was away on a year's sabbatical, communicating our life message into a symbolic analogy, the church was waiting to come unglued when I came back.

Nevertheless, the inner work of rest that had been coming to a completion during our time away held us in good stead. Part of me was sorely tested and grieved by the turmoil in the church and especially the personal implications to my leadership, but another part of me knew I could not be moved from my confidence and my peace. The journey had been too long and the lessons imbedded too deeply to be disregarded now. If I wasn't what some people thought I should be, what could I or should I do about it? Undoubtedly there were areas of my life and leadership that needed work and improvement, but that wasn't the greater picture. It simply was not all about me. It was about God and His purposes. I knew what Paul meant when he said, *"...by the grace of God I am what I am, and His grace toward me did not prove vain..."* (1 Corinthians 15:10).

Lyza and I did our best to stick together and cling to the Lord's revelation of 'rest' in our relationship as well. We experienced some strains from all these church struggles, and found ourselves deeply dependent on the Lord to keep us from falling into old patterns. Over the following months, as we went on to weather the most severe sifting and testing of the unity of our church (and of our very message) that we had ever gone through, we were aware that the Church is not a work of man's ability, wisdom, or effort, but it is a supernatural creation of God. It is dependent upon the workings of His power and grace, not upon one man or even many people's leadership. Our church and every other church needs to wait for the blessing of Abraham that comes down from above, from the Father. Jesus promised, *"...I will build my church; and the gates of hell will not prevail against it"* (Matthew 16:18 KJV). We were in good hands and we knew it.

In the midst of these church trials, we woke up one fateful morning to the news of the terrorist attack on the Pentagon and World Trade Center in New York. Life, it seems, will never be quite the same. The terrifying destructiveness stopped us in our tracks—suspended in the contemplation of this obscene intrusion. We have never felt so vulnerable in North America. Repeated over and over, the incredulous TV images of airliners full of people smashing into the World Trade towers, followed by the imploding buildings, left us in wounded shock. We watched the grief and we felt the fear and the anger. We also saw the heroism and the sacrifice, the humility and the re-forged unity, the renewed faith in God and the resolve. Human nature is flawed, but it is also designed to become refined, focused, and impassioned for good under trial.

Lyza and I sat on our front deck and surveyed the 180-degree view of the Gulf Islands. Our front deck? Was it possible that this home was ours? The smell of the beach smote our nostrils while gulls cried overhead and rode the spring breeze in pursuit of a predator eagle that was only minding his own business. We had sold our house on the golf course, occasioning the seventh (and we hope final) move since we had left the house near the beach over thirty years before. There was something deeply familiar and comforting about beholding the sight in front of us. We had begun our journey here by the beach and now, like a seafarer returning from a life of roving, we were home in our original port. It seemed too providential to be chance.

The sojourn in the big house in the prestigious subdivision that had absorbed our little five-acre farm had come to a natural end as the developers made a final deal with us to leave our claims on the house and pond behind. Up until this move, we had simply gone from one housing plan to the next step which opened up before us, but in this case, we had some money in our pockets and the whole peninsula of South Surrey/White Rock before us, with the options so varied and appealing we did not know what to choose. We could afford to live on an acre in the country in a decent house or a more upscale house in a subdivision, or we could build a house or buy some land.

As we contacted a realtor friend and started to look, the water began to exert a magnetic force upon us. Every time we looked at anything near the shore, a nostalgic peace descended. Finally we gave in to the pull of this gravity and made a list of water-view places within our price range. When we walked into this compact three-level house just a block above the east beach, both of us knew within ten seconds of walking into the place that we were 'home'. We could barely manage to heed our realtor's cautions not to express too much interest until we got back in the car with him. Afterward, as we sat in the car, discussing with the real estate agent how one proceeded from this point with the negotiations to buy, Lyza suddenly had a thought.

"Say, we must be pretty close to where we used to live, aren't we?"

We got out of the car to search out the addresses, and sure enough, as I pulled aside a branch of an overgrown laurel hedge, there was the street number of our old beach house (which had been bulldozed long ago). We had come full circle. The site where we had pitched our tent was almost directly across the street from this beautiful new home that we had just decided to buy!

We moved onto this piece of real estate overlooking the pier where my 'Man on the Beach' ministry had been birthed over thirty years ago. Although things were still mending from all the church struggles, we felt that we were moving on and that the true real estate, the surrender of our souls and the soul of our church to Christ's lordship, was settling in the spiritual realm. Faith and trust would always be the bread of the people of God. After all these years and all of these lessons and all of these illustrations of God's faithfulness and message, was there any other way that we could walk but into the inheritance that Jesus Christ secured eternally for us?

The inner spiritual journey into our inheritance is inextricably tied to the external circumstances of our lives and even the course of

278

nations and the world. It begins to make sense that there is a mystery of God at work in creation, in the history of the world, in our personal testimony and in the teachings of scripture that binds all of these things into a harmonious whole. God planned it all to reveal His glory and His purpose. His glory is defined as 'the unveiling of His loving character'. Therefore, life was designed to reveal the character of God. The character of God formed in us is the true and final inheritance. The character of God lost at the fall is being painstakingly re-instated to us through the tests of life and how we respond to them.

The purpose of life is to mature us and cause us to grow up in Christ—to make us useful to God in this life, and incredible as it may seem, to fulfill His further eternal purposes in the next. We only get glimpses of what these further purposes are, but they are described as an eternal inheritance beyond this world that exceeds anything we have imagined. Scripture reveals that overcomers are even promised to rule nations and cities, inherit the earth, judge angels and men, and be glorified with Christ in His future kingdom. The same cross that finally conquered our implacable enemy also won for us the eternal life in which to carry out the full purposes of humankind's destiny. This life is the 'boot camp' of life to come.

I thought again of Julie's eel bite in Hawaii and then of the awful trauma to the world from the terrorist attacks. Life will always be a battleground. It will never be safe or secure. There will always be a bite from the serpent when we least expect it. Just when we think we have gotten on top of everything, there is some unconquered giant that will show his ugly face on some battleground that we hoped was done with. Or the familiar pain in our heel flares up again to remind us that we are vulnerable, depending on a Strength that is far greater than our enemies. In that strength we find rest again and again. Through His ability we are shown how to place our feet on the serpent's head, crush him, and claim more ground. The world may fight many more wars, we may even find ourselves in a final Armageddon, but a final resting place for the world was already prepared long ago. We may face death, discouragement, and setbacks in our personal lives, but there is a place of rest prepared for us from the foundation of the world. Our Father has already written

His will and signed it in His own blood. We are His children, we are His heirs, the deed is done and the work is finished.

Appendix

The Journey into the Inheritance

The Ten Temptations

The Seven Pillars of Wisdom

The Inheritance Seminar

Journey Into the Inheritance

God's Process:

Promise   Problem   Provision

The Ten Temptations:

1. Pressures of Life
2. Power of Evil
3. Bitterness of Life
4. Hunger
5. Thirst
6. Idolatry
7. Counterfeit Service
8. Counterfeit Comfort
9. Counterfeit Leadership
10. Doubt & Fear

Seven Stages of the Spiritual Journey:

1. Passover in Egypt	2. Red Sea Crossing	3. Mt. Sinai Visitation	4. Wilderness	5. Crossing Jordan River	6. Conquest of Canaan	7. Rest in the Promised Land

The Ten Temptations

	The Place and Event	The Test	The Lesson	The Judgment
1	The Slaveries of Egypt, Exodus 5	The pressures of life	REDEMPTION To learn of redemption through the blood, our only escape	
2	Pharaoh's armies at the Red Sea, Exodus 14	The power of evil	WATER BAPTISM To learn of water baptism – the power of the cross over sin	
3	The Bitter Waters of Marah, Exodus 15	The bitter experiences of life – betrayal	HEALING To learn of the power of the cross to heal	
4	Hunger in the Wilderness of Sin, Exodus 16	Apparent lack of provision – insecurity	THE LIVING WORD To learn that man does not live by bread alone but by every word from God's mouth	
5	Thirst at Rephidim, Exodus 17	The loss of God's conscious presence - abandonment	THE PRESENCE OF GOD To learn that He never leaves or forsakes us and is working even when we can't see Him	
6	Idolatry at Sinai, Exodus 32	Counterfeit gods: The removal of our support system	THE BAPTISM OF THE SPIRIT To learn of the internalized God of the Spirit	The destruction of our idols and the poisoning of our lives.
7	Strange Firs of Nadab and Abihu, Leviticus 10	Counterfeit service: human and religious zeal	TRUE SPIRIT WORSHIP To learn the priestly ministry of worship in the Spirit	The destruction of our false zeal in God's fire.
8	Strange Flesh at Taberah, Numbers 11	Counterfeit comfort: The lusts of the flesh	TRUE FULFILLMENT To learn contentment and satisfaction in God's promises	The destruction of our flesh through overindulgence and disease
9	Rebellion at Hazeroth, Numbers 12	Counterfeit leadership: Disillusionment with leaders – usurping authority	SPIRITUAL AUTHORITY To learn to trust in God's sovereignty and power in our lives	The revelation of our own fleshly motivation and faults
10	Unbelief at Kadesh-Barnea near Jordan, Numbers 13	Counterfeit confidence: Fear of the giants – self-reliance	FAITH To learn to follow god fully by faith to the end	The consignment to wander in circles in the desert until we die.

The Inheritance Matrix:
The Seven Pillars of Wisdom
Proverbs 9:1

Creation Gen 1:1-30	History Old Testament Types	Christ New Testament Truths	Maturity 2 Pet. 1:4-5	Beatitudes Matt. 5:1-10	The Lord's Prayer Matt. 6:9-13	Prudence Basic Life Principles
Day 1 Dividing Light from Darkness	The Passover	Salvation Through the Cross	Faith	Blessed are … the poor in spirit	Hallowed be Thy Name	Design
Day 2 Dividing the Waters	The Red Sea Crossing	Water Baptism	Virtue	…they that mourn	Thy Kingdom Come	Responsibility
Day 3 Vegetation: Seed-Bearing	Mount Sinai	Spirit Baptism	Knowledge	…the meek	Thy Will Be Done	Ownership
Day 4 Dividing Day from Night – Sun to Rule	The Wilderness	Trials, Temptations	Temperance	…they that hunger and thirst for righteousness	Daily Bread	Success
Day 5 Animals of Sea and Air: New Kind of Life	The Jordan River	The Crucified Life	Patience	…the merciful	Forgive Us As We Forgive	Suffering
Day 6 Man to Have Dominion	The Conquest of Canaan	The Overcoming Life	Godliness	…the pure in heart	Lead Us Not Into Temptation; Deliver Us From Evil	Authority
Day 7 Day of Rest	The Inheritance – Rest from Fear	Rest, Abiding in Christ	Brotherly Kindness, Love	…the peacemakers	Thine is the Kingdom, the Power and the Glory	Freedom

The Inheritance Seminar

To more deeply delve into the revelation of the inheritance and how it applies to our lives, John and Lyza have developed a teaching format to further explore these truths, make the personal applications and receive the power for transformation through prayer.

This seminar increases understanding of life's purpose, brings hope for the future, and brings perspective of the past. It becomes a preparation for receiving and living in the inheritance God has provided for us. In addition to the ten tests of life and the meaning of the fundamental Bible metaphors, the seminar covers the seven pillars of wisdom hidden in scripture that confirm the mystery of the inheritance and the meaning of life.

For more information about the Inheritance Seminar
or to order additional copies of "The Inheritance"
please contact:

White Rock Christian Fellowship
2265 152ⁿᵈ Street, Surrey, British Columbia, Canada
Phone: (604) 531-8301
Email: wrcf@hotmail.com

(also available online at www.amazon.com)